Superb SHOPS

SUPERB SHOPS
Edition 2007

Work Conception: Carles Broto
Publisher: Carles Broto
Editorial Coordinator: Jacobo Krauel
Graphic designer & production: Pilar Chueca, Carolina Ferreira
Text: contributed by the architects, edited by William George and Marta Rojals

© Carles Broto i Comerma
LINKS INTERNATIONAL
Jonqueres, 10, 1-5
Barcelona 08003
Spain
Tel.: +34 93 301 21 99
Fax: +34 93 301 00 21

info@linksbooks.net
www. linksbooks.net

Superb SHOPS

index

introduction

When designing commercial spaces it is necessary to consider not just the types of activities that will be carried out in them, but also the different locations, functions and environments that they will require. All commercial premises, however, need a basic infrastructure that creates an efficient working environment and facilities that ensure excellent customer service.

There have been considerable developments in the area of commercial spaces in recent years, mainly caused by the trend towards increasing numbers of shopping centers appearing in cities, following the influence of the American model. The proliferation of these centers has gone hand in hand with developments in new ways of understanding commercial premises. These include changes in the way internal spatial divisions are conceived (they were far more schematic and conventional in the past), the systematic use of light and color as integral elements of the architecture, the use of prefabricated materials and the widespread tendency to use transparent spaces, with few visible separations.

In order to provide a representative vision of the most innovative recent designs, we have tried as far as possible to show the great diversity of commercial spaces and their almost infinite decorative possibilities, as a kind of graphic guide to current and future trends in interior design for customer service spaces.

We have also made a considerable effort to show not just the overall design of each project, but also the most significant construction details, which in some cases are an essential part of the character of the finished space. For this reason we have included all kinds of graphic material, such as photographs, plans, elevations and axonometric views and sketches, together with a description of the work as it was conceived by the architect.

Studio 63

Miss Sixty Tokyo

Tokyo, Japan   *Photographs: Seishi Maeda*

Welcome to the world of Miss Sixty. Here you can find a glamorous world of fantastic scenery and an imaginary reality. An organic space designed with curved walls, sculptured counters, soft and cozy surfaces with bright colors, all made to create a reality bigger than life. A space that gives you the freedom to be who ever you would like to be. The freedom to be yourself.

This is the new concept of the "Miss Sixty" shops designed by studio 63 situated in Florence Italy. Together with the client, Vicky Hassan, the architects have tried to create a dream world inspired by the styles, designs and glamorous entertainment world of the 70's. The reference to the 70's was input by the client and evoked a profound and thorough research that was made later by the architects.

The organic forms of the furniture, the colorful bright colors with the shiny varnish, the heavy velvet drapes and the accent lighting, were all made in order to create a warm, feminine and glamorous atmosphere. An atmosphere that reinforces the miss sixty brand as a young and glamorous women's wear.

The architects were mostly inspired by the graphic designs of the 70's but not only. They have challenged themselves to transform two-dimensional patterns into three-dimensional structures. Taking patterns from wallpapers and textiles and transforming it into furniture. Quoting designs by Verner Panton as well as the music and performance of David Bowie.

Although the concept is of a chain shop, every shop has its own characteristics related to the structure of the space and the location of the shop. Each wall of every store is thought of as a composition on its own. The contour made by the infinite line of the shelves giving even the merchandise the opportunity to become part of the design.

The miss sixty-chain shops are to be spread all over the world, From Tokyo to Los Angeles, from Berlin to Hong Kong. Using the references of the 70's reassures a widely recognizable image with an intelligent common denominator.

Although the concept is of a chain shop, every shop has its own characteristics related to the structure of the space and the location of the shop. Each wall of every store is thought of as a composition on its own.

The miss sixty-chain shops are to be spread all over the world, From Tokyo to Los Angeles, from Berlin to Hong Kong. Using the references of the 70's reassures a widely recognizable image with an intelligent common denominator.

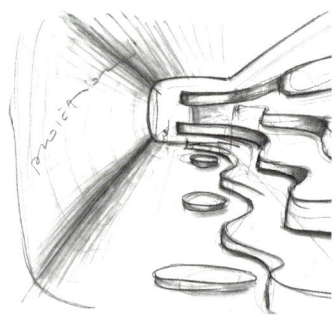

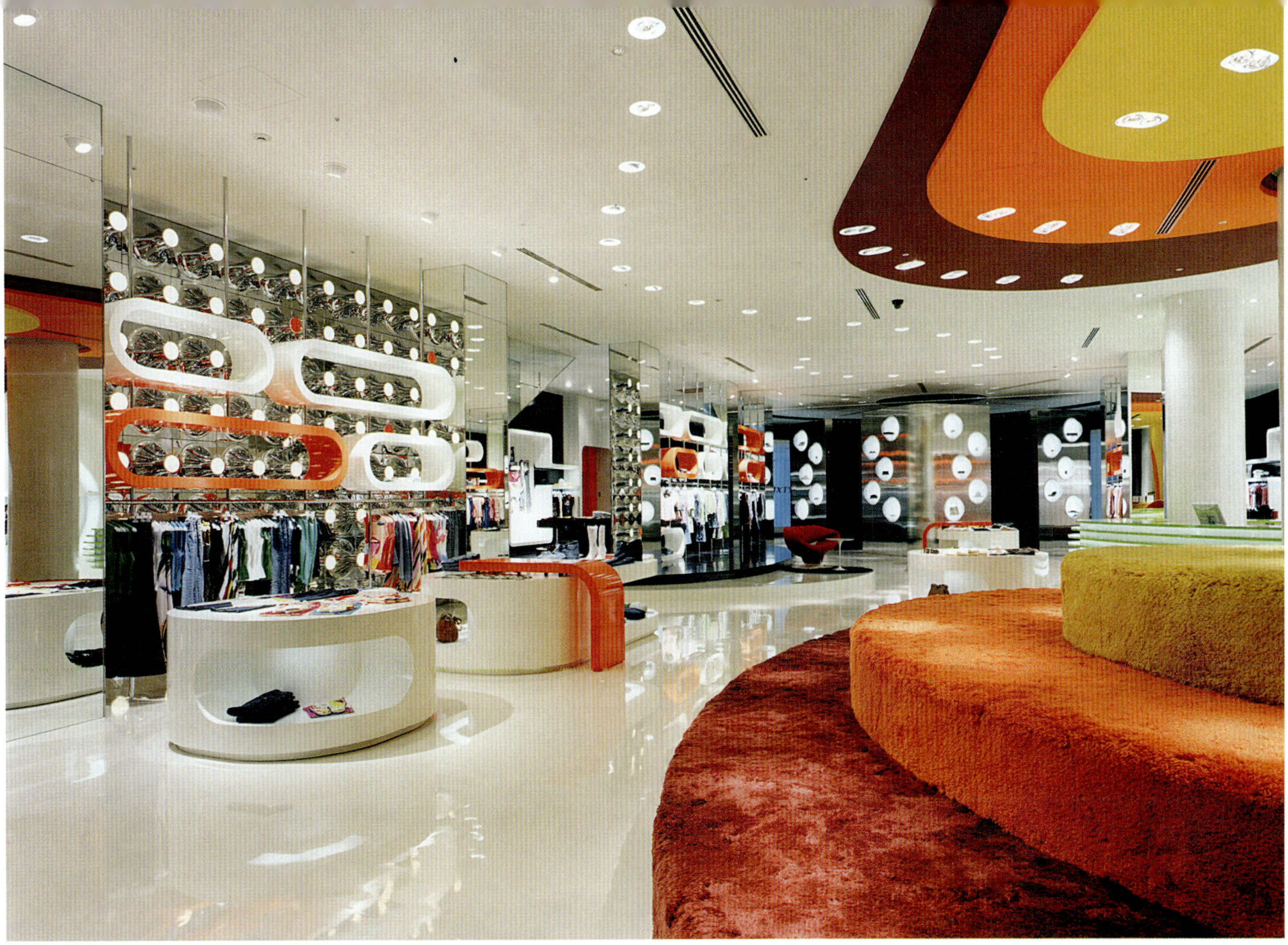

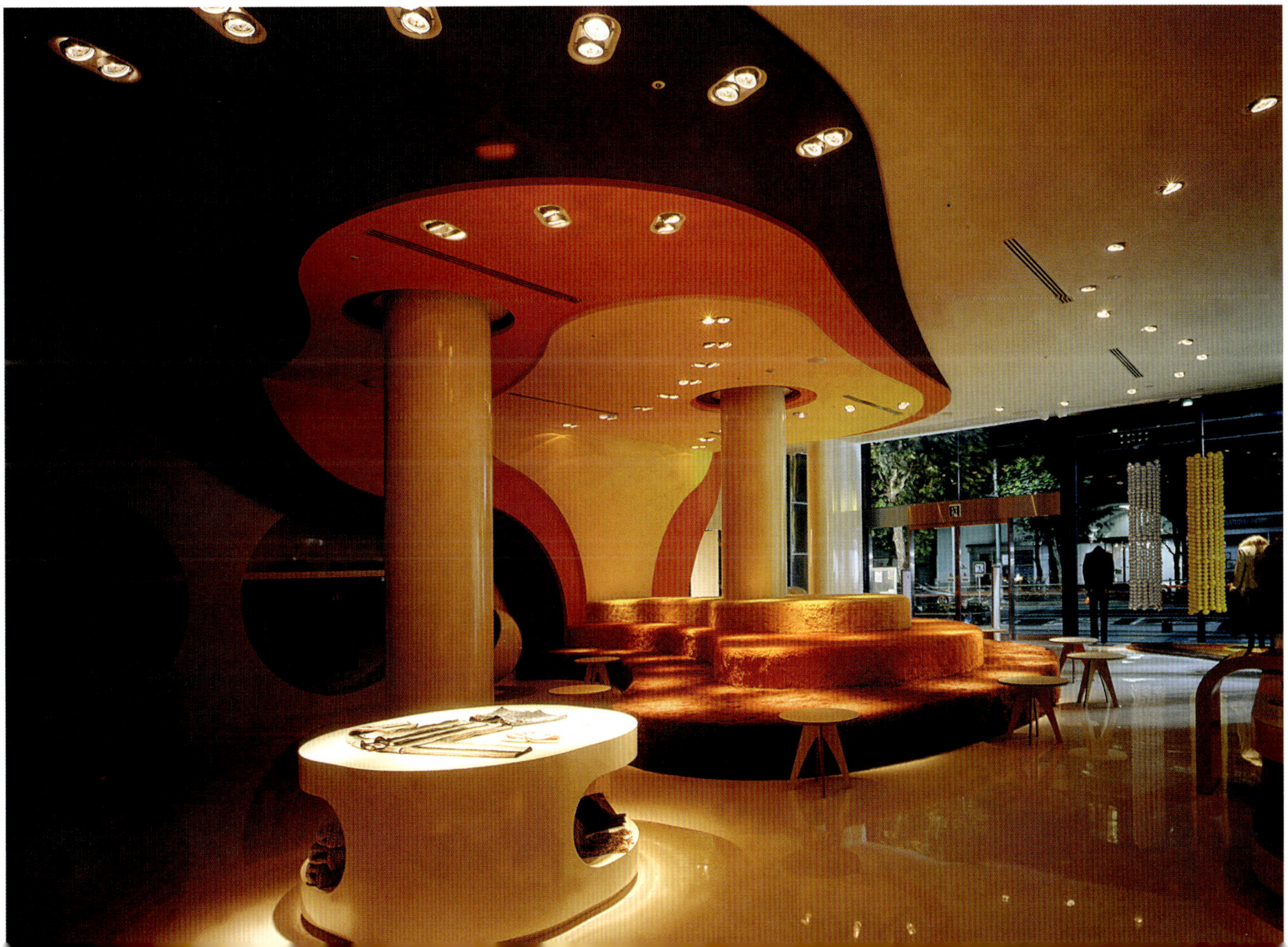

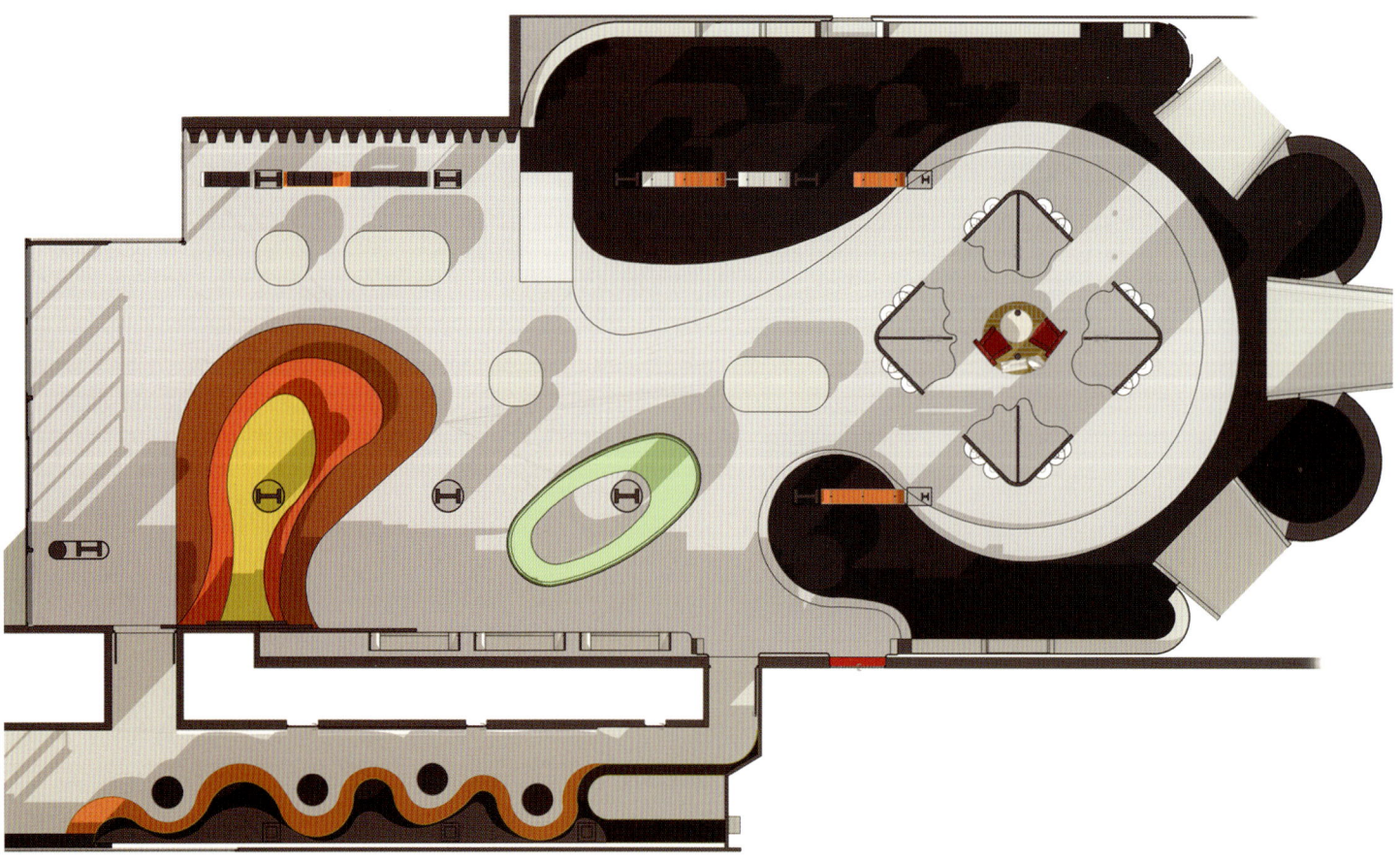

Ground floor plan

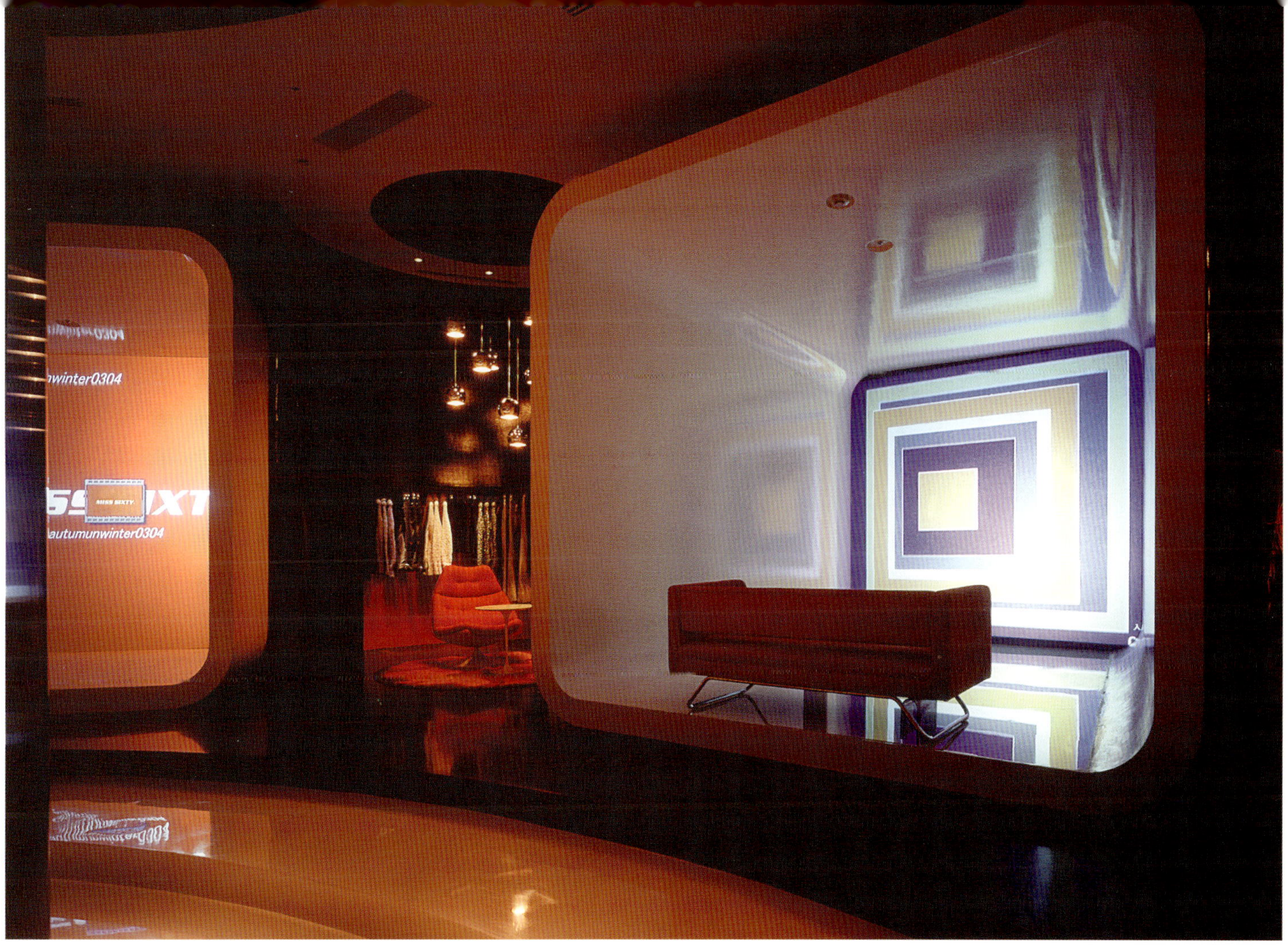
winter0304
autumunwinter0304

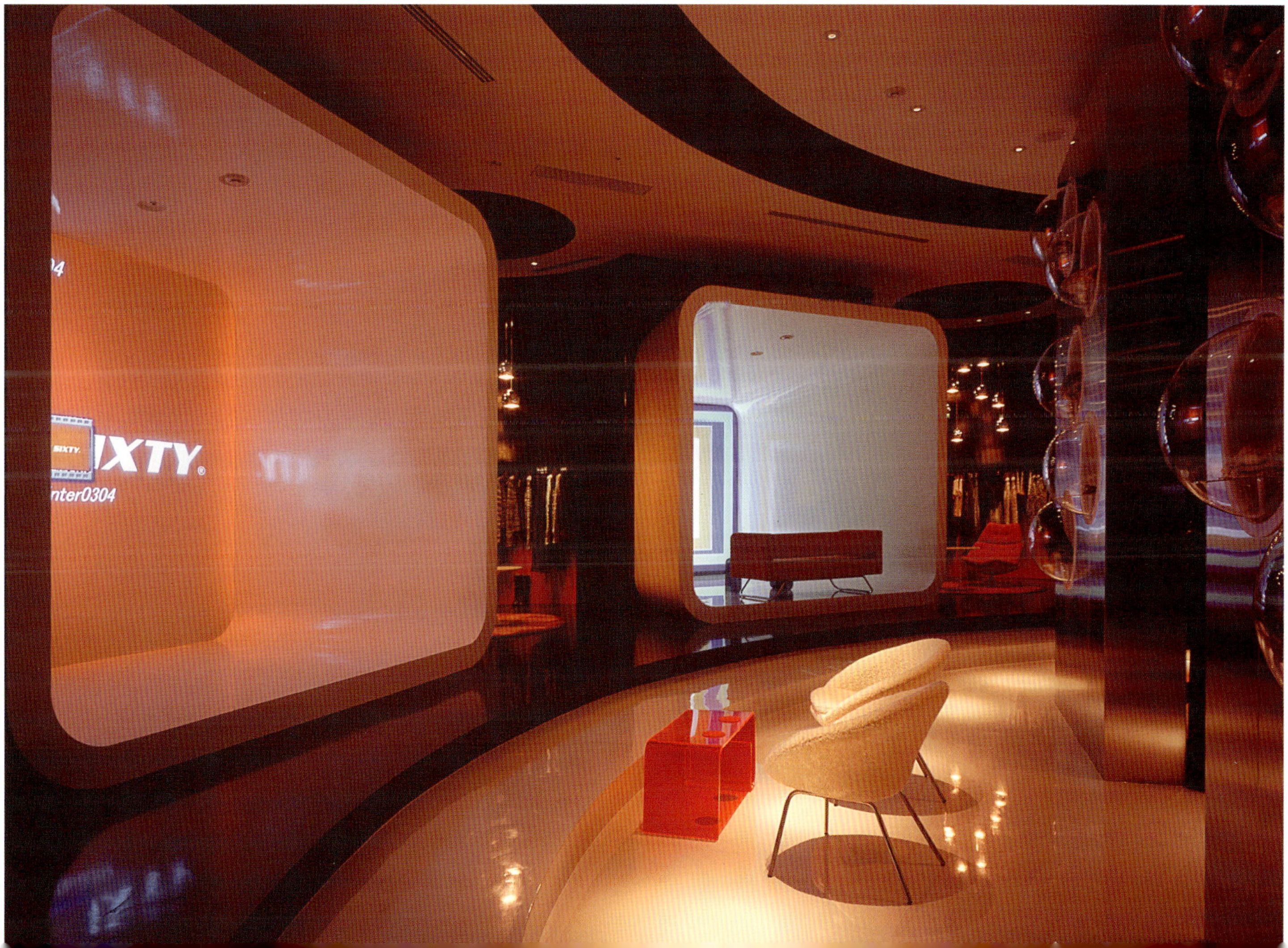
IXTY.
nter0304

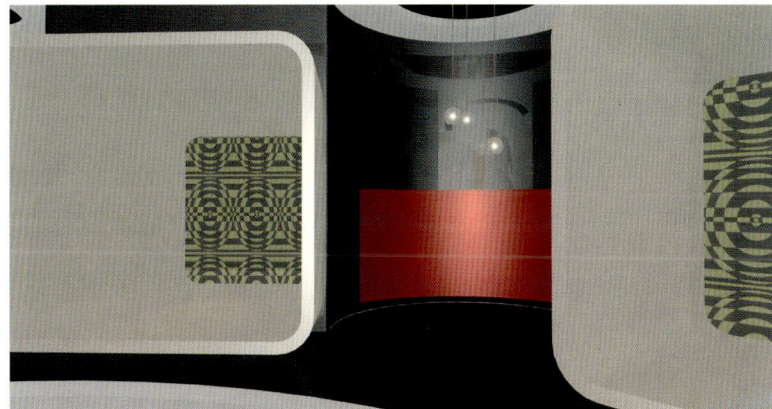

The organic forms of the furniture, the colorful bright colors with the shiny varnish, the heavy velvet drapes and the accent lighting, were all made in order to create a warm, feminine and glamorous atmosphere. An atmosphere that reinforces the miss sixty brand as a young and glamorous women's wear.

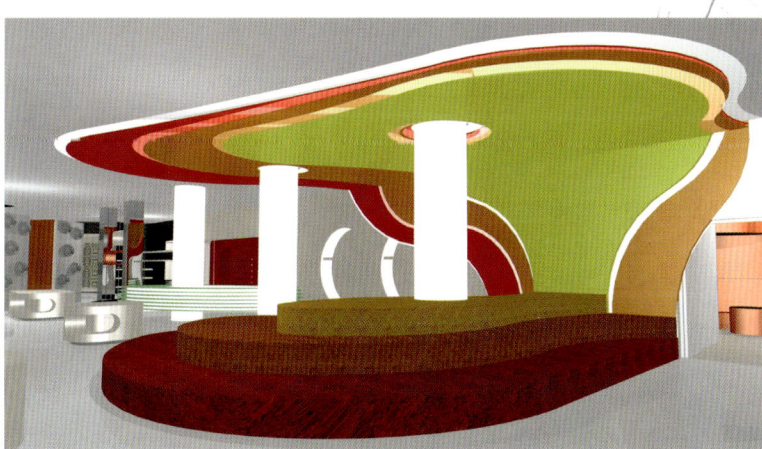

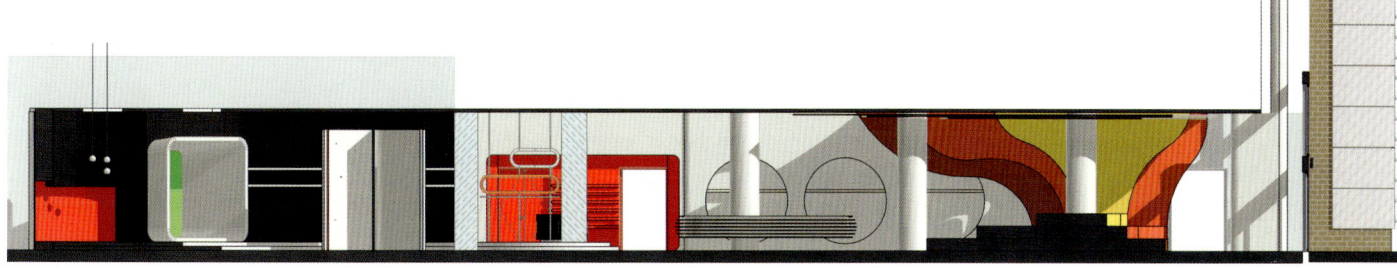

Longitudinal section

Vincent van Duysen

Natan Boutique

Brussels, Belgium

Photographs: Alberto Piovano

The idea behind the Natan boutique project, in an old building in Brussels, was to create a bright but intimate atmosphere. The space is defined through white elements: load-bearing walls, pillars and beams, a mezzanine that seems to float in space, the marble staircase within an angular balustrade and the light wall of the shop window parallel to the façade. Although abstract, the minimalist white surfaces -some of them mobile- delimit the spaces where the customers, protected from the street, can try on the garments while they enjoy a view to the exterior through a horizontal opening in the wall. The street thus becomes a shop window for the customers.

The display elements match the rest of the space in color and materials, which gives uniformity to the whole and highlights the interplay of volumes and forms created between the vertical circulation space and the mezzanine.

The lighting system, spotlights fitted into a hung ceiling and perimeter lighting, help to enhance the brightness of the boutique. The hung ceiling does not touch the wall, and, as if suspended in the air, it momentarily breaks the uniformity of the space. This arrangement forms part of the interplay of volumes and geometries of the design: lines that cut through each other, juxtaposition and overlapping of bodies. The mezzanine highlights the vertical dimension of the space and creates an interplay of heights on the ground floor. Windows with black shutters on the outside and white ones on the inside soften the impact of the entrance to the boutique and use the metaphor of color to show the contrast between the hustle and bustle of the street and the clear peacefulness of this space.

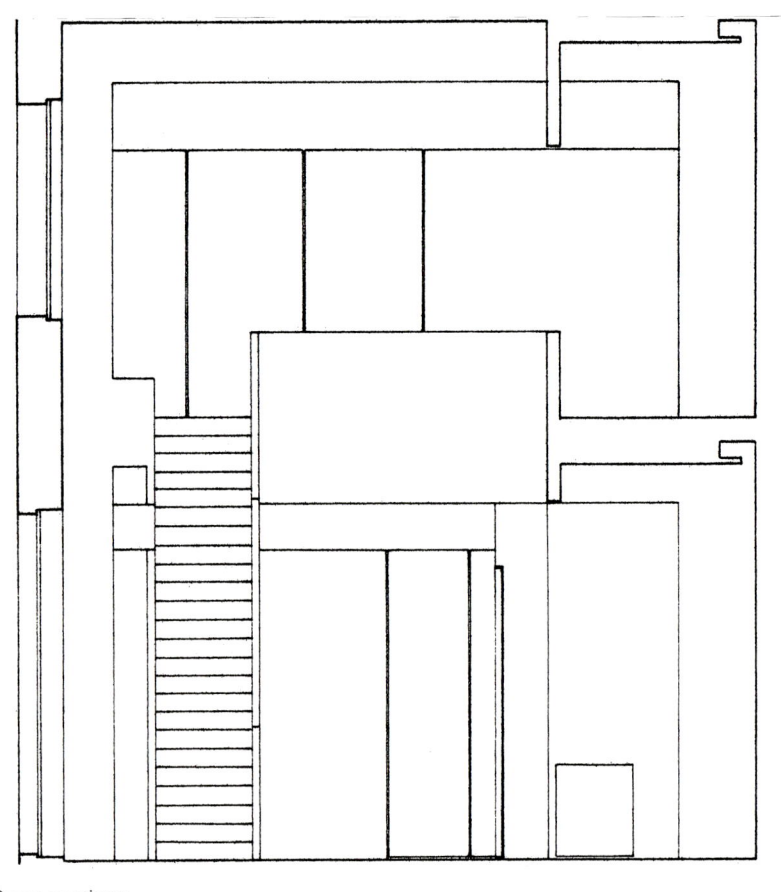

Cross sections

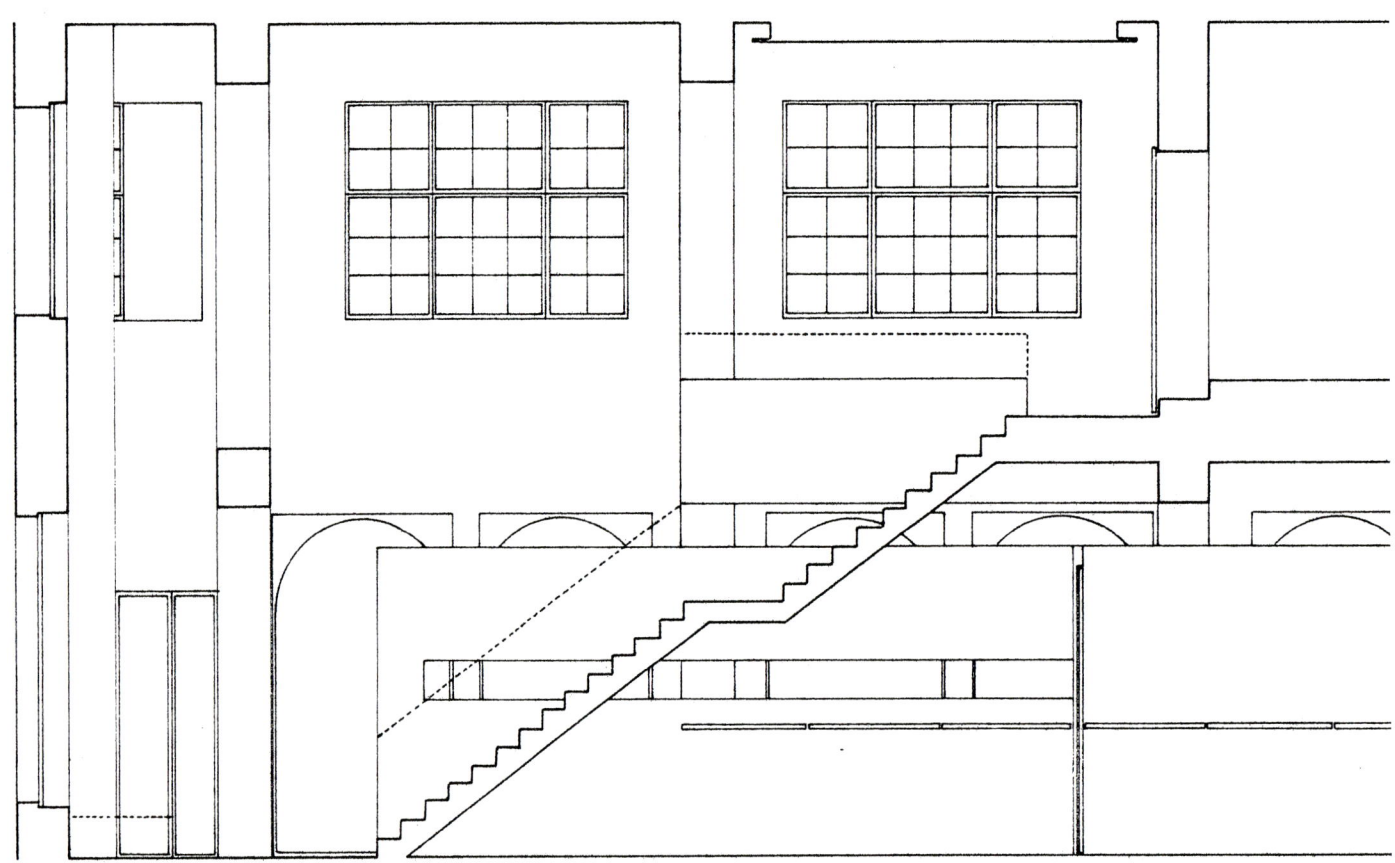

Longitudinal section

The location of the building that houses the boutique, at the corner of two streets, had a decisive influence on the design concept. The aim was to isolate the boutique by giving it a high degree of autonomy in order to prevent the urban environment from invading the interior space.

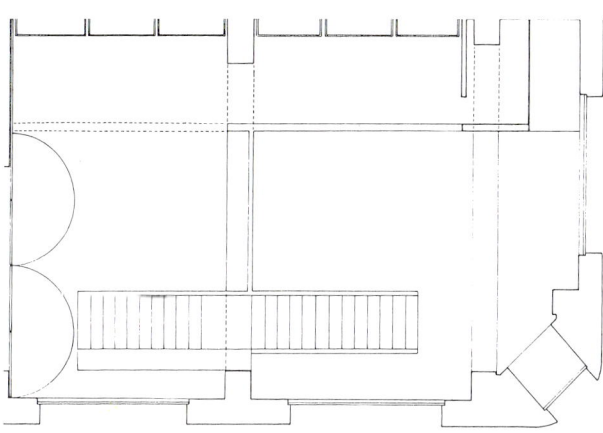

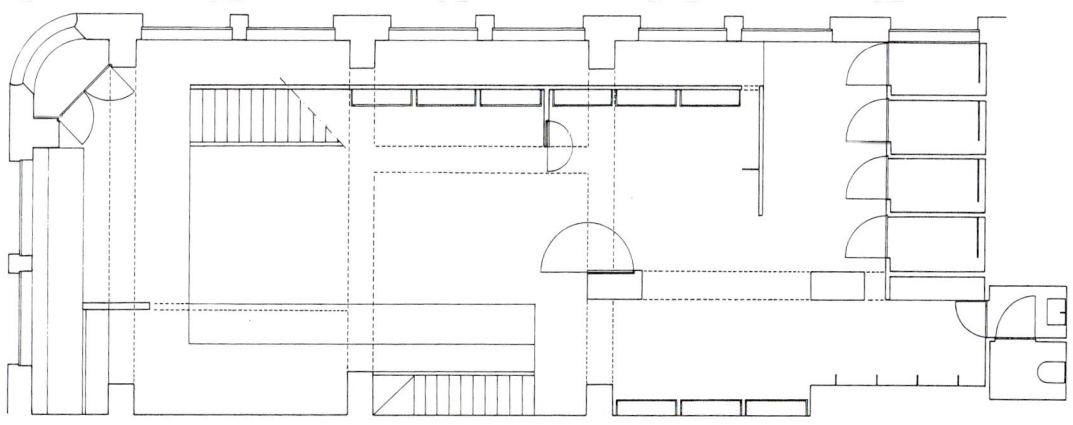

Ground floor plan

Gordon Kipping & Frank O. Gehry

Issey Miyake Tribeca

New York City, USA

Photographs: Paul Warchol, Gordon Kipping

Located on 119 Hudson Street at the corner of N. Moore Street, this is a new showcase for Issey Miyake Men's and Women's collections. The shop was designed by architect Gordon Kipping, principal of the New York City office of G TECTS LLC. Miyake, always fascinated by Gehry's vision and approach, contacted the architect who agreed to sign on in conjunction with Kipping.

The design was born after Miyake's visit to the Gehry studio in Los Angeles, where he described his vision of a Gehry "tornado" whipping through the space and transforming everything in its path.

The original warehouse building was designed by the prominent New York architect Thomas R. Jackson and completed in 1888. G TECTS LLC led a team of preservation experts and conservation consultants to determine the building's original condition and direct the subsequent restoration, primarily of the façade.

The use of glass is extensive throughout the project. Transparency enabled spatial and programmatic connections where vertical separation and security concerns necessitated physical separation. The re-moval of the original wood plank flooring to expose the original building joists enabled the insertion of a new glass box building into the cellar floor. To emphasize this new construction, a five foot wide border of glass flooring was inserted between the glass box and the existing structure.

The cash desk is a double-cantilevered stainless steel box hovering precariously over the glass floor border. Stainless steel display platforms on concealed wheels contain stock in drawers and alternately function as runways for the presentation of collections. Glass display cases and shelving offer display for more precious merchandise.

Alejandro Gehry produced two murals for the project. Inspired by his father's architecture and Miyake's clothing, and with elements of his own personal style thrown into the mix, the hand-drawn and computer manipulated collages serve to draw the eye to the farthest reaches of the retail area, down to the cellar lounge and back to the turbulent sprawl of his father's sculpture. The murals mark a gallery space that will feature a rotating display of work by young artists.

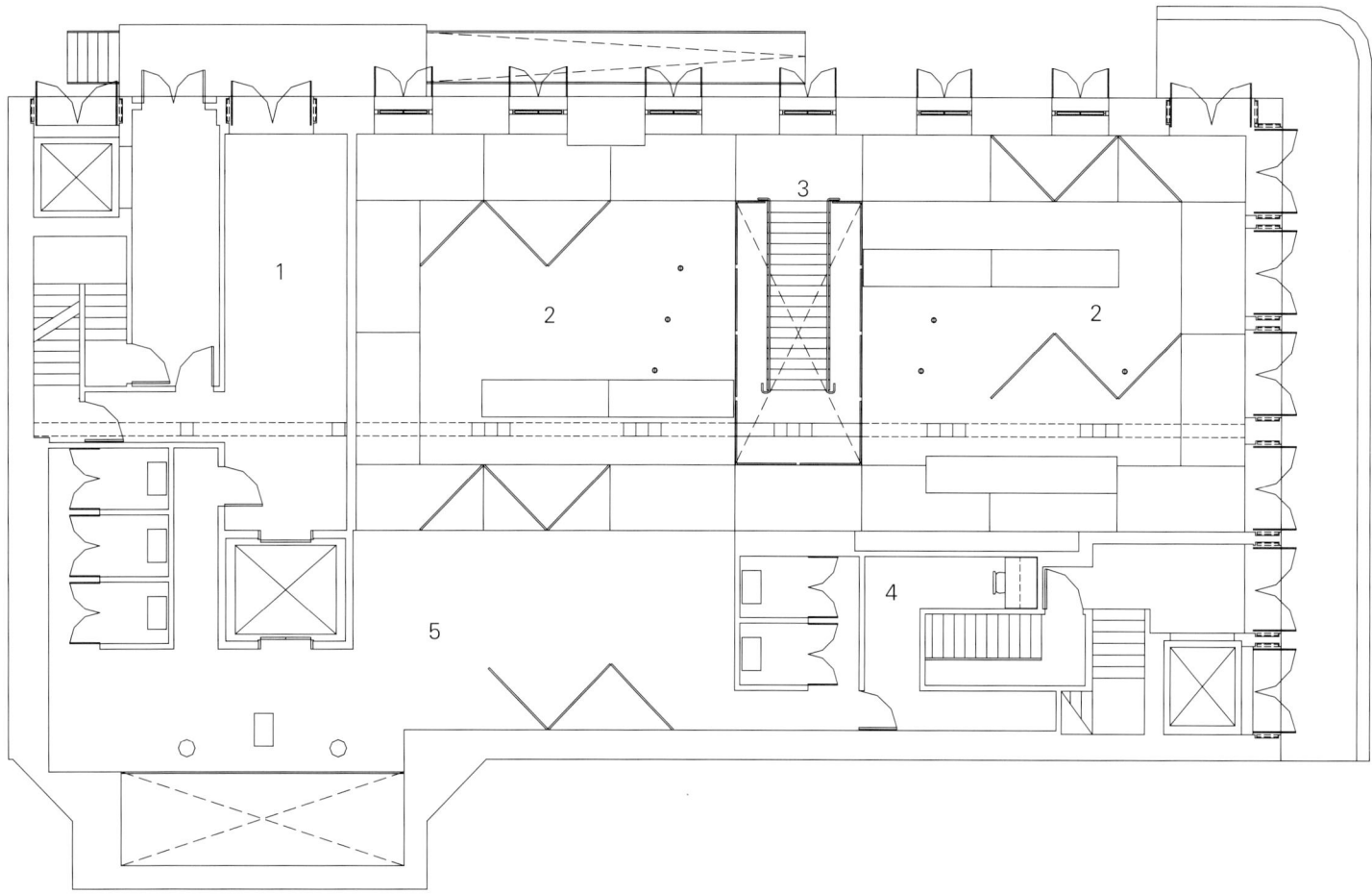

Ground floor plan

01. Entrance lobby

02. Showroom

03. Stairway

04. Offices

05. Collections

06. Reception

07. Customer lounge

08. Toilets

09. Press

10. Fitting room

11. Administration

The ground floor is the main selling area with 2876 sqft of retail space, with the rest of the space dedicated to storage and service space and the entrance lobby. The cellar floor features a 700 sqft showroom, ample retail space and a customer lounge.

Part of Frank Gehry's titanium 'tornado' sculpture is seen on the preceding page. The piece extends from a shaft emerging from the cellar floor to a turbulent sprawl engulfing the ceiling of the ground floor. Built from ultra-thin gauge titanium, it was shipped to the site in flat 4 x 8 foot sheets. There, Gordon Kipping and a team of architect volunteers bent it to match the project model and adhered it to a steel armature with Velcro pads.

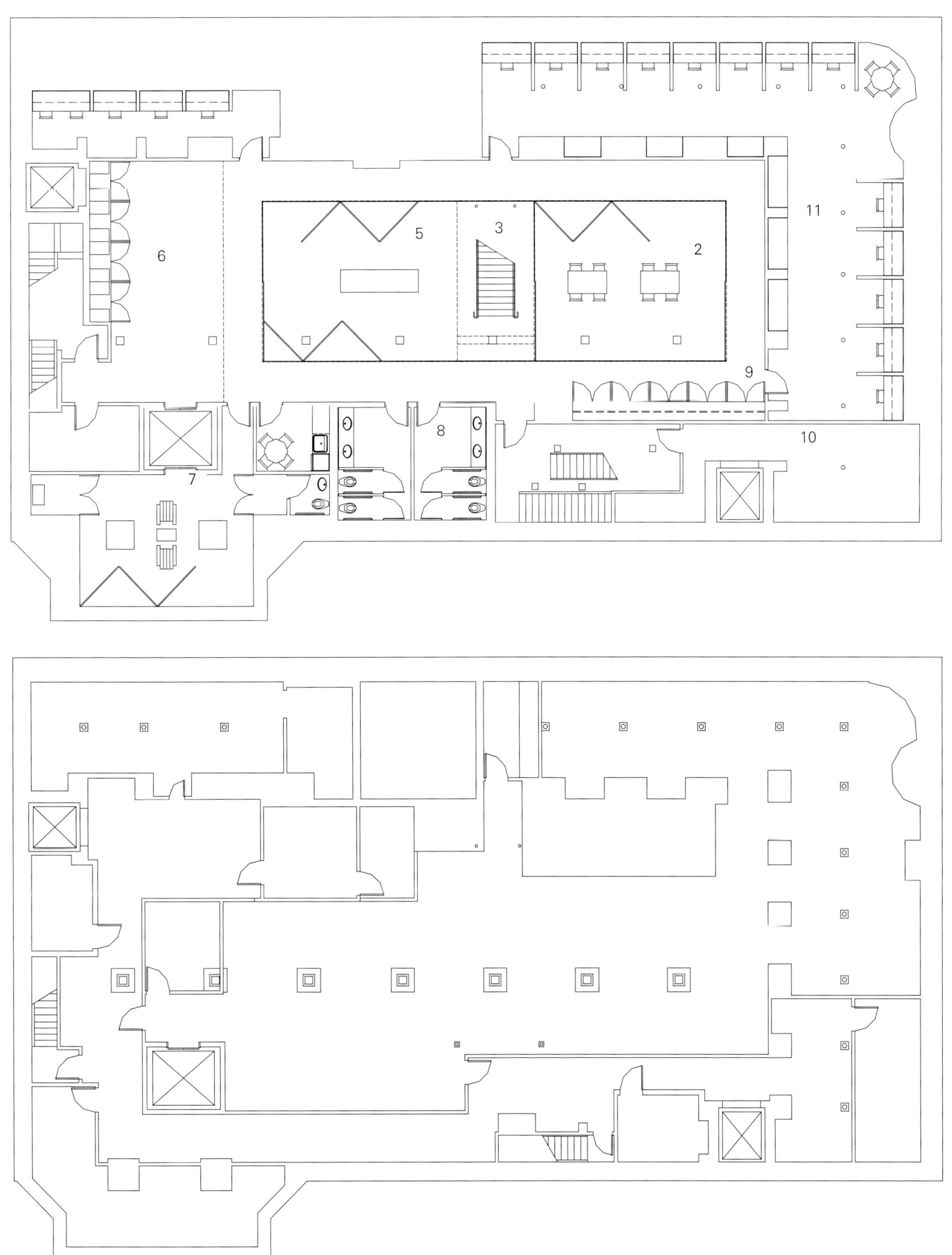

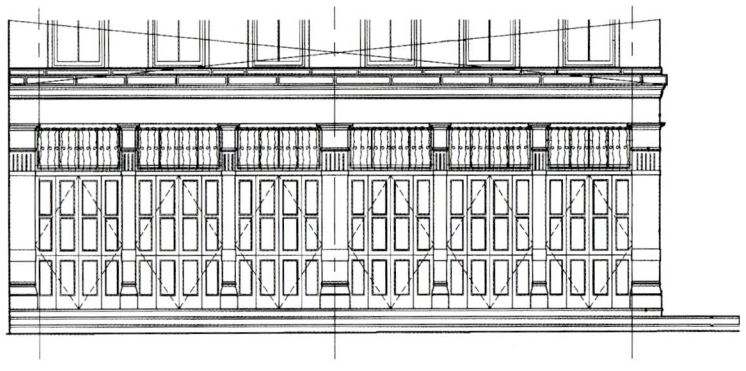

East elevation   Elevation (Shutters closed)

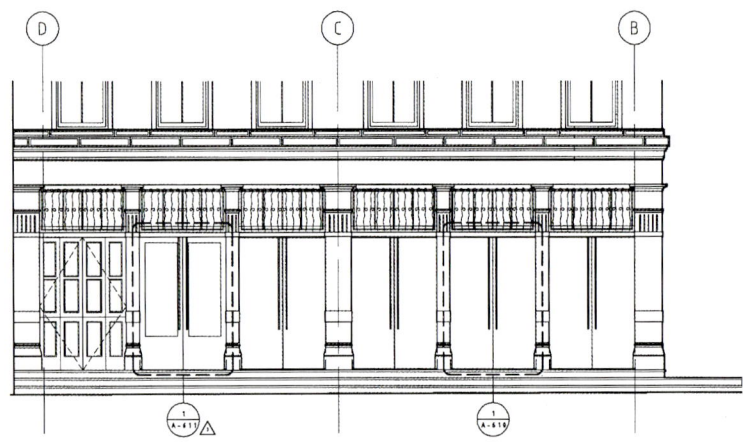

Elevation (Shutters open)

The cast iron ground floor façade of the late 19th century building was brought to a bare metal finish and sealed with a clear coat. Granite and Bluestone courses on the N. Moore Street façade were stripped and re-caulked. The stepped vault with glass lens sheathing on Hudson Street was cleaned, repaired and painted. The six story building façade was cleaned and repainted.

All fixtures, which were custom designed by G TECTS LLC, are moveable for flexibility. Benches and tables are bent from stainless steel sheet.

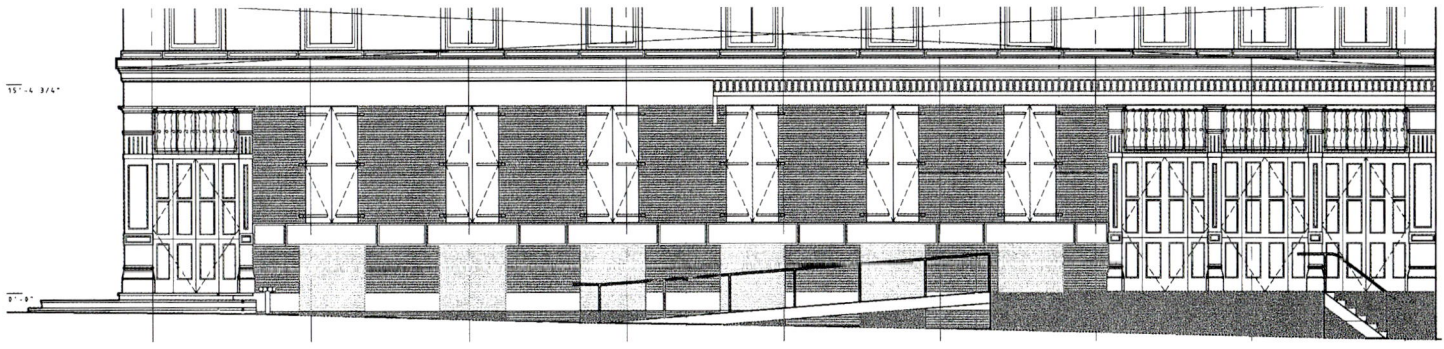

Elevation (Shutters closed)

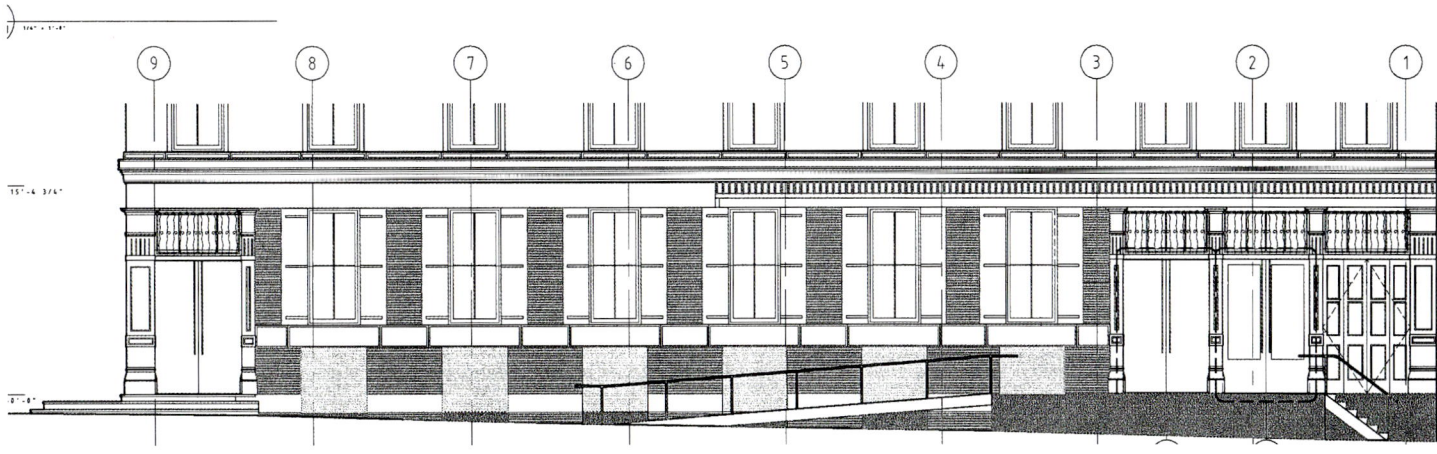

Elevation (Shutters open)

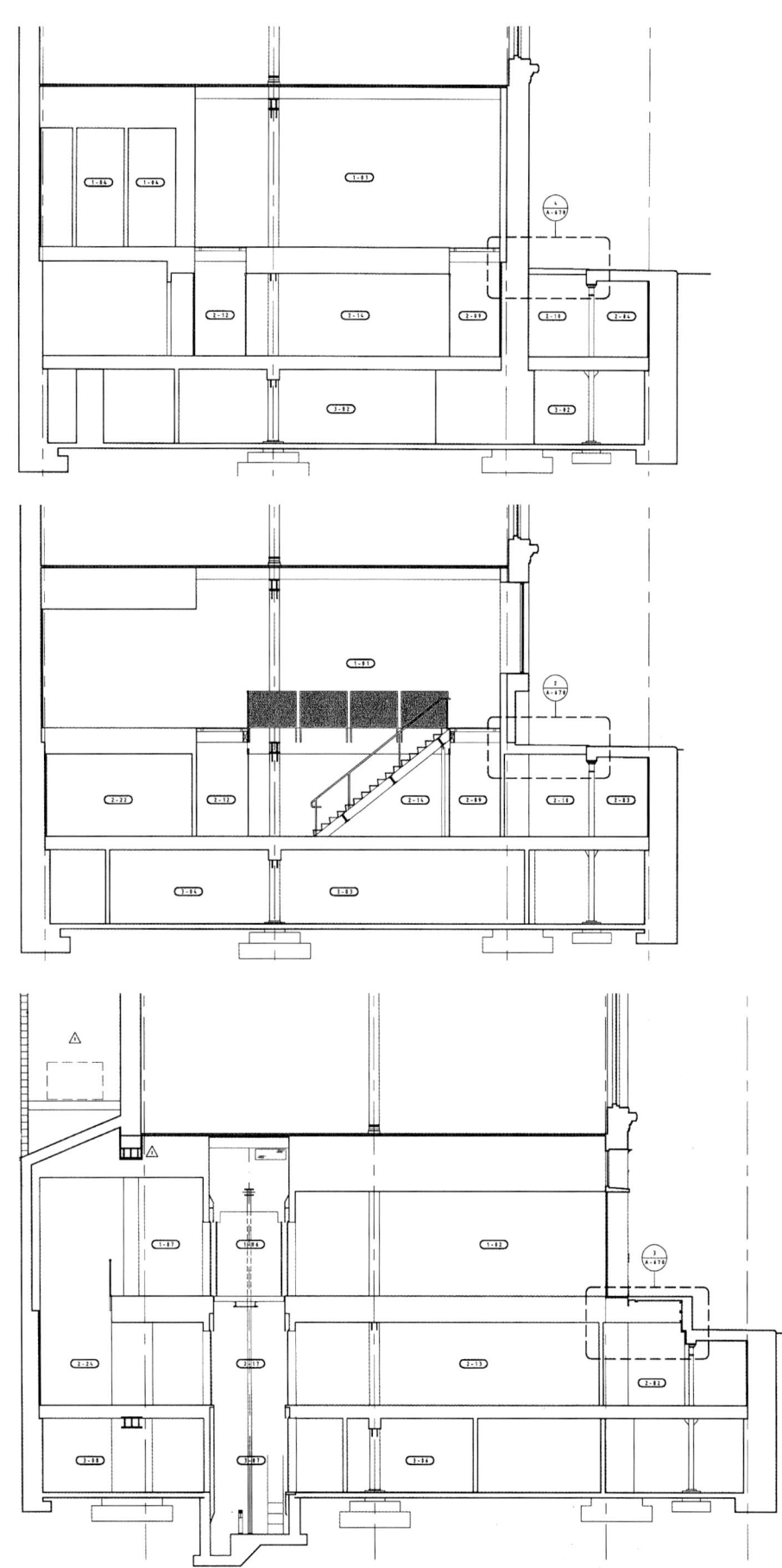

Cross sections

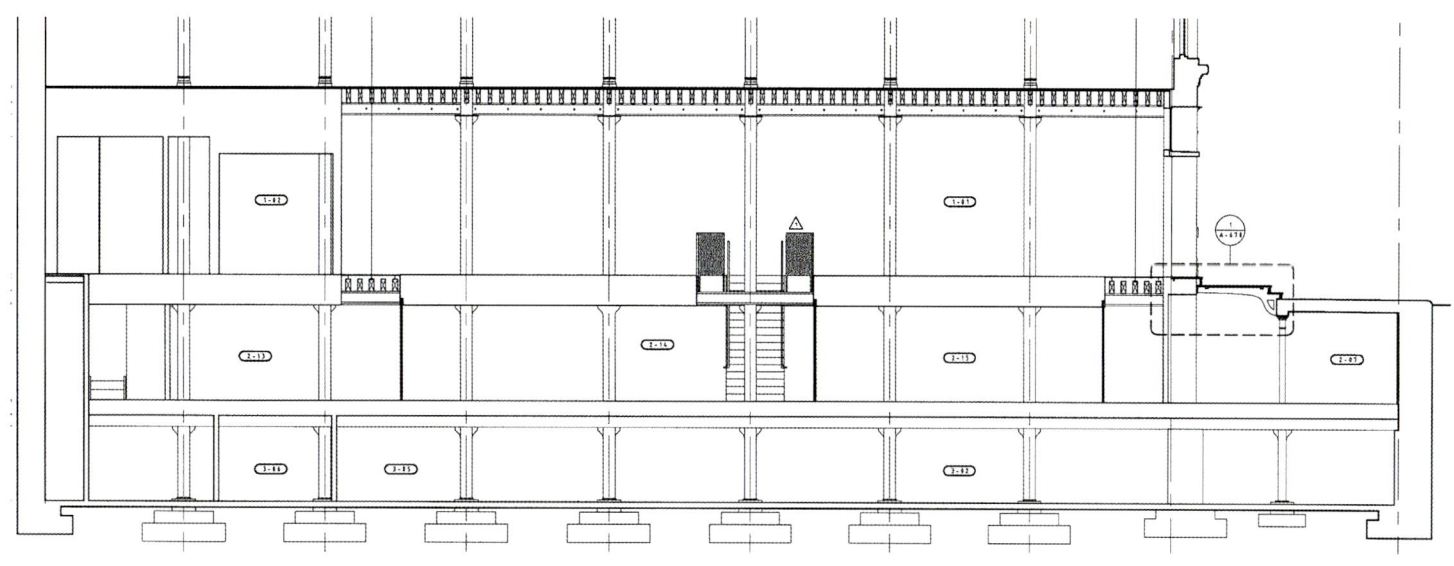

Longitudinal section

Support detail, section

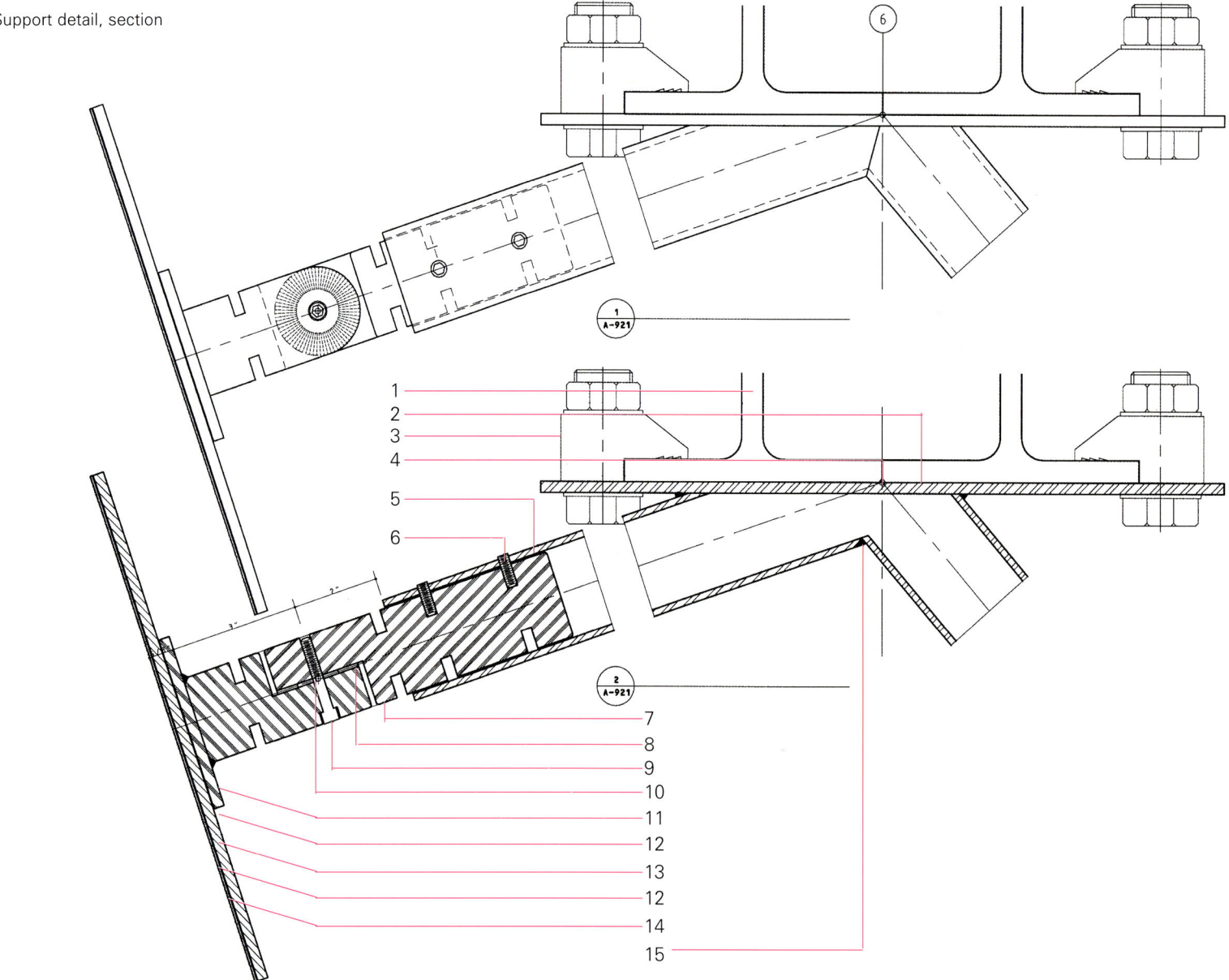

01. Existing cast iron beam

02. Steel plate

03. Type B MLB100 clamp by lindapter

04. Point of intersection of secondary support, centerline & cast iron beam

05. Secondary support, 2"dia. Schedule 40 steel pipe

06. ¼" -20 dia. by ¾" long socket set screw, w/ ratchet locking action

07. Stainless steel 2 piece elbow

08. Adjacent elbow surfaces w/ radial saw tooth serration

09. ¼" -20 dia. by 2" long socket head cap screw

10. Point of projected intersection of secondary support centerline & elbow pivot point

11. ¼" stainless steel plate

12. Adhesive

13. ¼" neoprene sheet

14. Industrial Velcro pad

15. Full penetration groove weld all around

16. Point of projected intersection of primary & secondary support centerlines

17. Primary support

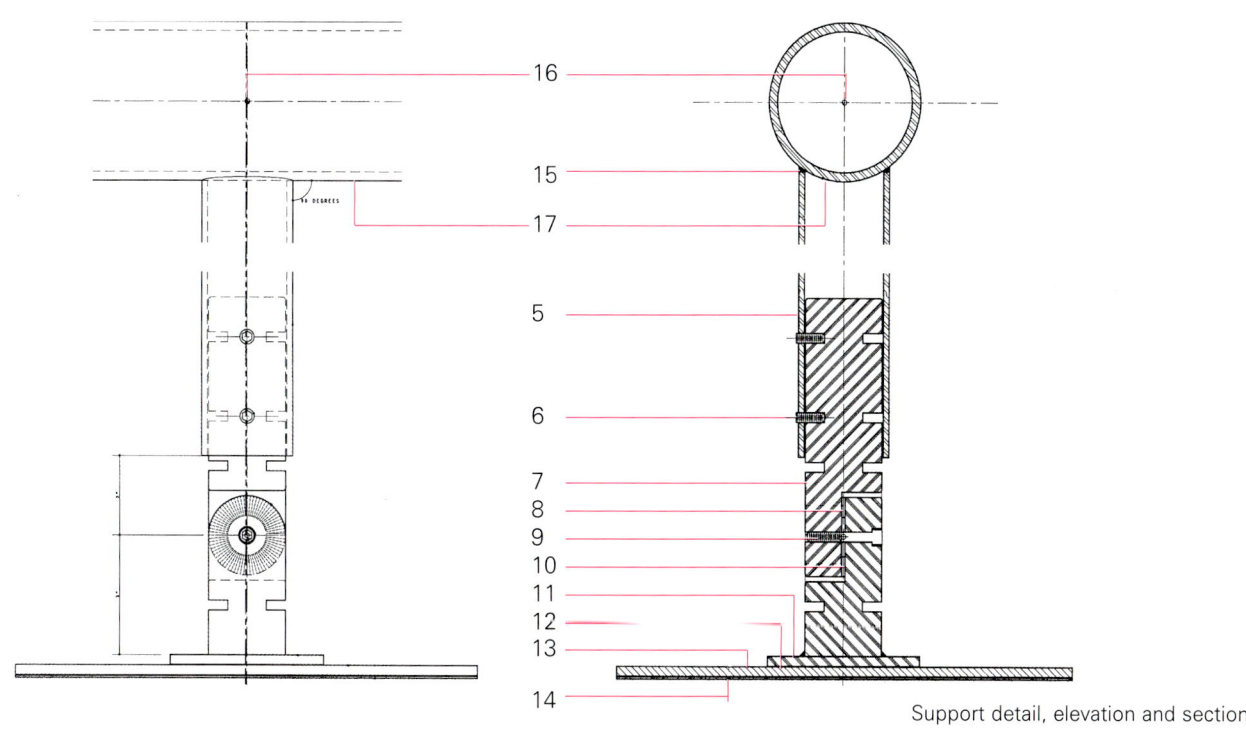

16

15

17

5

6

7
8
9
10
11
12
13

14

Support detail, elevation and section

Corneille Uedingslohmann

Little Red Riding Hood GmbH

Berlin, Germany *Photographs: Joachim Wagner*

The story of Little Red Riding Hood is the world of fashion label LRRH. With its newly opened flagship store in Berlin Mitte, it offers an area for fashion, accessories, books and music within the context of the Grimm narrative. The inventory consists of: mannequins with wolf heads, clothes, shoes and jewelry. It also features beautifully illustrated books from different countries, which show the well-known fairy tale, along with magazines like 'Alert' and 'Parkett' alongside the latest CDs.

With the opening of its flagship store, LRRH gives life to a completely new sales concept, which is a symbiosis of fashion, art and modern media spread over two stories. The newest Prêt à Porter creations of the label are presented beside selected assortments of fashion, accessories, recent books, radio plays and music. The planned exhibitions which will rotate every three months will include artists from fashion, media and performance art. With every new presentation LRRH hopes to allow the artists to represent themselves from their own standpoint as well as show the connection between the performer and the label.

The spatial realization of the store was conceived as a three-dimensional scene of this fantastic fairy tale.

It comprises one space divided into two levels. With a size of only 33sqm on the ground floor, the entrance is reduced to its bare function. The stairwell flows by a large projection screen that depicts the surreal images akin to the world of the fairy tale and into the basement which is ten times larger.

The interior of the construction is formed from white fiberglass and is a contrast to the heterogeneous surrounding of the Friedrichstrasse and fades out the external world in favor of that of the fairy tale one in the basement.

The cross section of the wall covering is constantly changing and forms niches, curvatures and recesses for the presentation of merchandise. The production quality of the individual elements is exemplary. In Germany there are hardly any examples of this technology in a continuous form especially in this order of magnitude. Even if design and conception as well as the computer files represent an ideal basis for a file-to-factory procedure, such a process remains to be one of prototypes, compromise and persistence. The use of a 3-D plotter, as in the stereo lithography, is for this type of project somewhat unrealistic due to the fact that they can only produce small objects.

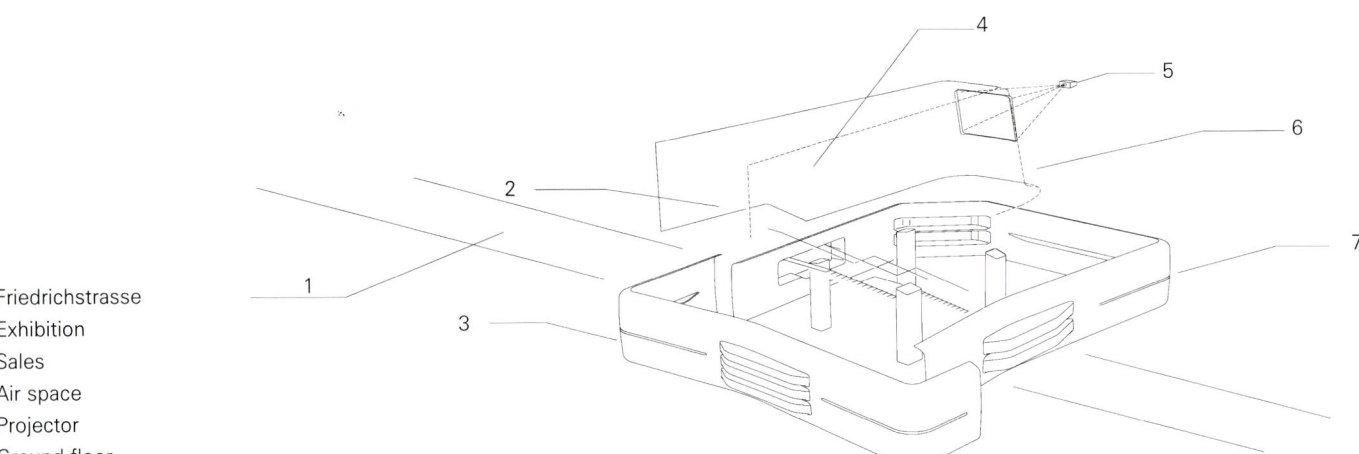

1. Friedrichstrasse
2. Exhibition
3. Sales
4. Air space
5. Projector
6. Ground floor
7. Basement

The exposed ceiling with its visible ductwork and lighting fixtures increases the dreamlike effect of the wall coverings due to their strong contrast. The flooring is also left raw with an unpolished lacquer finish and functions mainly as a backdrop for the precisely planned and constructed wall surfaces. The computer-generated 'continuous loop' fiberglass form was prefabricated into 7 meter sections and positioned on-site.

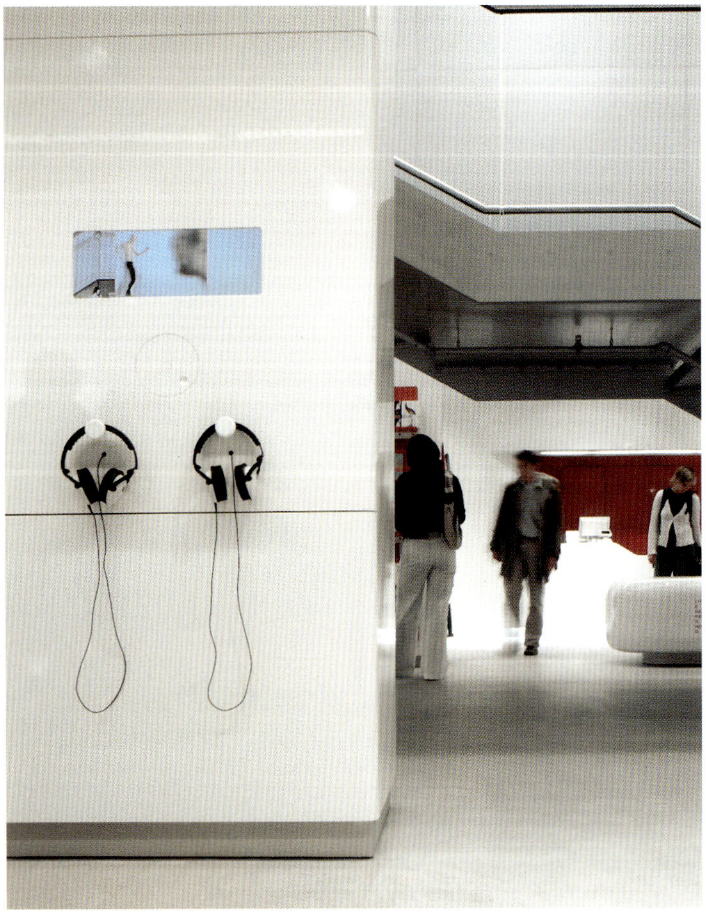

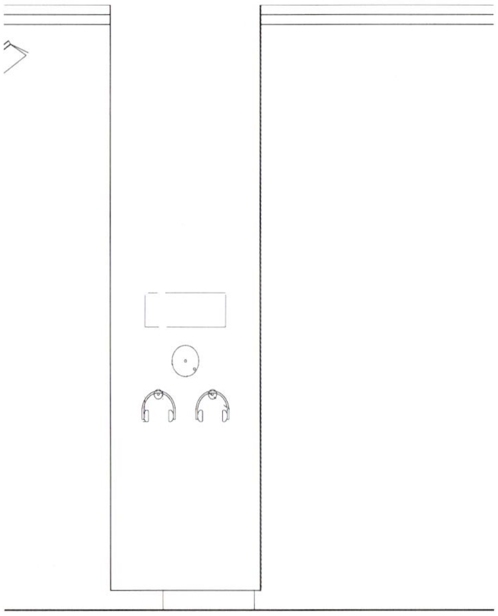

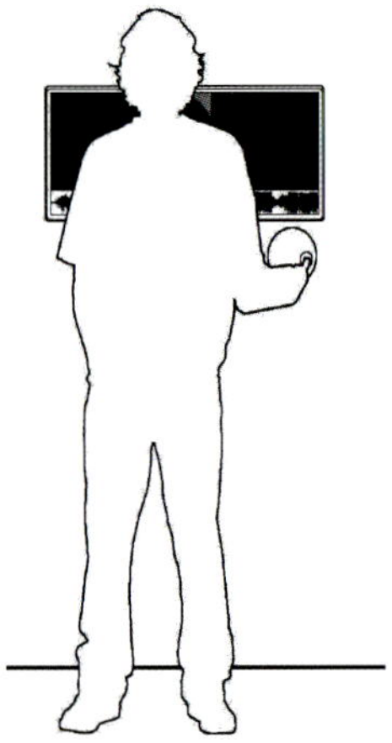

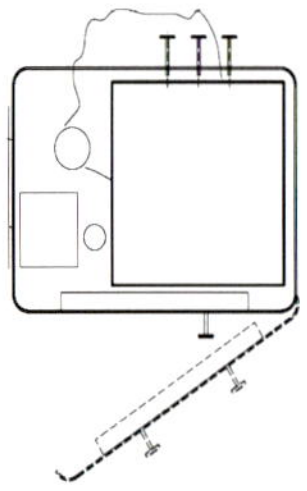

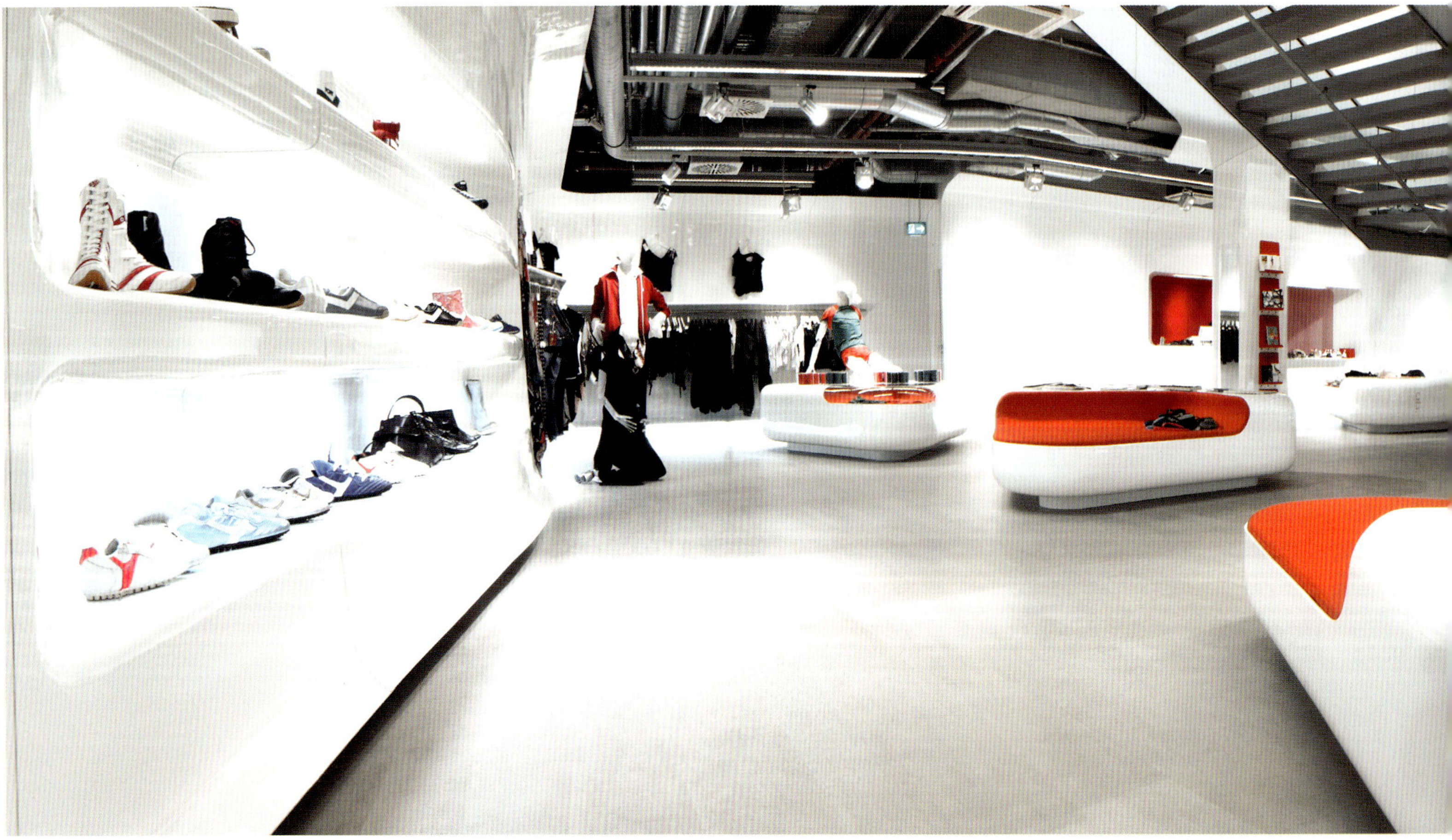

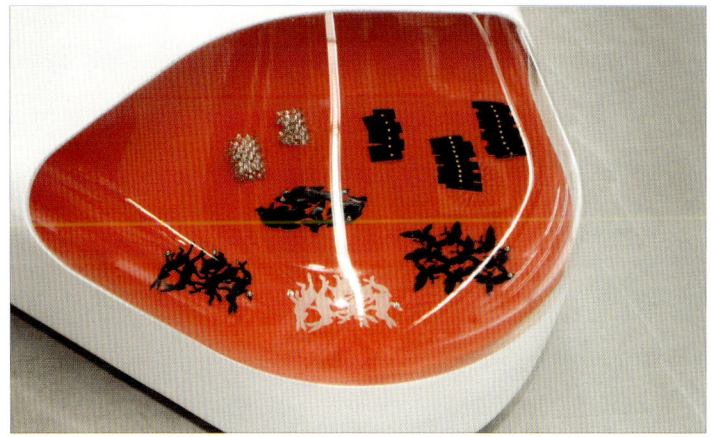

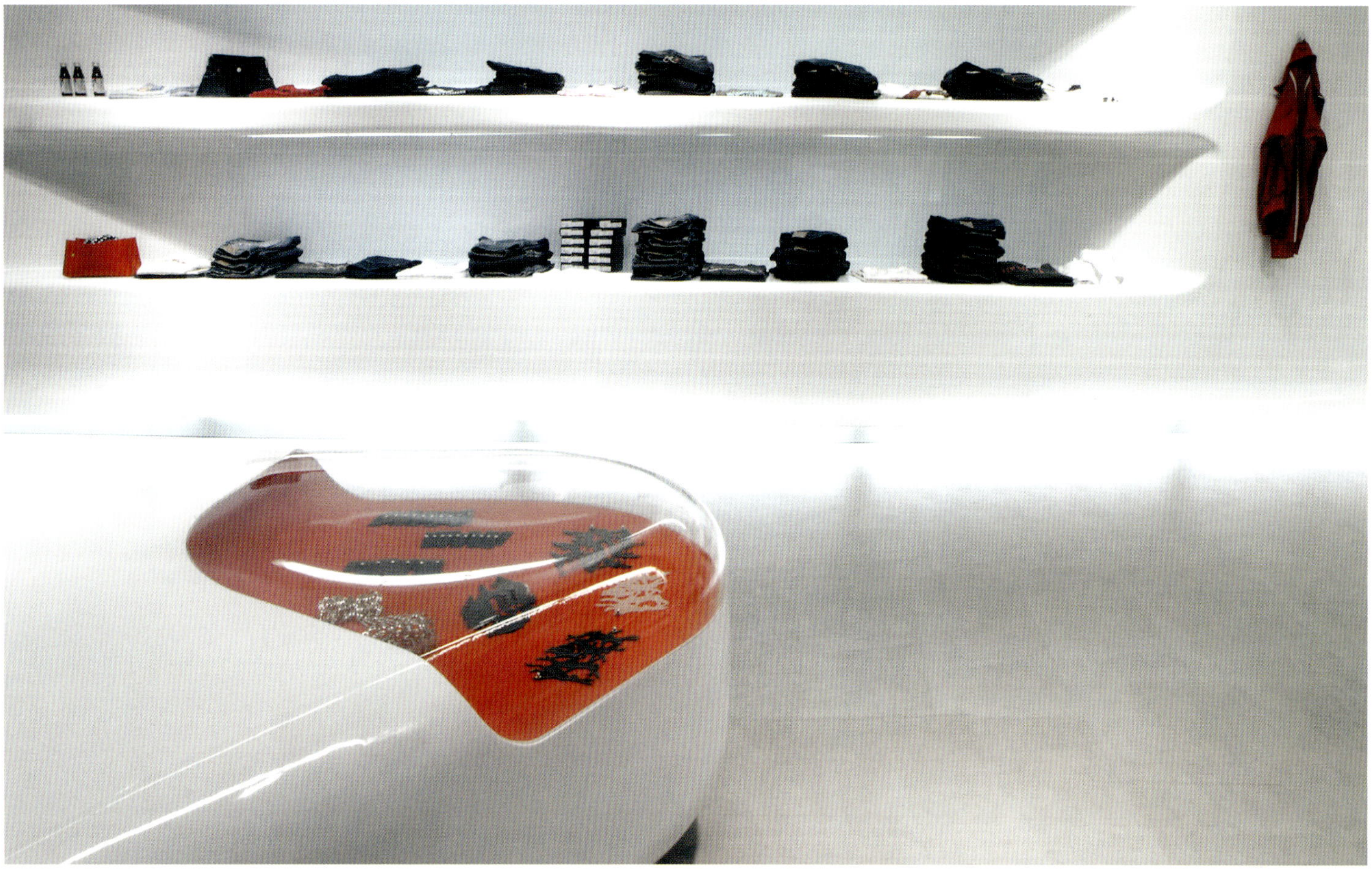

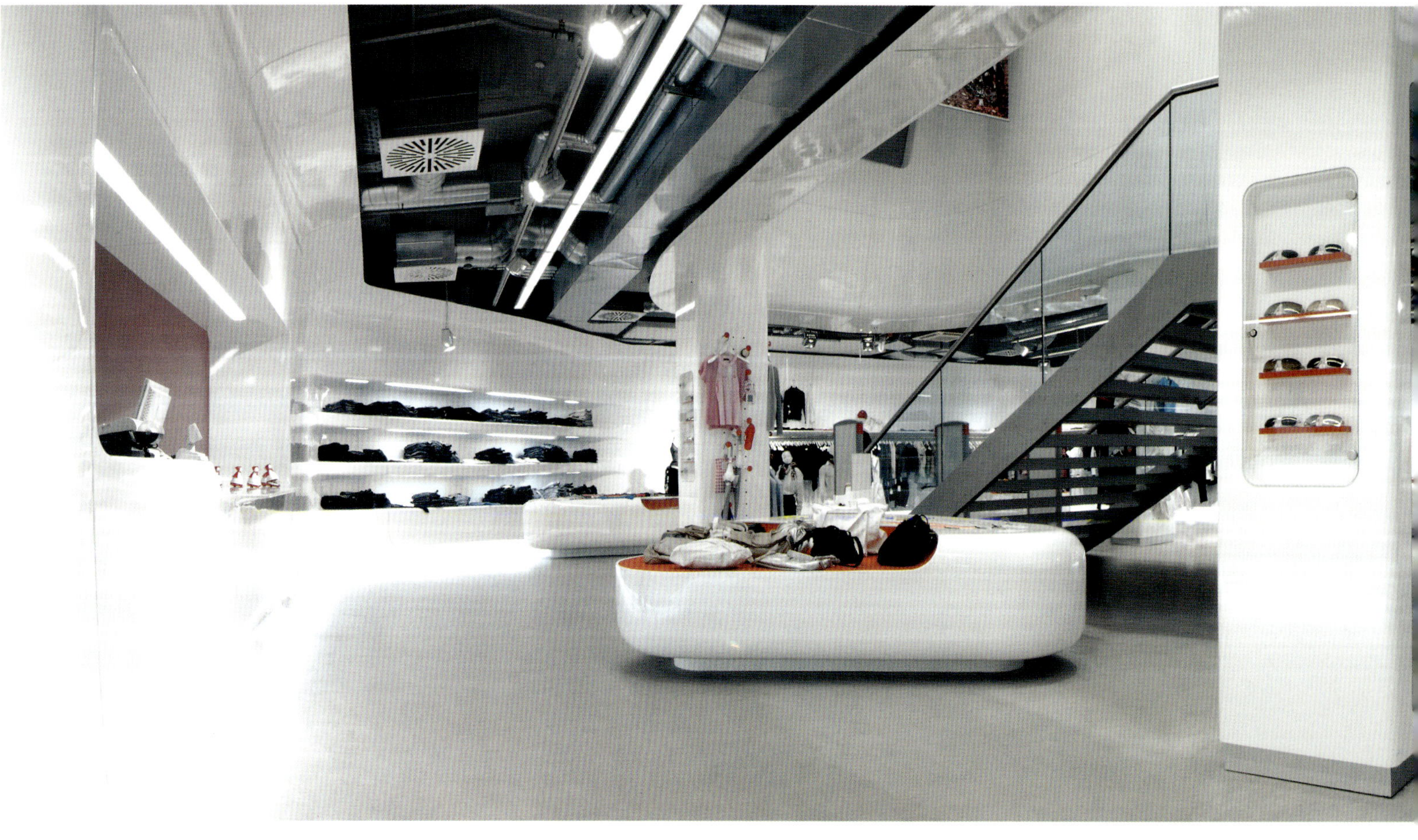

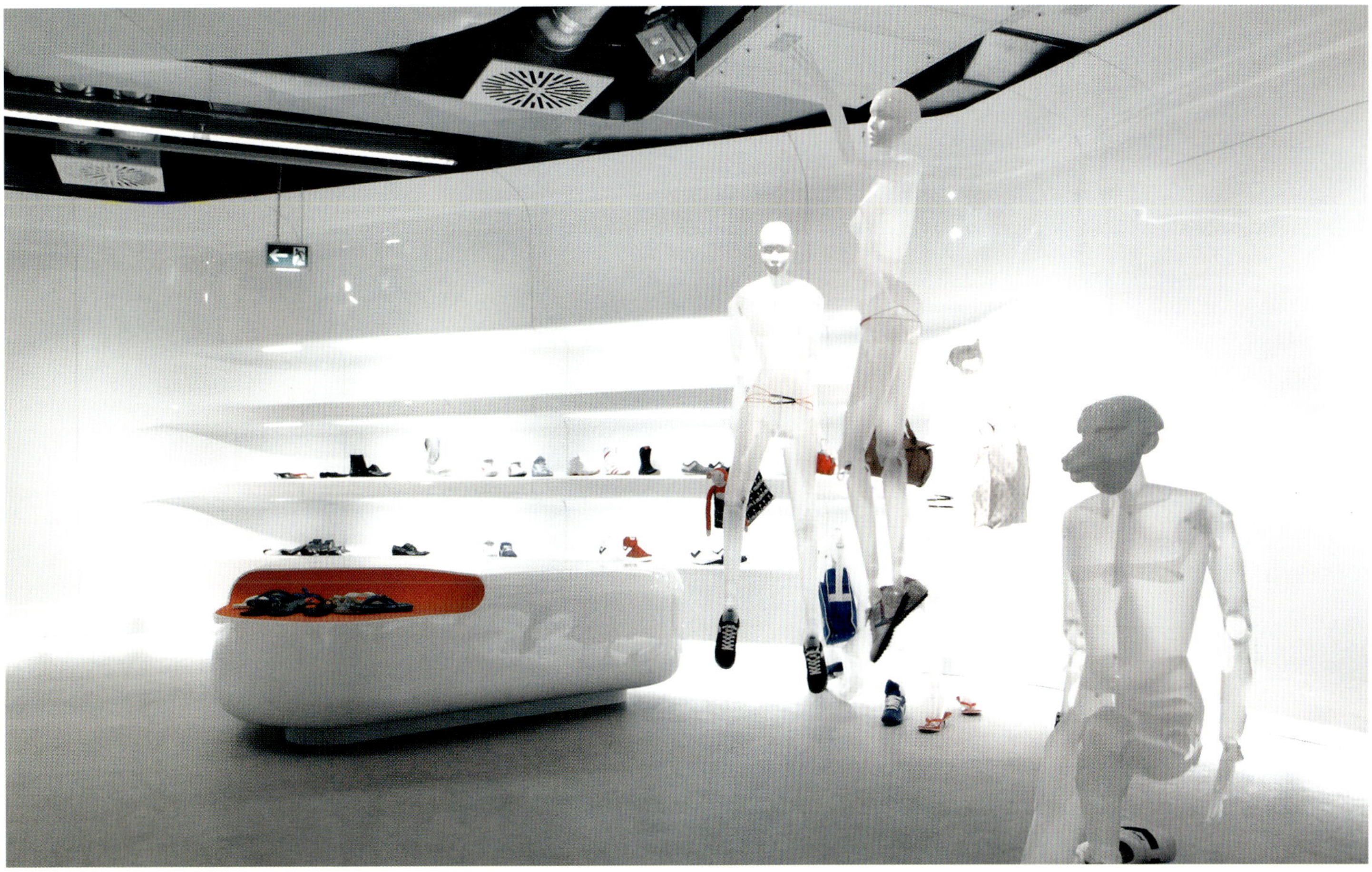

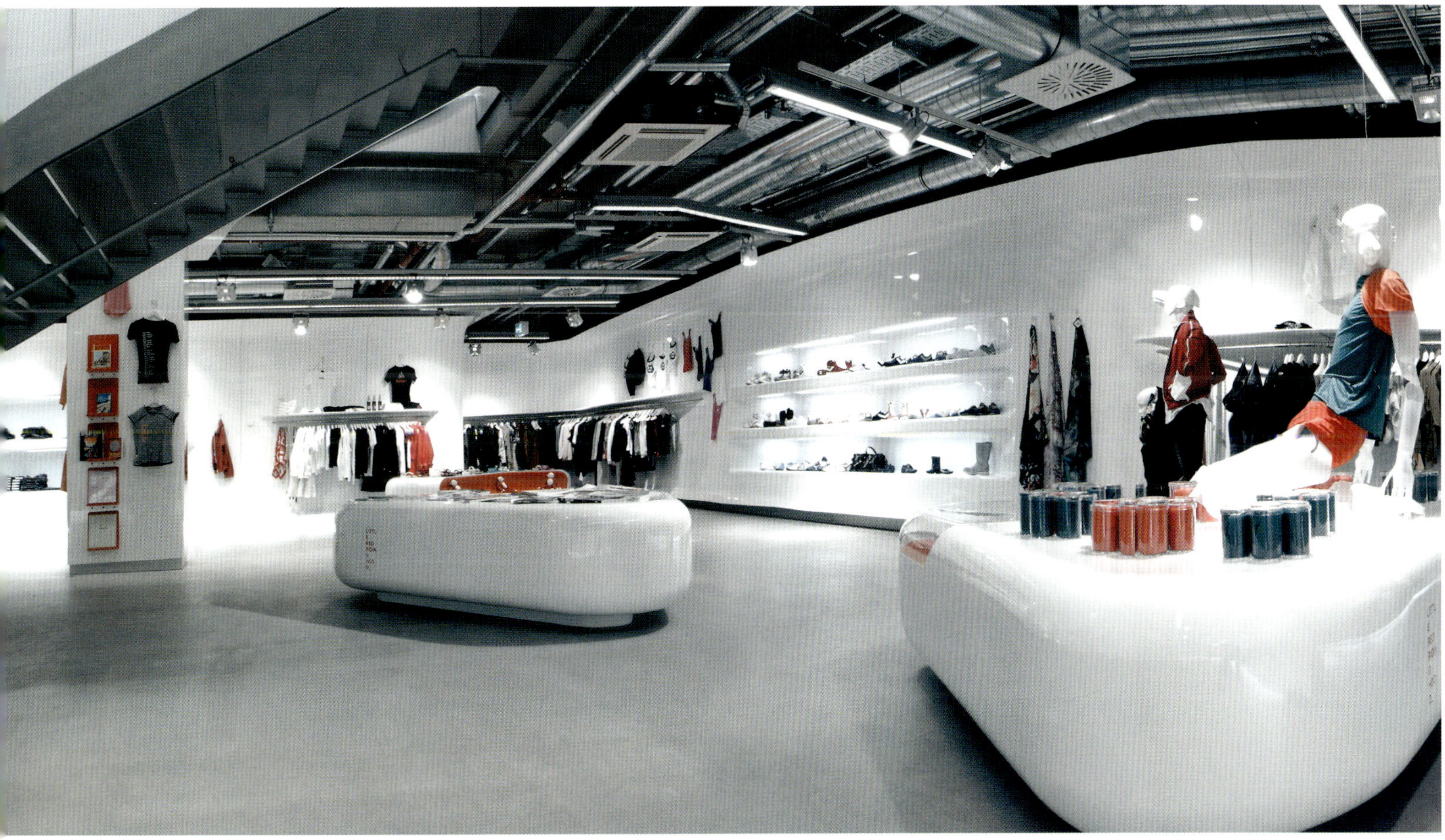

Renzo Piano Building Workshop

Maison Hermès

Tokyo, Japan *Photographs: Michel Denancé*

The French Group Hermès chose a 6000 sqm building in Tokyo's Ginza district for its Japanese headquarters. This project was both aesthetically and technically challenging. How, in the architectural diversity of Tokyo, could a "landmark" building be conceived, one that would also comply with Japan's strict earthquake standards?

The idea of a "magic lantern" like those hung in the doors of Japanese houses soon arose; a facade made entirely from 45x45 cm glass blocks successfully imparts this aspect of the design.

The innovative anti-seismic system was inspired by traditional Japanese temples that are still standing despite frequent earthqakes. The back-bone of this building is made up of a flexible steel structure that is articulated at structurally strategic locations with visco-elastic dampers, from which cantilevered floors extend to support the suspended glass-block facades.

The entire building can move during earthquakes, thanks to predefined displacements, uniformly distributed throughout the structure.

A small, open square at the center connects the street to the subway station via a long escalator. A mobile sculpture by the artist Susumu Shingu overlooks this space from atop the building.

The floor plan of this 15-floor-building measures 45x11 meters. As a response to Japan's strict seismic controls, the backbone of the building is made up of a flexible steel structure that is articulated at structurally strategic points with visco-elastic dampers, from which cantilevered floors extend to support the suspended glass-block facades.

Ground floor plan

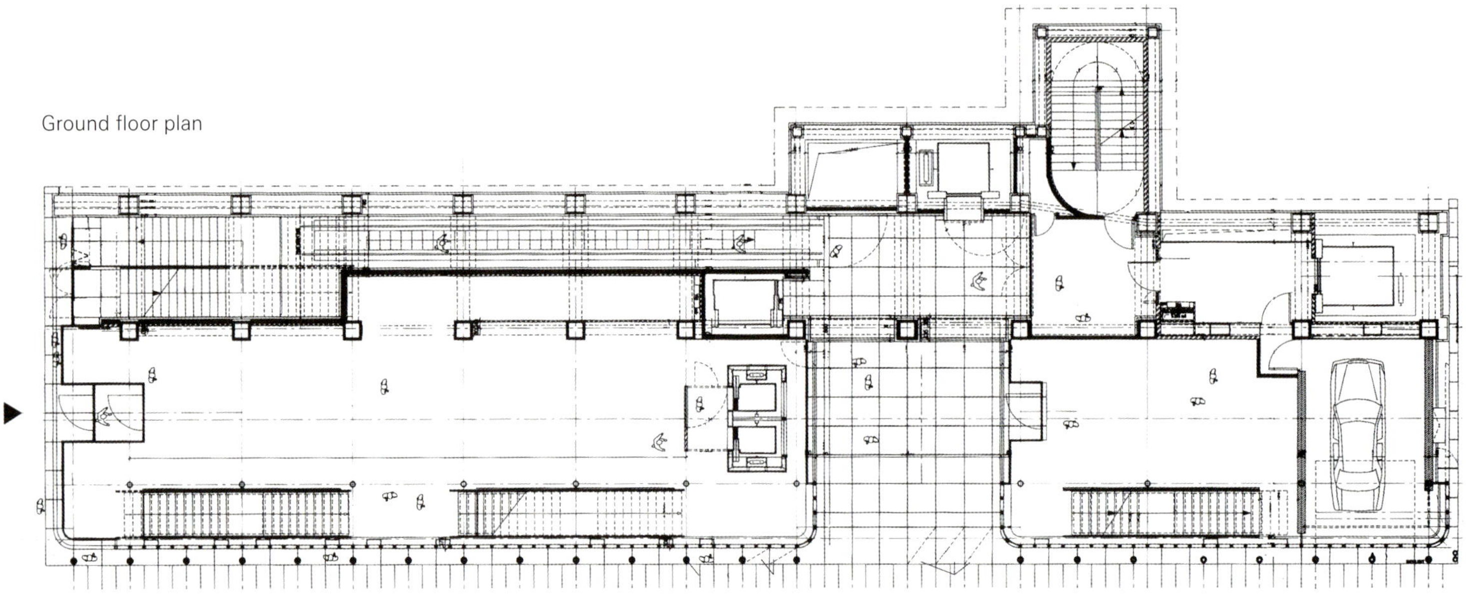

Second floor plan

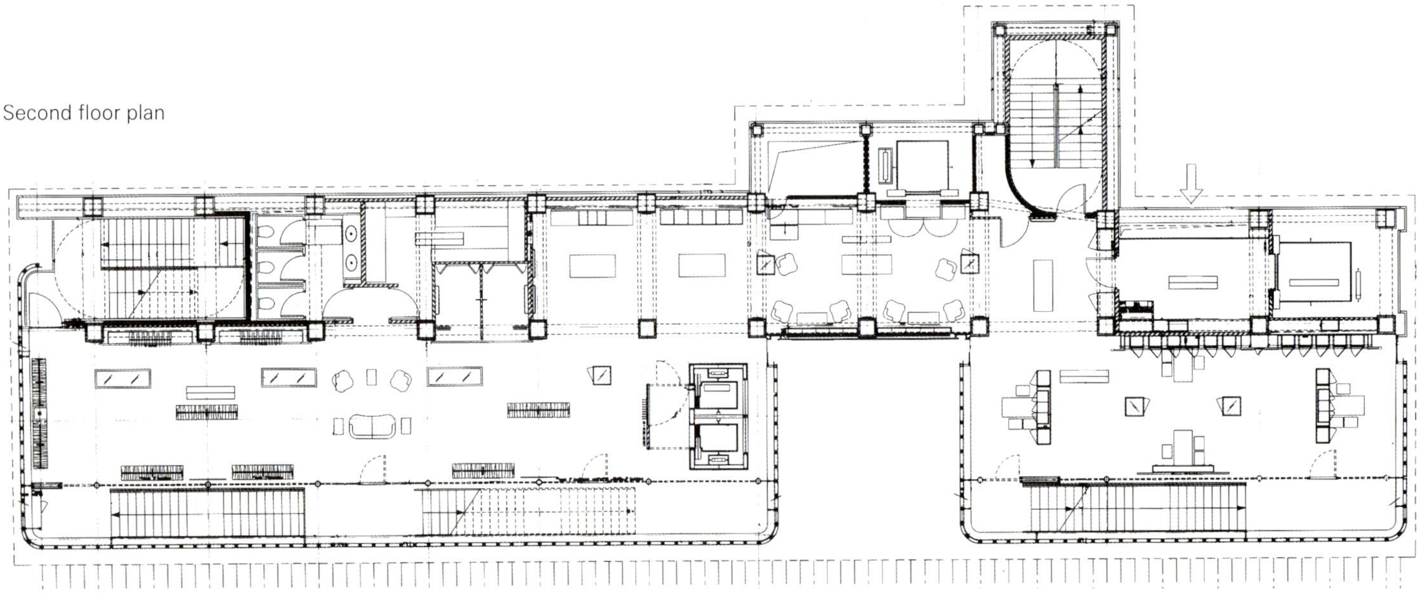

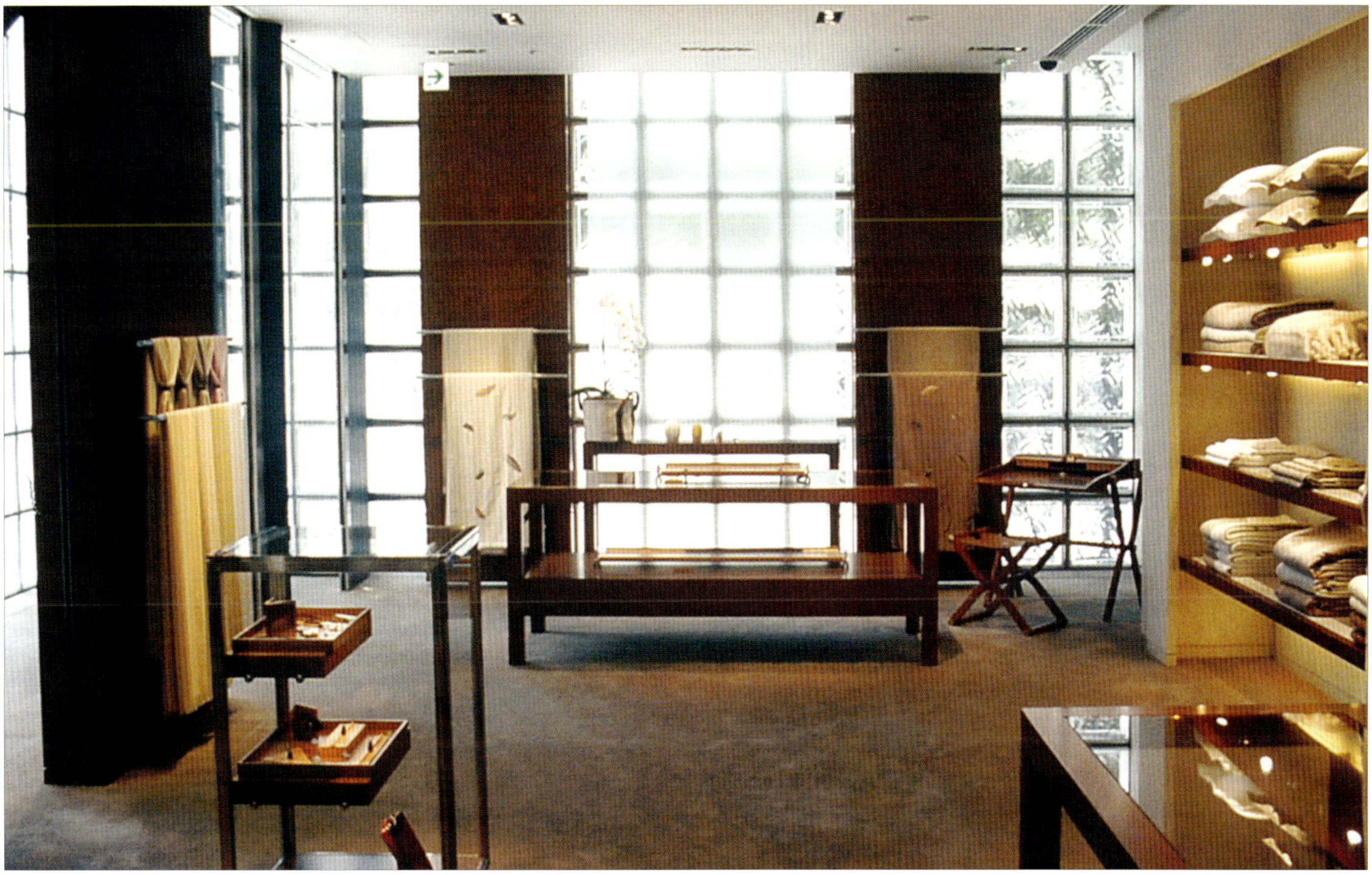

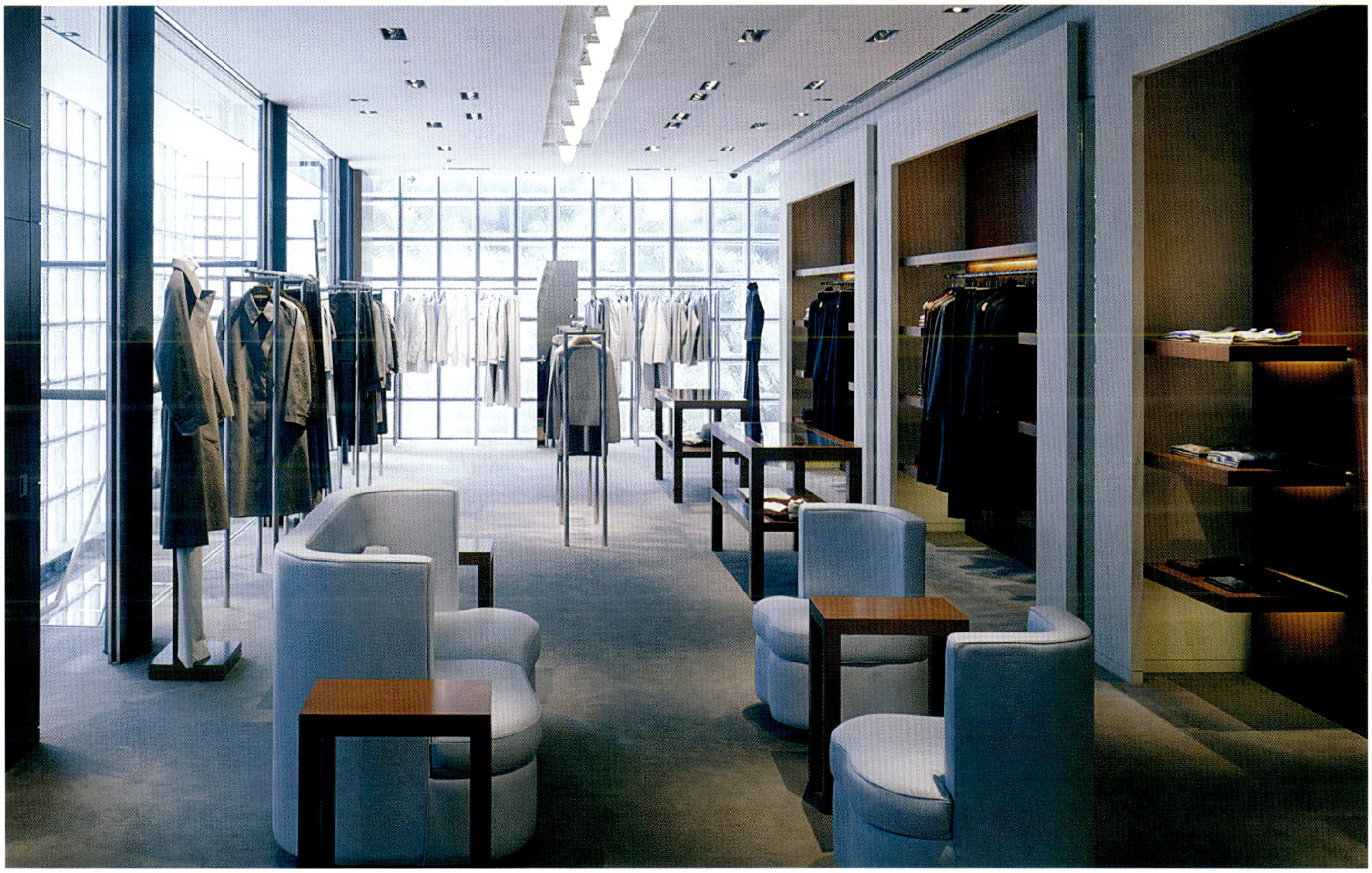

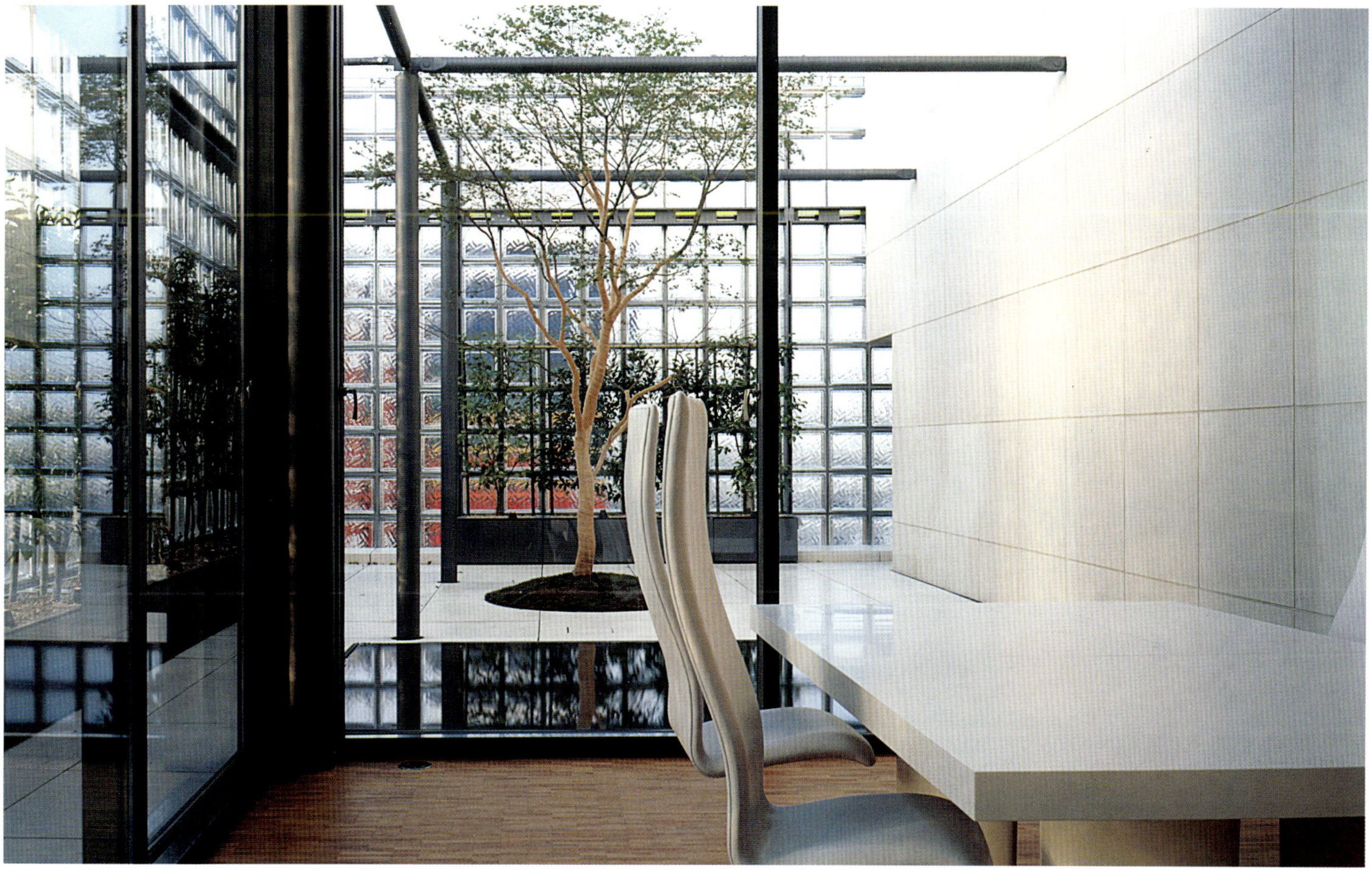

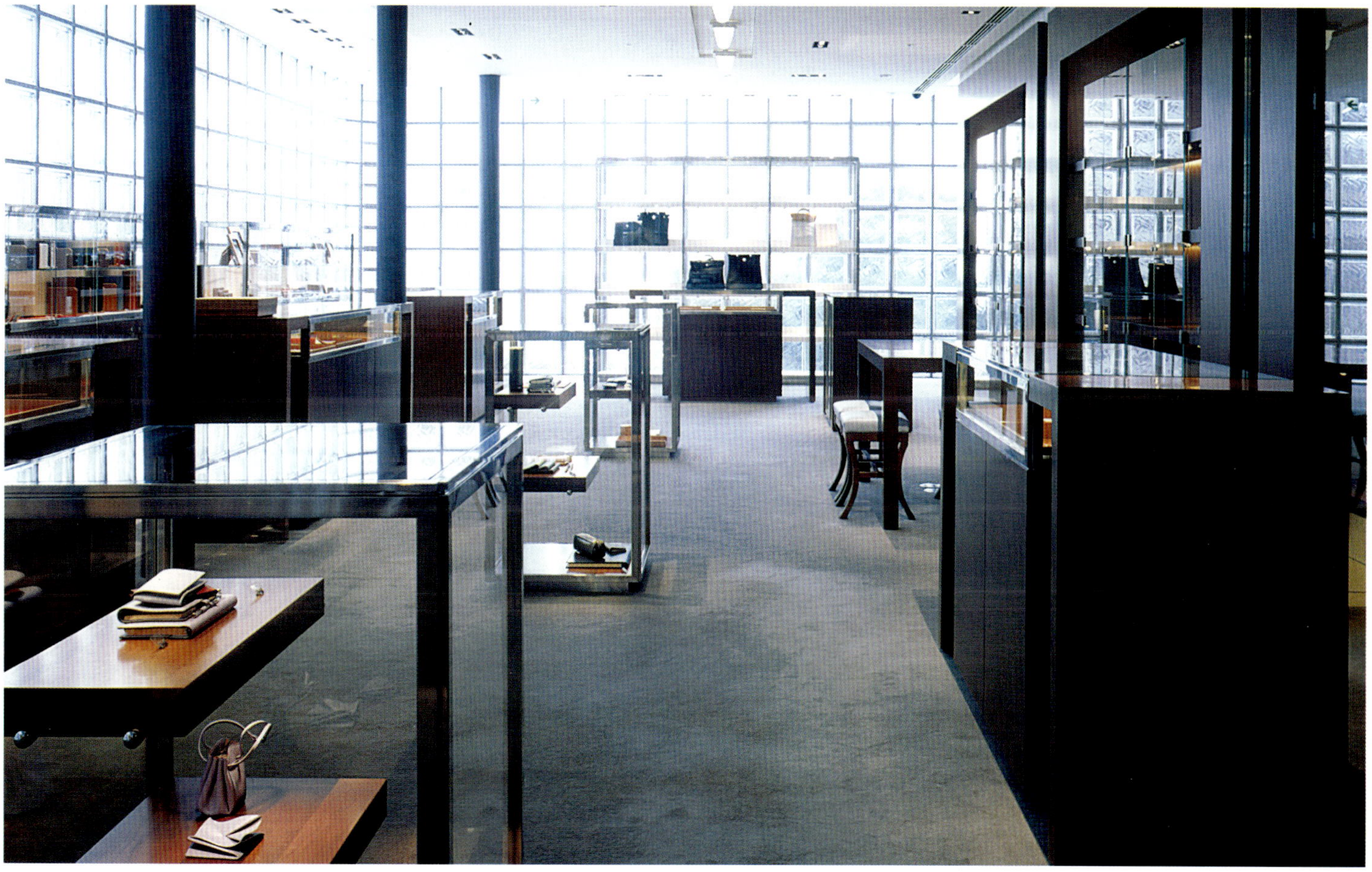

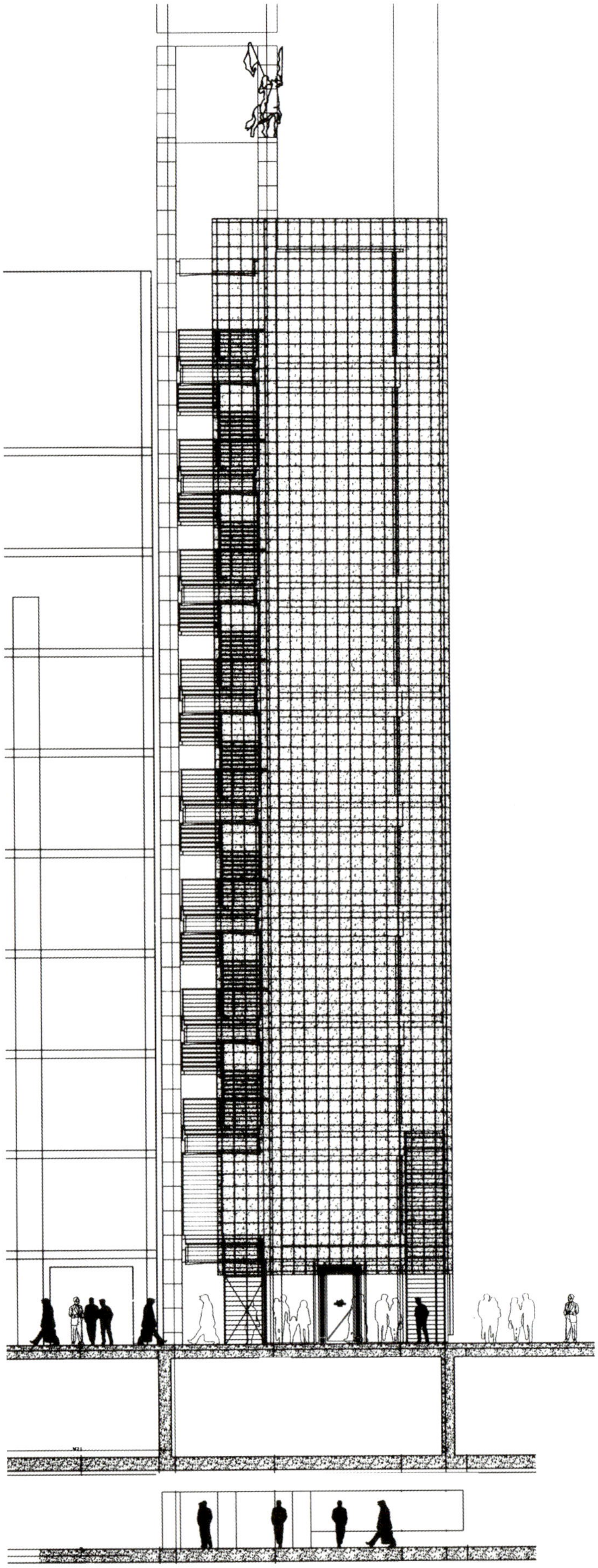

North elevation

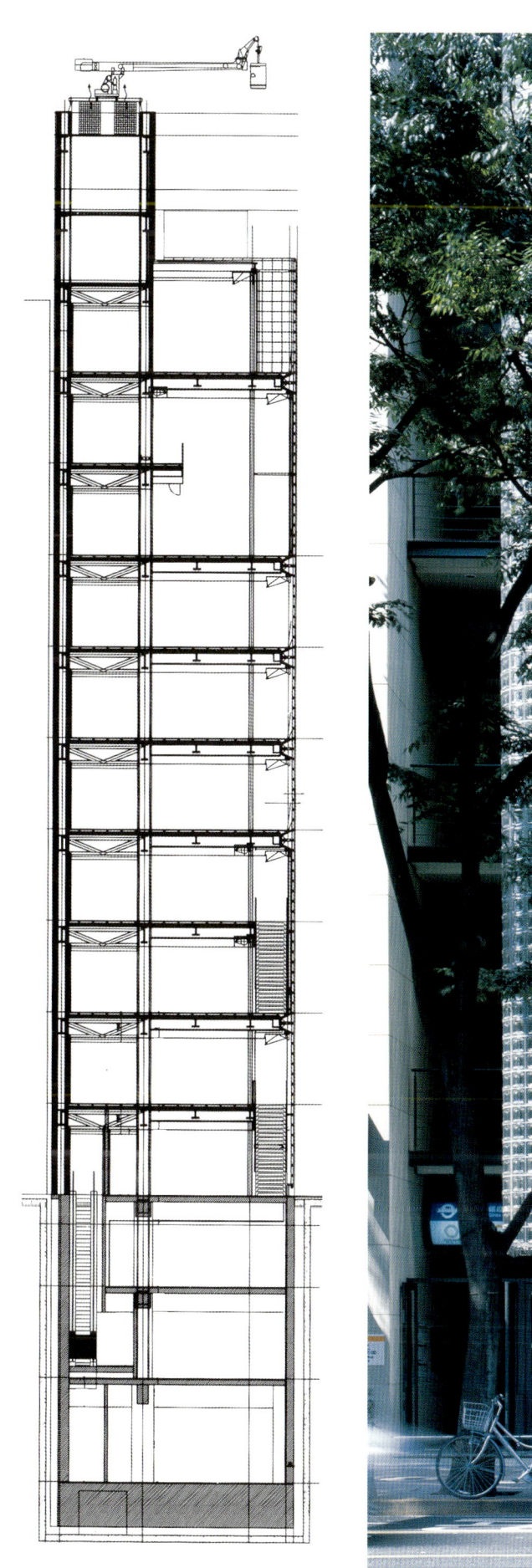

Cross section

The façades are entirely made up of 45x45 cm glass blocks, which give it the desired "magic lantern" effect, inspired by traditional lamps hung in the doorways of Japanese houses. In the event of an earthquake, the whole building has been designed to move, according to pre-defined displacements uniformly distributed throughout the entire structure. Each element of the construction would absorb a given portion of the shock.

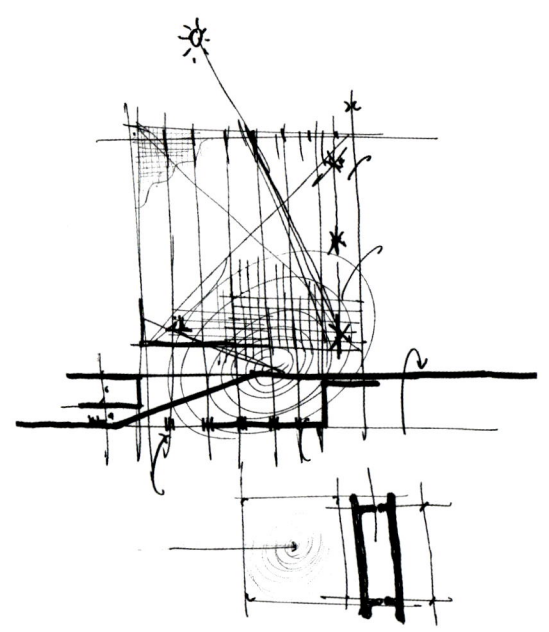

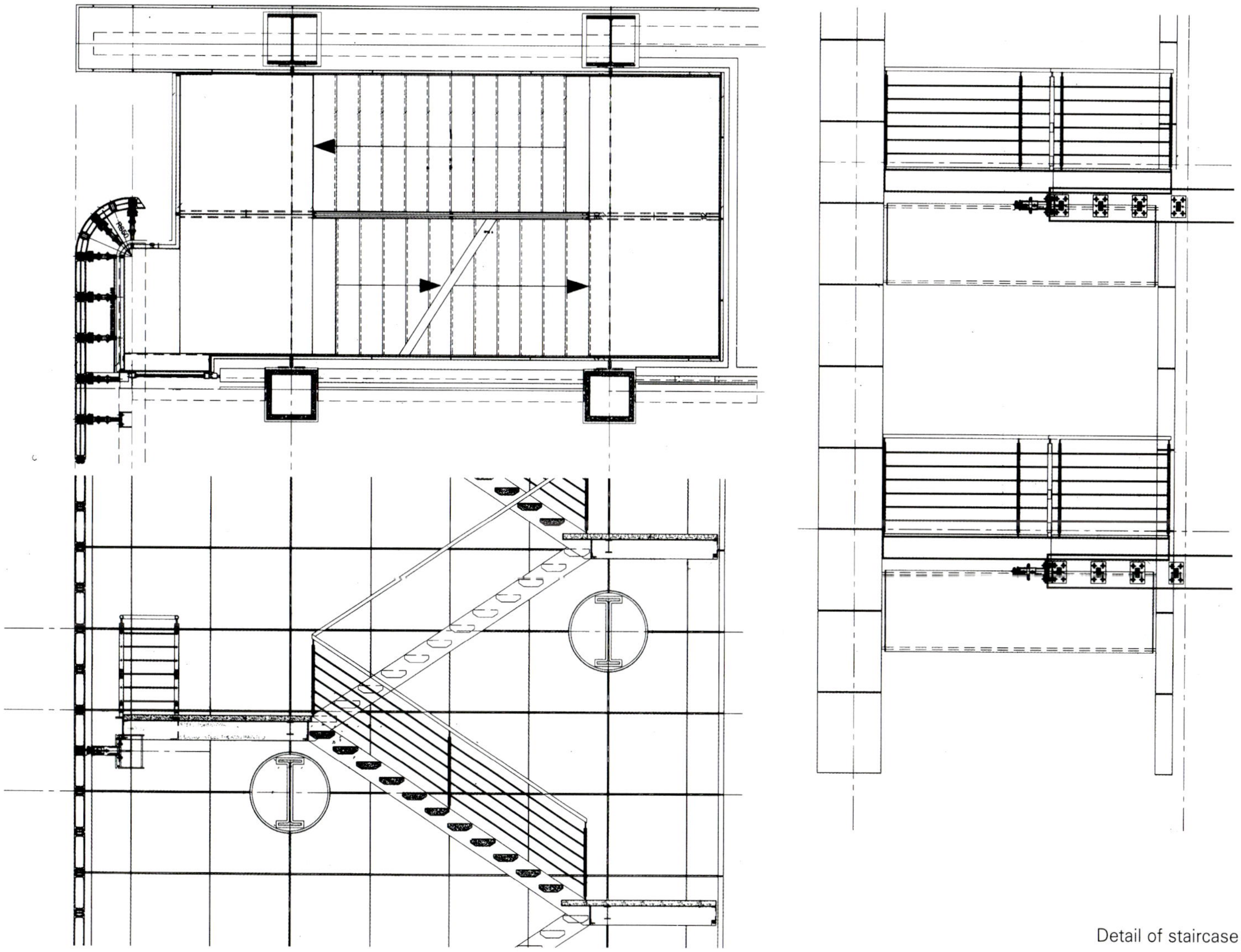

Detail of staircase

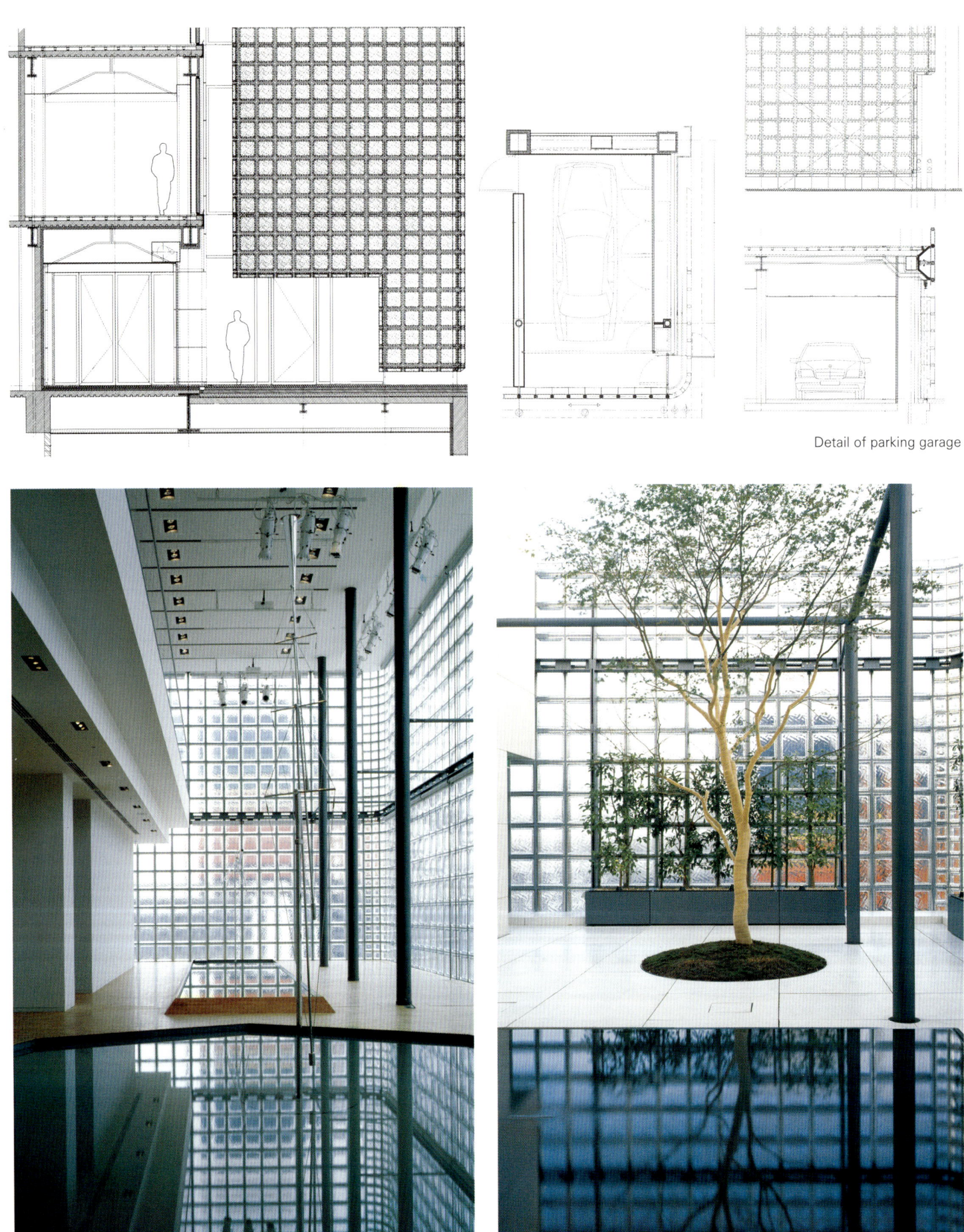

Detail of parking garage

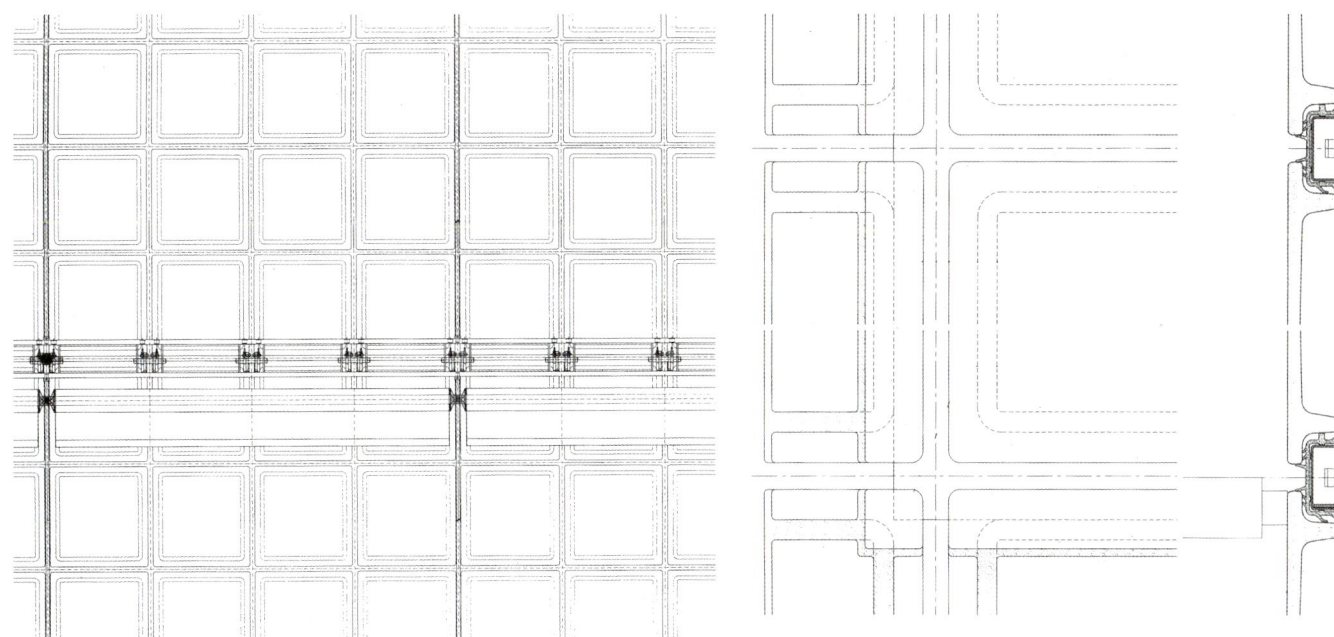

Details of glass-block wall

Giorgio Borruso Design

Fornarina

Las Vegas, USA   *Photographs: Benny Chan/'Fotoworks'*

Our objective was to create, inside the chaotic bustle of Mandalay Bay and its host city, an oasis; a place of rest for the retina and the mind, a place to retire and feel comfortable. We designed a sophisticated system composed of integrated "organs" to invite the visitor inside and expose him or her to a series of "marvelous" products encased in clear silicon rings or displayed on unexpected floor undulations created from custom made textured vinyl containing tiny flecks of color.

Along the perimeter a mantle of vinyl rears up to become the wall and wedges underneath an outer surface. The overlap generates an eyelid. From inside the eyelid light flows down the wall to animate the product within the space. This line of demarcation represents the tentative juncture of two different worlds: the floor where walking becomes an experimental and tactile sensation, and the "sky", sometimes raining strange light objects, bulbs of

glass suspended from magenta filaments, or large tentacles with an obtrusion of eyes which observe and at the same time indicate where to concentrate our vision, suggesting we abandon ourselves inside materials, clothes, and shoes. Dressing. Changing. All in an oneiric experience.

These four large lighting elements which hang from the ceiling in the middle of the store which reaches a maximum height of 29 feet are composed of an aluminum and polycarbonate structure wrapped in a membrane of fabric and are internally illuminated. These tentacles support a grid of directional lights.

The visual and tactile experience in the store becomes very important. One becomes aware of this through the texture and consistency of a variety of materials. The signature Fornarina Magenta is present as an accent in a neutral context where the product becomes the true vector of color.

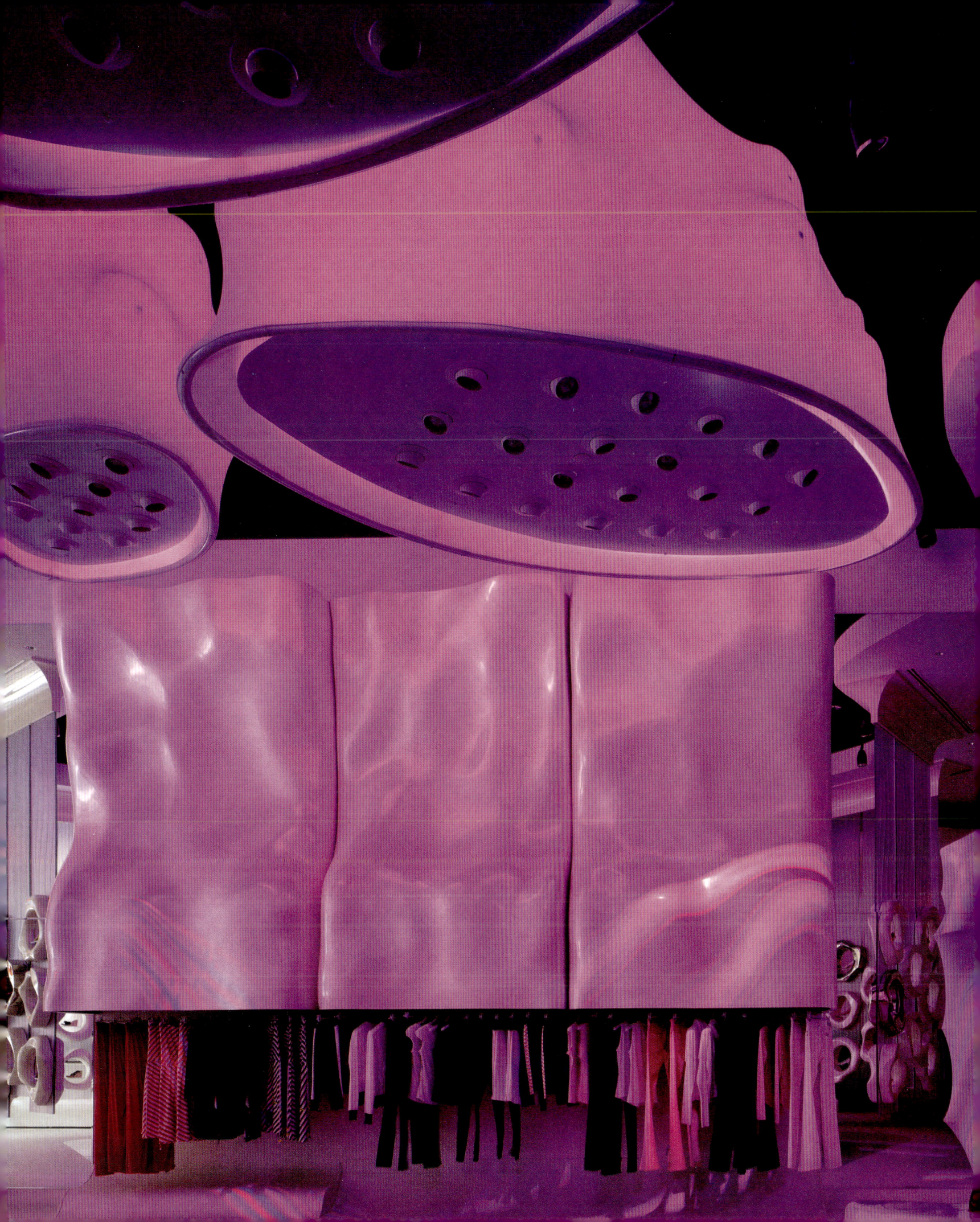

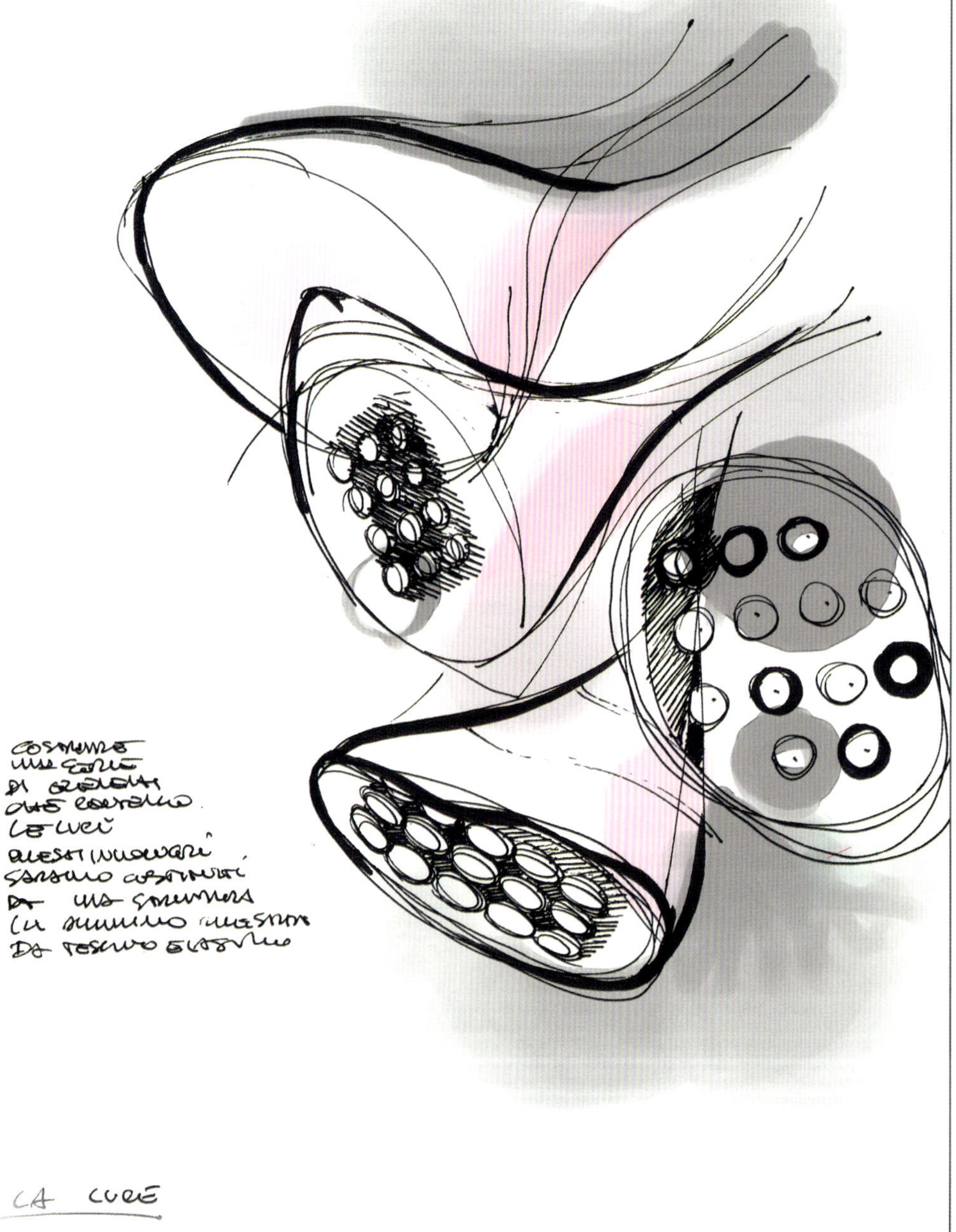

COSTRUIRE
UNA SERIE
DI QUELCHE
CHE CONTROLLO
LE LUCI
ALLEST (NUOVARI'
SARANNO COSTRUITI
DA UNA STRUTTURA
(LA SUMMIMO ALLESTION
DA TESCURO ELASTICO

CA CURÉ

Giorgio Borruso

Fornarina®
Mandalay Place - Las Vegas

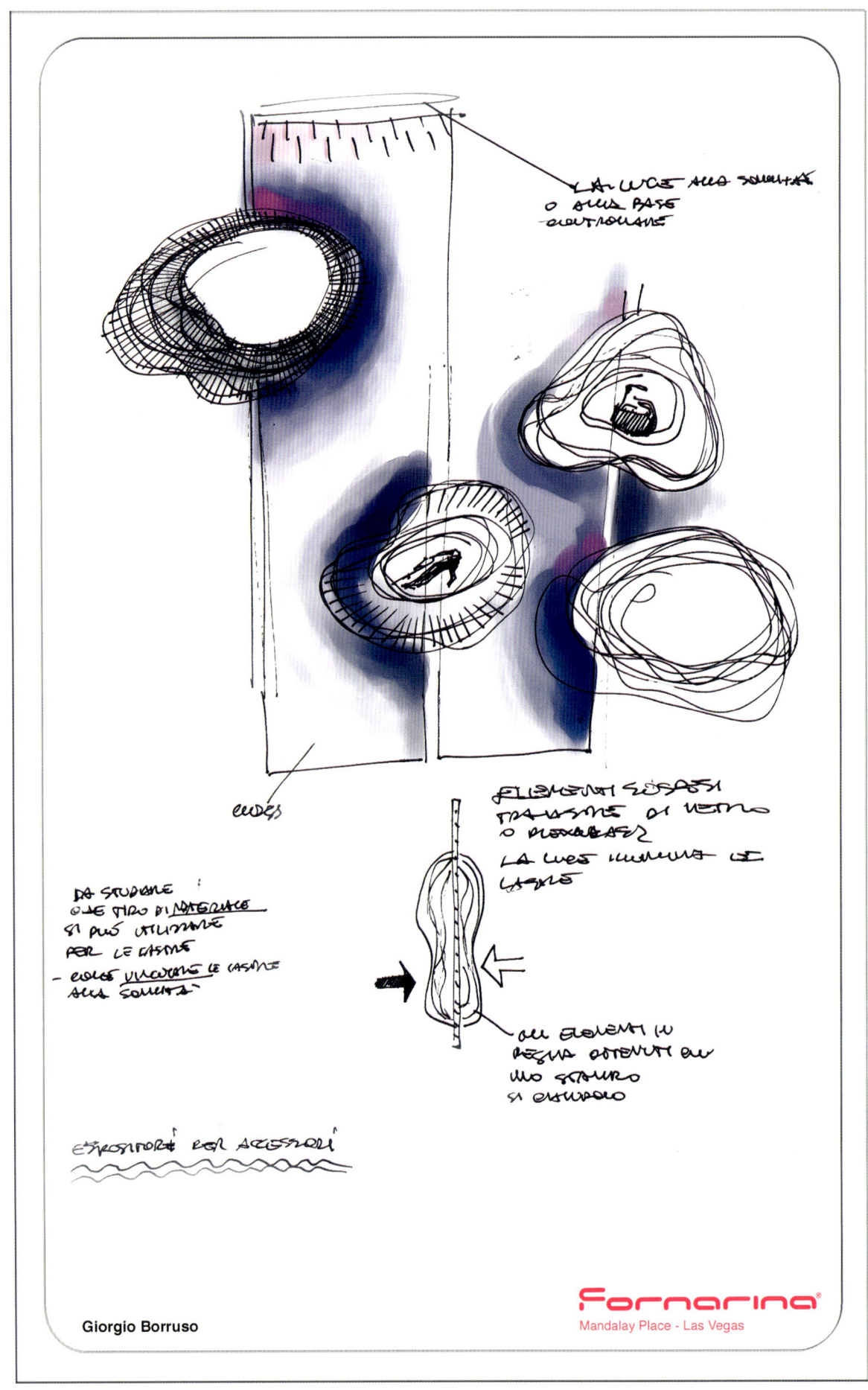

Giorgio Borruso

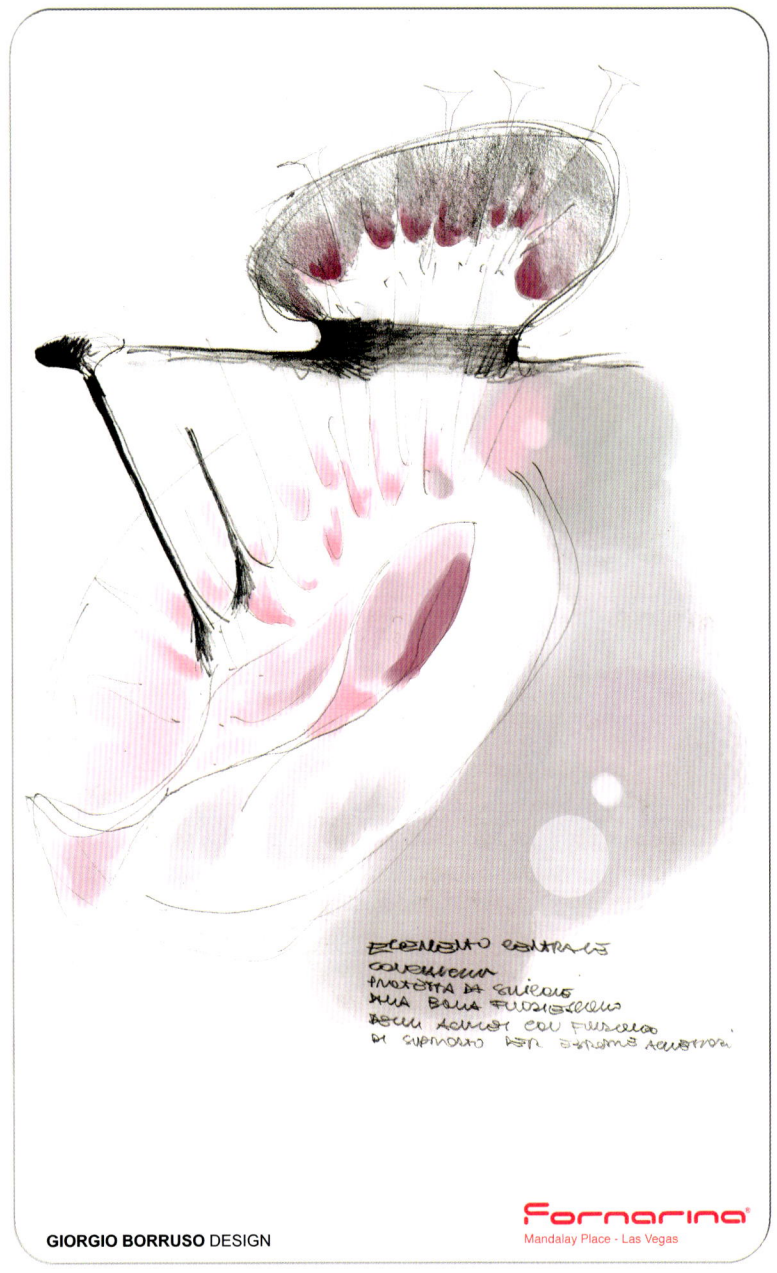

GIORGIO BORRUSO DESIGN

Fornarina
Mandalay Place - Las Vegas

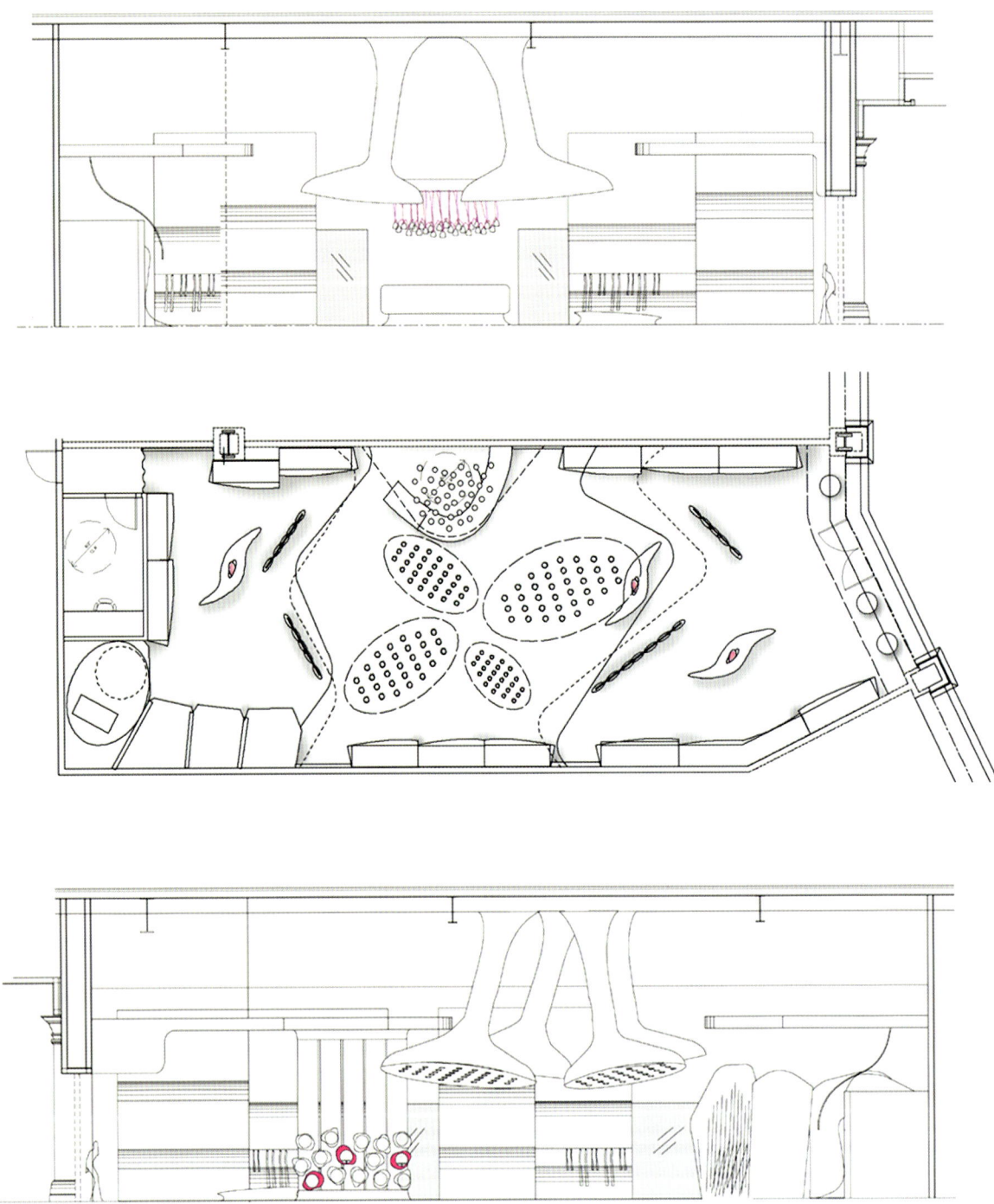

Floor and elevations

Marta de Renzio

Kickers

Milan, Italy

Photographs: Margherita del Piano

The new Italian office of the Kickers footwear firm is located in Milan, in an old industrial building. This type of space proved particularly suitable for housing both the public and private spaces of the firm: the offices on the first floor, and the warehouse and shop on the ground floor.

The old premises of Caprona Aerei offered a great advantage: four glazed facades that allowed a large amount of natural light to enter the building. These extraordinary lighting conditions influenced the decision to empty the space, eliminating the internal divisions and treating the interior walls as translucent divisions. These were made in wood and vitreous resin, a material that acts as a catalyst and diffuser of natural light. Through the planimetric layout of these walls, new perspectives have been obtained that function as guides to the different routes and let the visitor guess the depth of the spaces. The decision to transmit the image of a luminous box is expressed by means of the material used in the floor: brilliant white epoxy resin forming a homogeneous surface. The introduction of notes of color, warm orange tones, is reserved for the walls that serve as a background for the perspective of the long circulation spaces and the graphic play of the mobile wall that contains, on the opposite side, the footwear display.

The general lighting of the offices consists of small, industrial-type suspended lights in satin-finish aluminum, while each table is illuminated locally by desk lamps. In the circulation spaces, large fitted spotlights with low-consumption bulbs were used. The show room is lighted by suspended, industrial-type halogen lamps. The display wall is illuminated by swiveling iodine lamps that do not alter the colors of the products.

Ground floor plan

The rehabilitation and recovery of the building was based on the urban and historiographic analysis of the typical morphologies and typologies of industrial architecture, incorporating and highlighting the aspects that adapted most naturally to the desired image and functional characteristics.

The panel designed for the project is a fundamental element of the design. The circulation space is marked by low-consumption Reggiani lights fitted into the false ceiling.

The architects have unified a multi-use space by using light, color and bright, clear materials. While bright colors have been used for the walls of the circulation areas, in the show-room white is dominant and the products on display are the main features of the space.

DeuxL, Vudafieri Partners

PUCCI

Ginza, Tokio, Japan / London, England
New York, EE UU

Photographs: Santi Caleca
(Pucci London and Pucci New York), contributed by the architects

Among last century's great fashion names, Pucci is of the few still firmly on the cutting edge in the twenty-first. This trail-blazing retro-future boutique chain has opened on New York's 5th Avenue, London and Tokyo. The shops adhere to an identifiable design trend, featuring pop geometries, spirals, floral prints and brilliant pastel tones. The interiors are manifestly "liquid", unharnessing a universe of blues and purples onto the walls, ceilings and floors. The lighting adds to the association with the sea and sky.

The objective is to transmit a feeling of lightness to the customer: in the New York shop a floor-to-ceiling screen acts as backdrop for the mannequins in the show-windows, while hiding the bustle in the street, sheltering the shoppers from external stimuli that might break the spell.

Pucci's new shops are truly pop, from the carpets- of Emilio Pucci's own collection- to the studied lighting. The ceiling is governed by large oval luminaires pierced by spotlights, a note of sci-fi about to touch down. The luminaire design, which varies from one project to the next, combines diffuse light with spots that are not aimed directly at the products. The bright light above and the built-in lighting of the shelves glances off the glossy surfaces of the counters, walls and floor, reflecting Pucci's characteristic tone-chart. This language of light is carried on by the walls of the shops, which are sheathed in backlit translucent sheeting, to make a glowing ethereal stage for Pucci's multicolored creations.

The shop's femininity is underlined by the curves and absence of sharp edges. The gently rounded surfaces are finished in high gloss. Most of the furniture is transparent polished Plexiglas, emphasizing the ambient levity. Other accessories such as cupboards and shelves are volumes of white acrylic.

The interplay of light with materials that seam to defy the laws of gravity make the objects on show appear to float on air; the clothing is draped on transparent hangers that hang from the ceiling (Boeing uses them for airplane curtains); The delicate handbags of the Pucci collection are suspended on fine threads inside their own transparent packing; lighting underneath the translucent counters and shelves reaffirm the global levity that rules these establishments. in high gloss. Most of the furniture is transparent polished Plexiglas, emphasizing the ambient levity. Other accessories such as cupboards and shelves are volumes of white acrylic.

Tokyo

The prevailing aesthetic in the shop can be guessed from the exterior façade, where the show window performs as a great screen that invites the passers-by to enter and discover for themselves the futuristic universe that awaits inside.

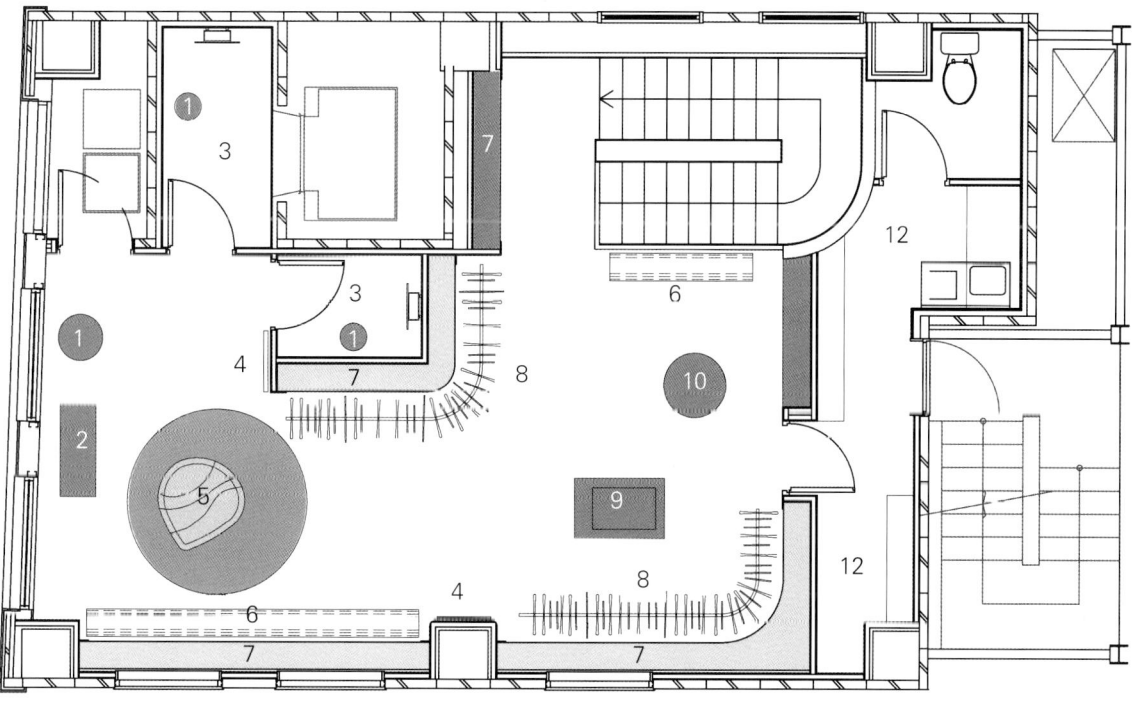

First floor plan
1. Pouf
2. Open desk
3. Fitting Room
4. Mirror
5. Pouf
6. Plexishelves shoes
7. Fabric wall
8. Hangers
9. Desk
10. Small table
11. Oval niche
12. Storage

Ground floor plan
1. Doormat
2. Podium
3. Plasma Monitor
4. Fabric Wall
5. Plexishelves
6. Desk
7. Accessories Shelving
8. Mirror
9. Small Leather Goods
10. Wrap
11. Cashdesk
12. Storage

London

At night the exterior of the Pucci shops are like a recreation of the most chic of Italian capriccios, as well as a prelude of the ethereal ambience inside, where the predominant tones are reminiscent of candy floss.

1. Accessories Shelving
2. Plexishelves
3. Fabric wall
4. Mirror
5. Hangers
6. Video Cravattes
7. Cash
8. Foulard niche
9. Fitting room
10. Bench
11. Mirror door
12. Services rises
13. New staircases
14. Delivery room

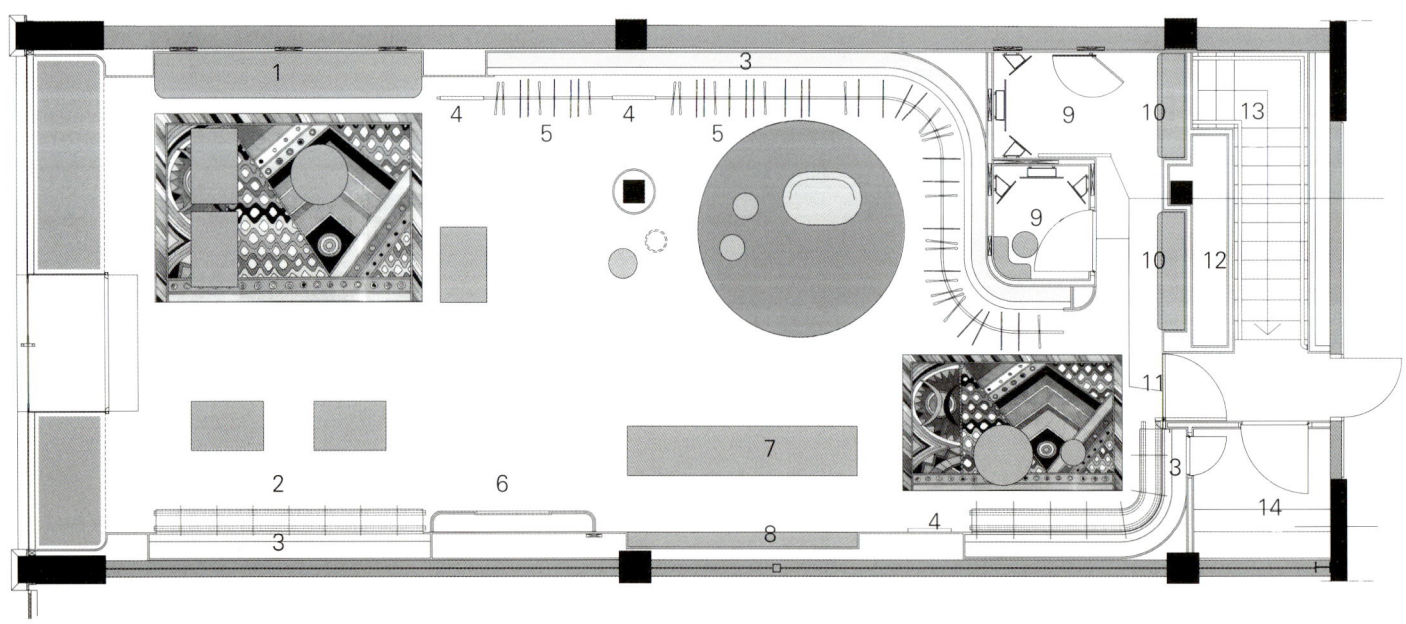

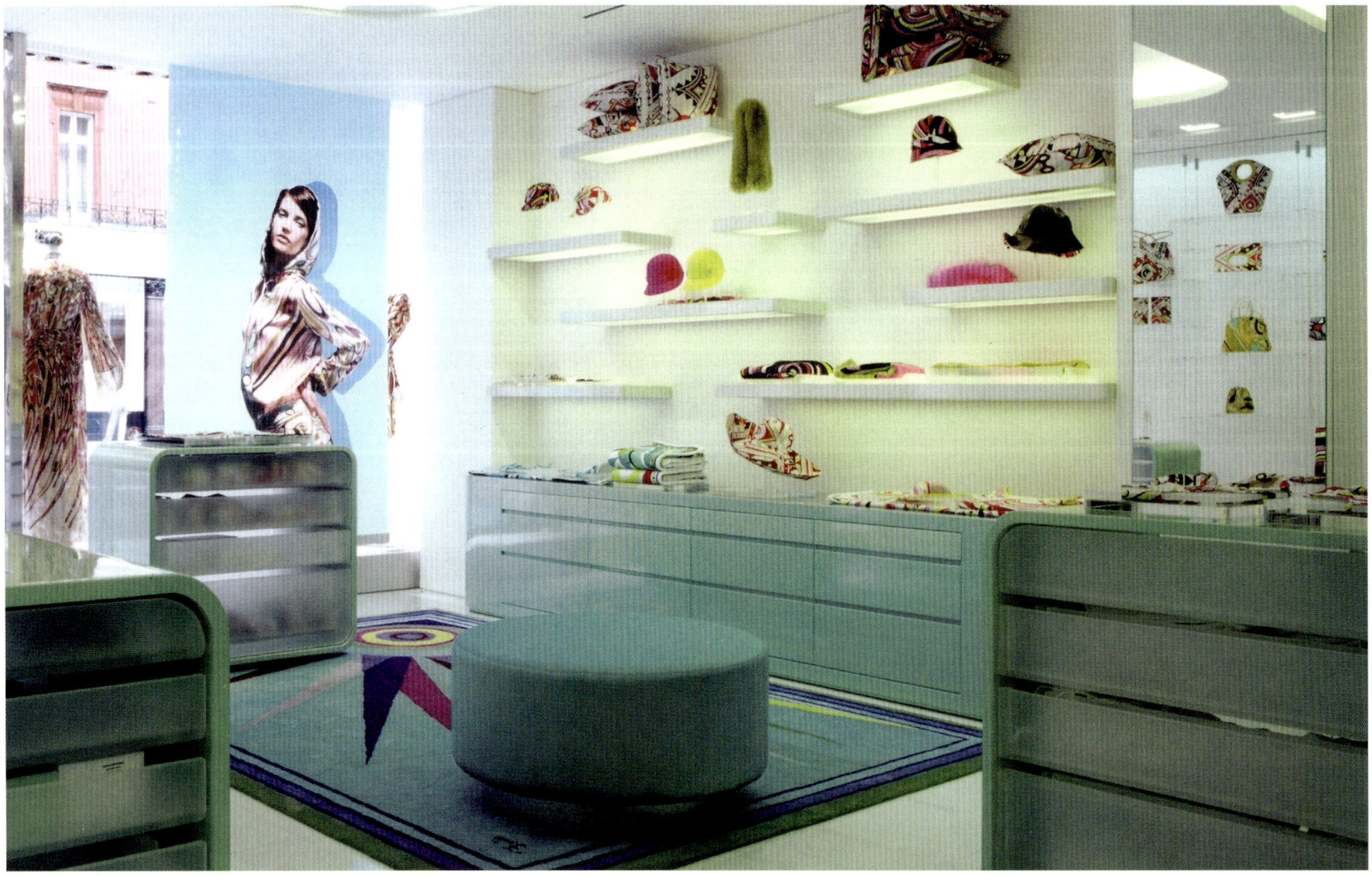

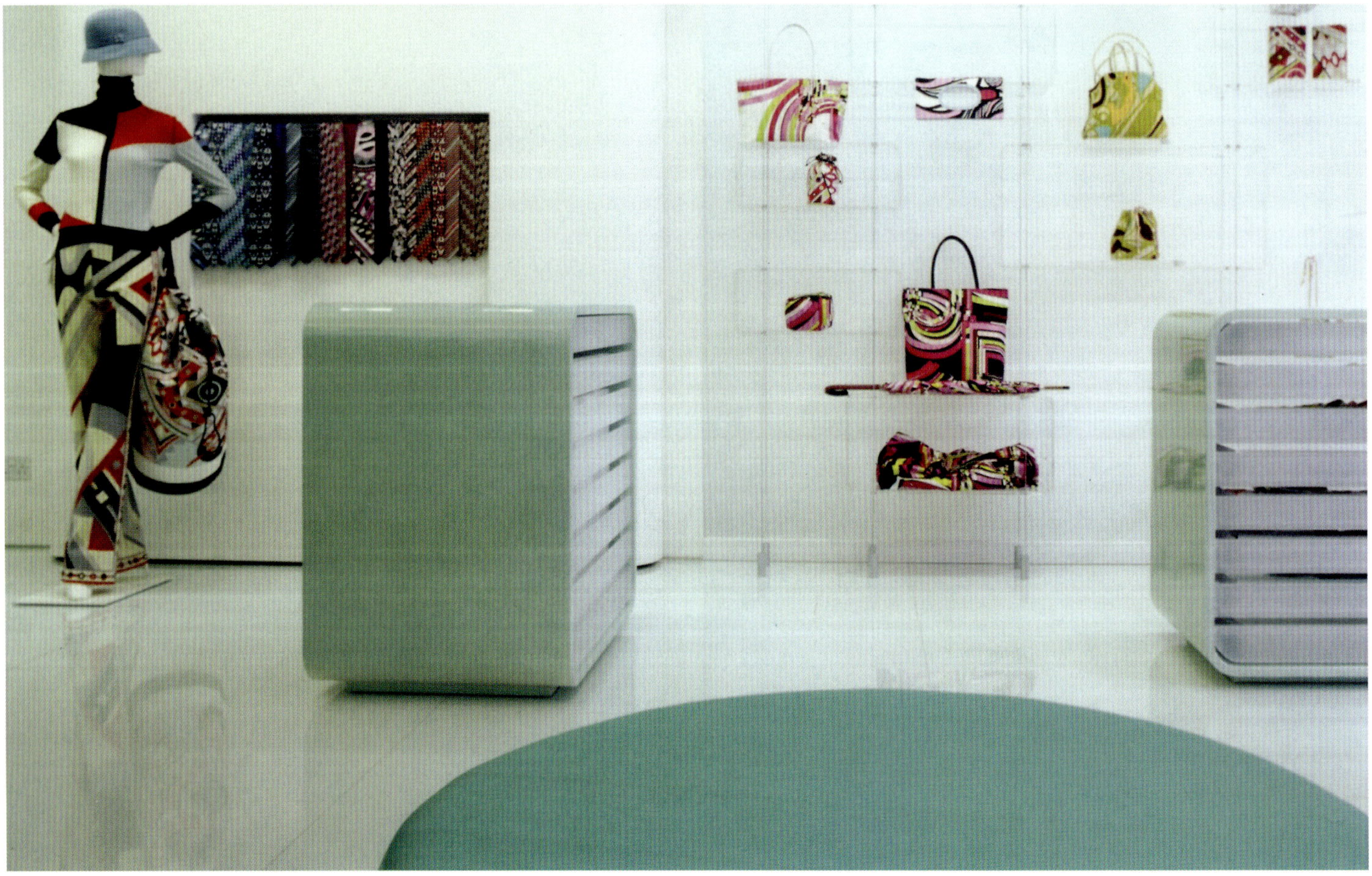

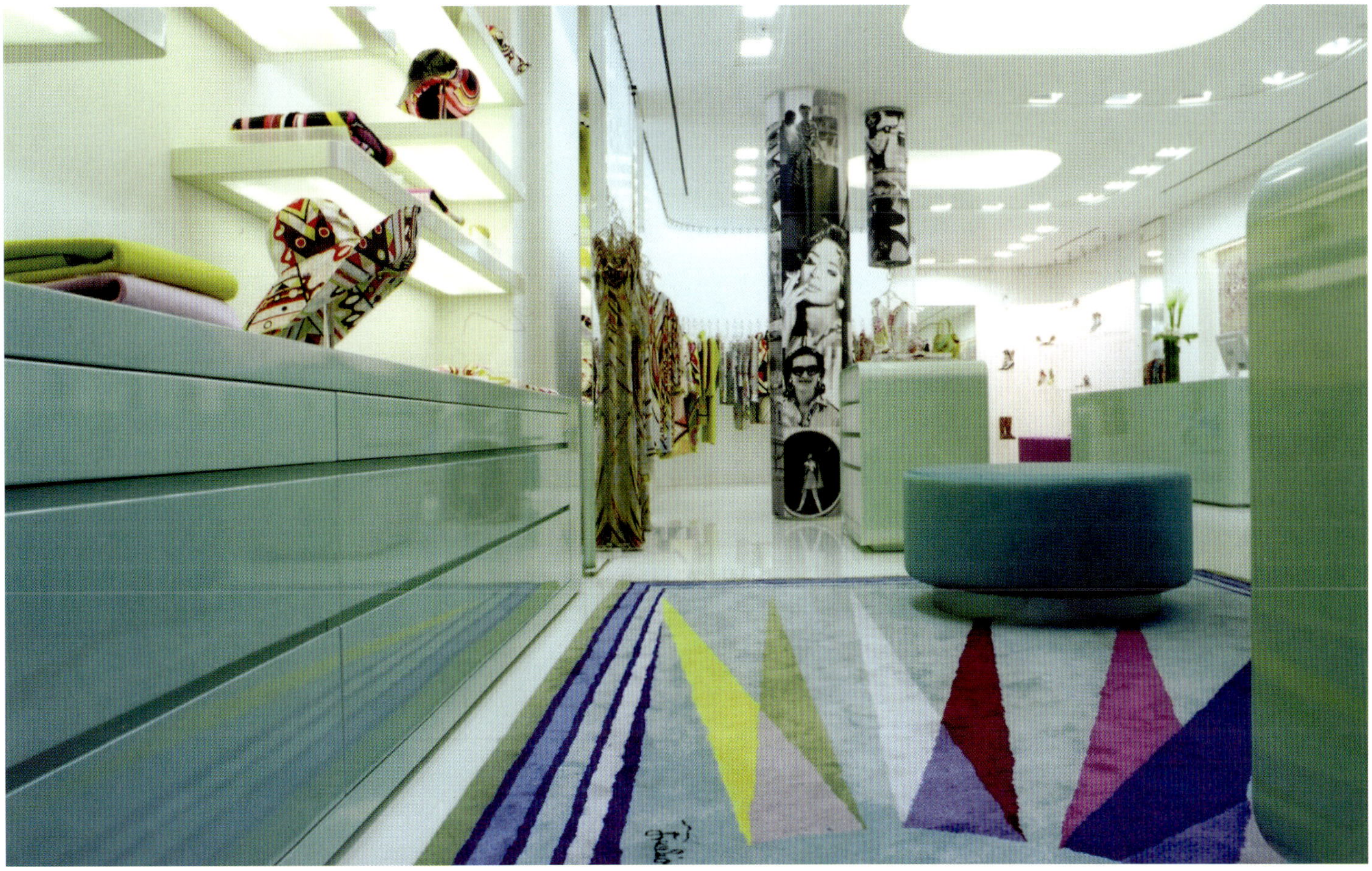

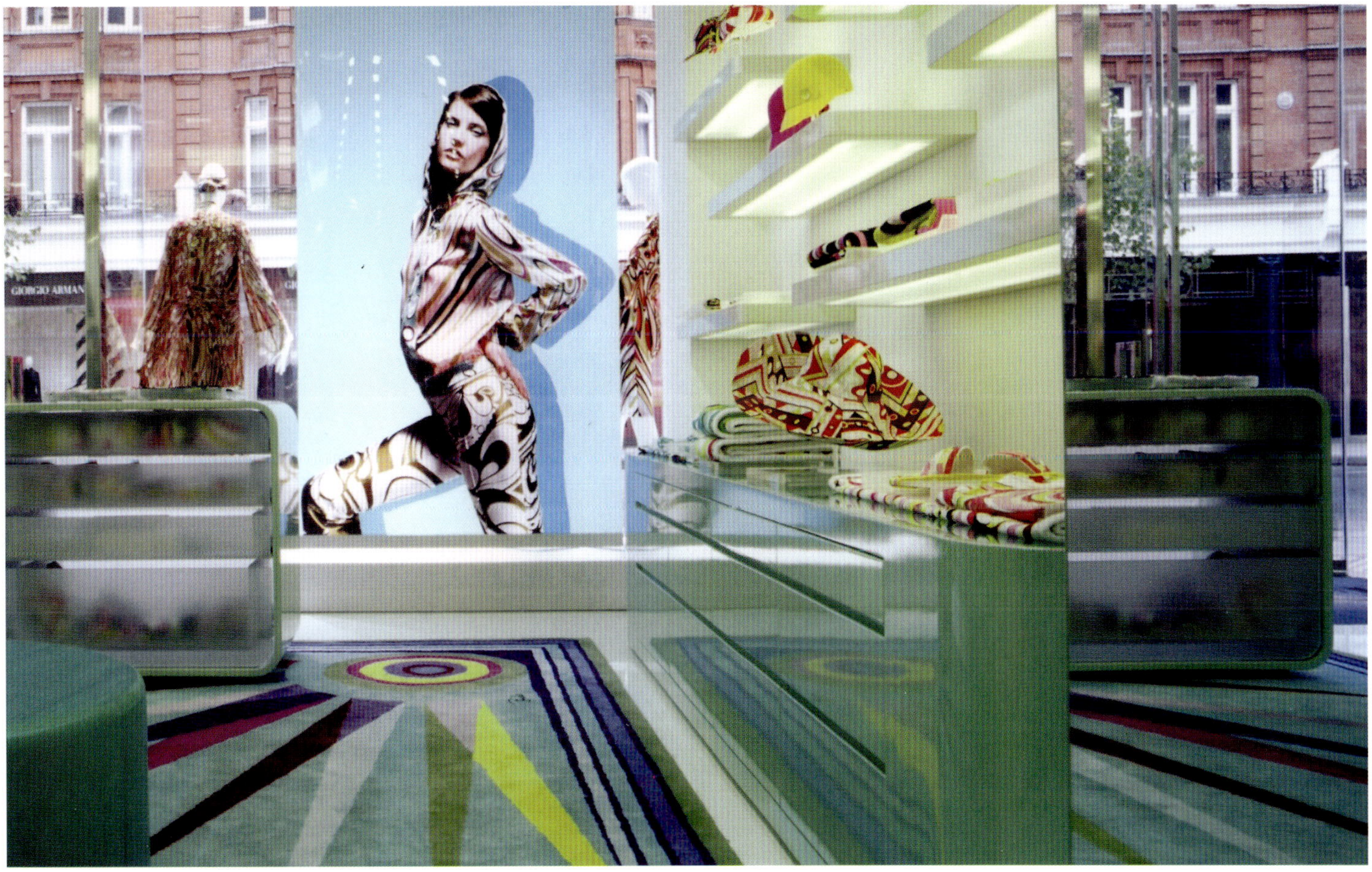

New York

One of the features of Pucci's New York shop is a mosaic of photographs that complements the new products hanging from upholstered pedestals along the walls. This background is regularly brought up to date, ensuring that the visitor is completely enveloped in Pucci's psychedelic paradise of color.

1. Decorative wall panels
2. Pouf
3. Ricomposed Stone Quartz
4. Desk
5. Plexishelves
6. Fabric wall
7. Accessories Shelving
8. Mirror
9. Hangers
10. Tie/Foulard Bar
11. Plasma Video
12. Foulard niche
13. Cash
14. Rug
15. Carpet
16. Mirror door
17. Fitting room
18. Storage

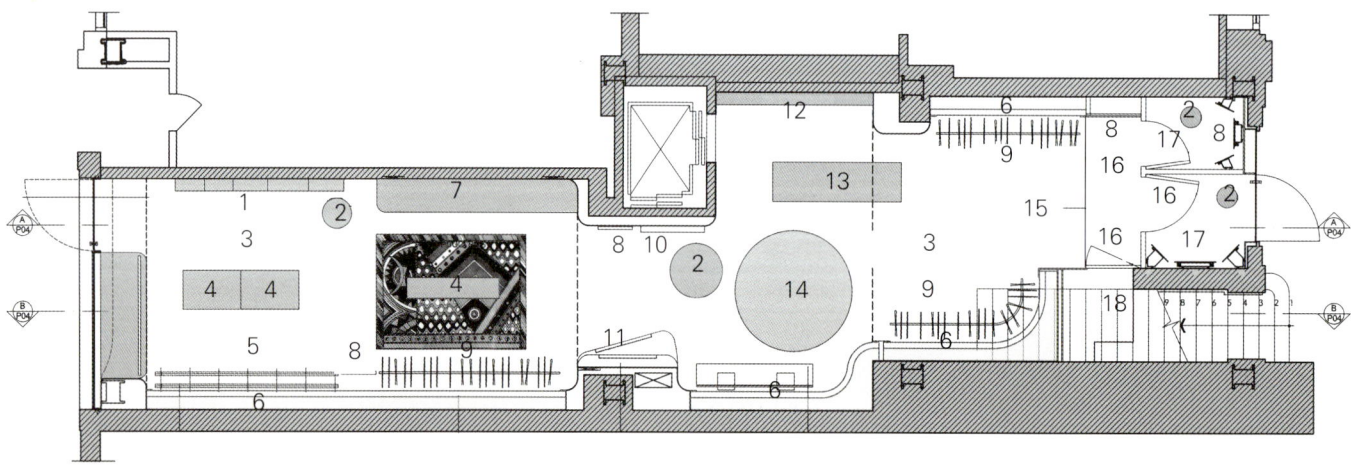

Ground floor plan

② SECTION

Sections

3Deluxe

D'Fly Jewelry Store

New York City, USA   *Photographs: James Wilkins*

The New York jewelry store D'fly owes its heterogeneous spatial impact to the contrast between emphatically tech-functional features and the organic forms of "genetic architecture".

Even a first glance through the shop window enthralls the passer-by: a fascinating and uniquely intense, nearly lab-like atmosphere cast almost entirely in white. The interior of the shop has the feel of an artificial implant on 47 Greene Street - the original shell is a listed building in the style typical of Soho.

The optical effects are further enhanced by the pneumatic noises made by sixteen remote controlled showcases which, when their opening mechanism is triggered, evoke an almost industrial high-tech atmosphere. Artificial muscles help raise their heavy glass lids 40 cm, enabling the selected piece of jewelry to be removed.

The shop is clearly divided length-wise into three consecutive zones. In the front third, as part of the genetic architecture evident throughout the shop, there is a small lounge, adding a touch of coziness and private charm to the otherwise rational atmosphere. The soft lighting, with its gradually changing color tones, emphasizes that this is an area where you can relax and enjoy taking your time.

The diagonal front of the desk directly opposite skillfully steers customers toward the middle section of the room, where attention is focused solely on displaying the goods. Here, the lighting turns sober, guiding the eye more to the products. Architecturally, the area is accentuated by projections on the walls and ceiling that seem to grip the room in the middle like a clasp. The showcases, arranged lengthwise at eye height, emphasize the unifying character of this section of the room.

Once through, you reach the try-on area, characterized once again by "genetic architecture" and colorful, moving light. A bamboo garden integrated into the rear wall lends the place a special charm. The try-on counter provides further technical finesse: by means of a remote-controlled extending mechansim, three mirrors slide silently out of the counter's corpus. They form a surprisingly private setting for both customer and personal sales advisor for the duration of the fitting. The innumerable reflections of the bamboo plants can be seen in the mirrors and the glass of the neighboring showcases, bringing the shop owner's home country of Taiwan to mind.

Ground floor plan

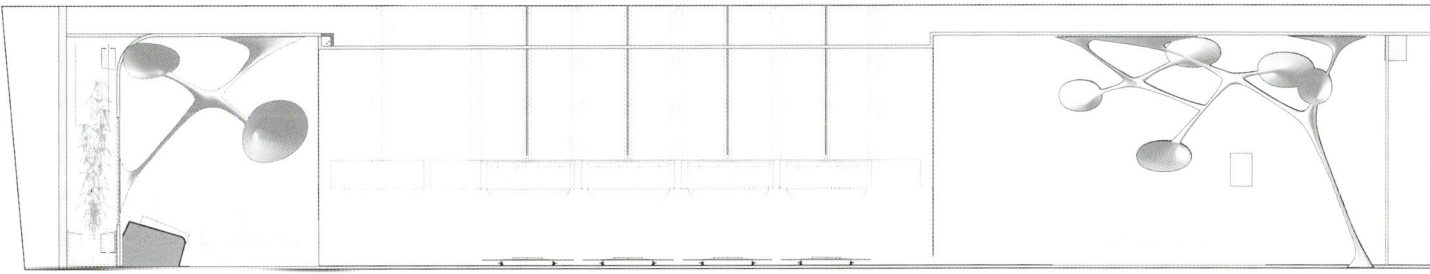

Section AA

Section BB

Each of the sixteen custom-designed display cases is lit from within by a combination of halogen and fluorescent lamps set into the light boxes, which are composed of stainless steel elements and tempered glass. A peripheral slit has been left open to let heat from the lamps escape. The glass doors of the display cases are remote control operated, thereby eliminating the need for keys.

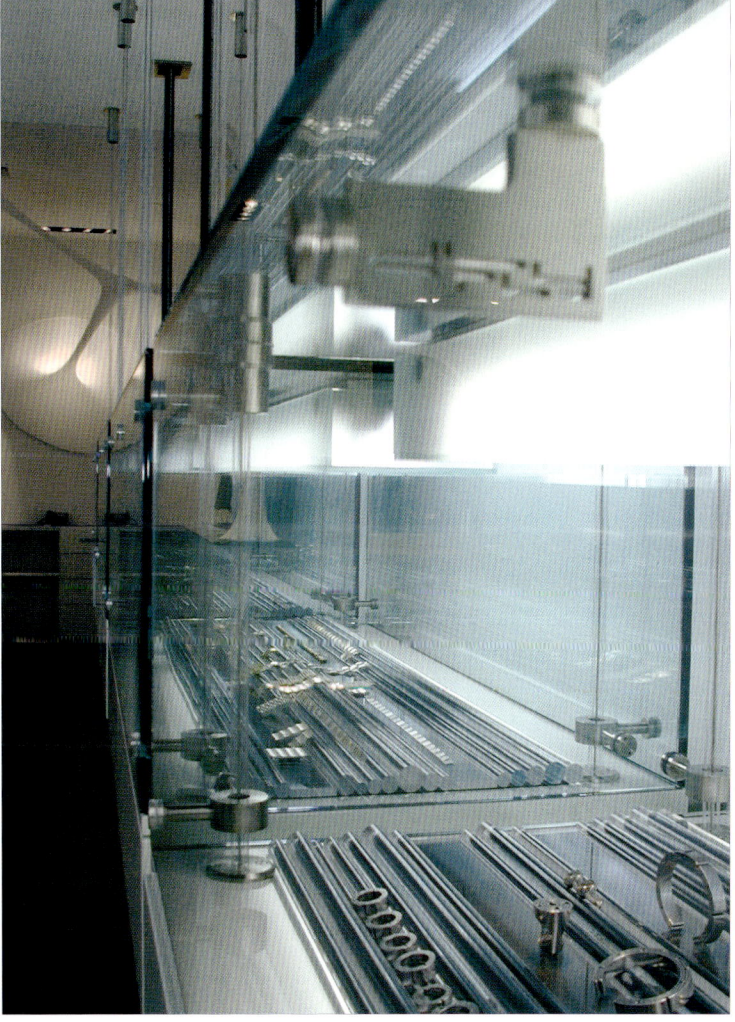

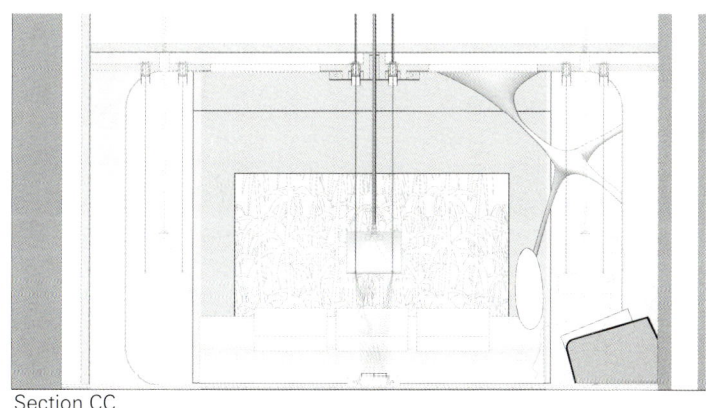

Section CC

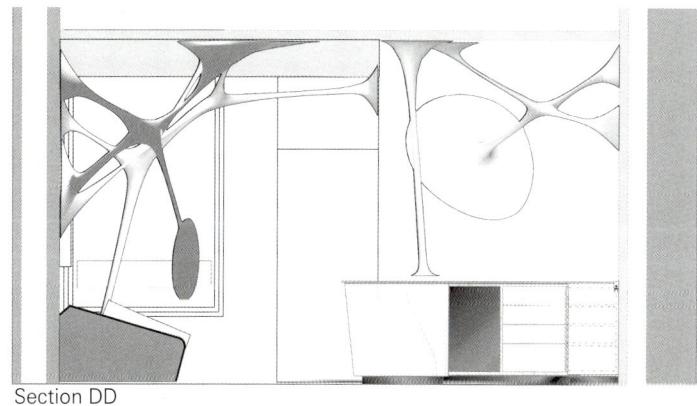

Section DD

Wulf & Partner

Adidas Factory Outlet

Herzogenaurach, Germany

A factory sales outlet in the country does not immediately suggest itself as an ideal location for ambitious architecture. But adidas is a is a world-class firm, and wanted to put itself ahead of the competition with a pioneering, dynamic building that also has the quality of an effective sign. They had to bring off a balancing act between high ambition and simple, factory-style execution. The design relates to Marc Angélil's master plan and is intended to implement its basic idea: "The dynamic that was hitherto concealed in the landscape elements is transformed into dynamic building structures ..." This has produced a dynamically curved, but calm and relatively compact building, drawing an artificial topography from the terrain. Landscape and movement are the design catalysts.

In the interior, the dynamic continues in spatial terms, and prompts visitors to walk through the space in a three-dimensional loop, hence seeing the maximum number of sports goods. An upward-curving "earth layer" contains the car park and delivery areas. It is important for the general impression that the parking deck and the sales building run together and become a design unit. A large open car park or an unrelated multi-storey structure would have been unwelcoming and counter-productive.

A forum-like forecourt is defined by curved steps for sitting on. This continues into the building's interior, and is taken up by a gallery edge. The boomerang-shaped building seems to want to rotate, and is held in place by a glowing core. This thrusts through the roof in the form of a tower, and provides advertising facilities and a projection screen. It is entirely covered with fabric.

The industrial glass façade follows the curved upward spiral of the floor levels unobtrusively. It has a double shell, is smooth inside and outside, and has no framing.

The peripheral ceiling supports, protection against sunlight and the necessary insulation for the protruding concrete slab, are concealed in the gap, which is 60 cm wide. This measure gives the interior a sense of fluent grandeur. The visible concrete ceiling is supported by bell-shaped columns. They follow the soft dynamic and provide a memorable design constant for the changing décor.

© Wulf & Partner

© Roland Halbe / ARTUR

© Wulf & Partner

© Roland Halbe / ARTUR

Visitors arriving by car drive past the forecourt to the parking deck, so that they have taken in the whole complex before "disappearing". Access to the forecourt and entrance is via the open terrace steps. The entrance is the focal point of the arena, and encourages the constant game of seeing and being seen.

© Wulf & Partner

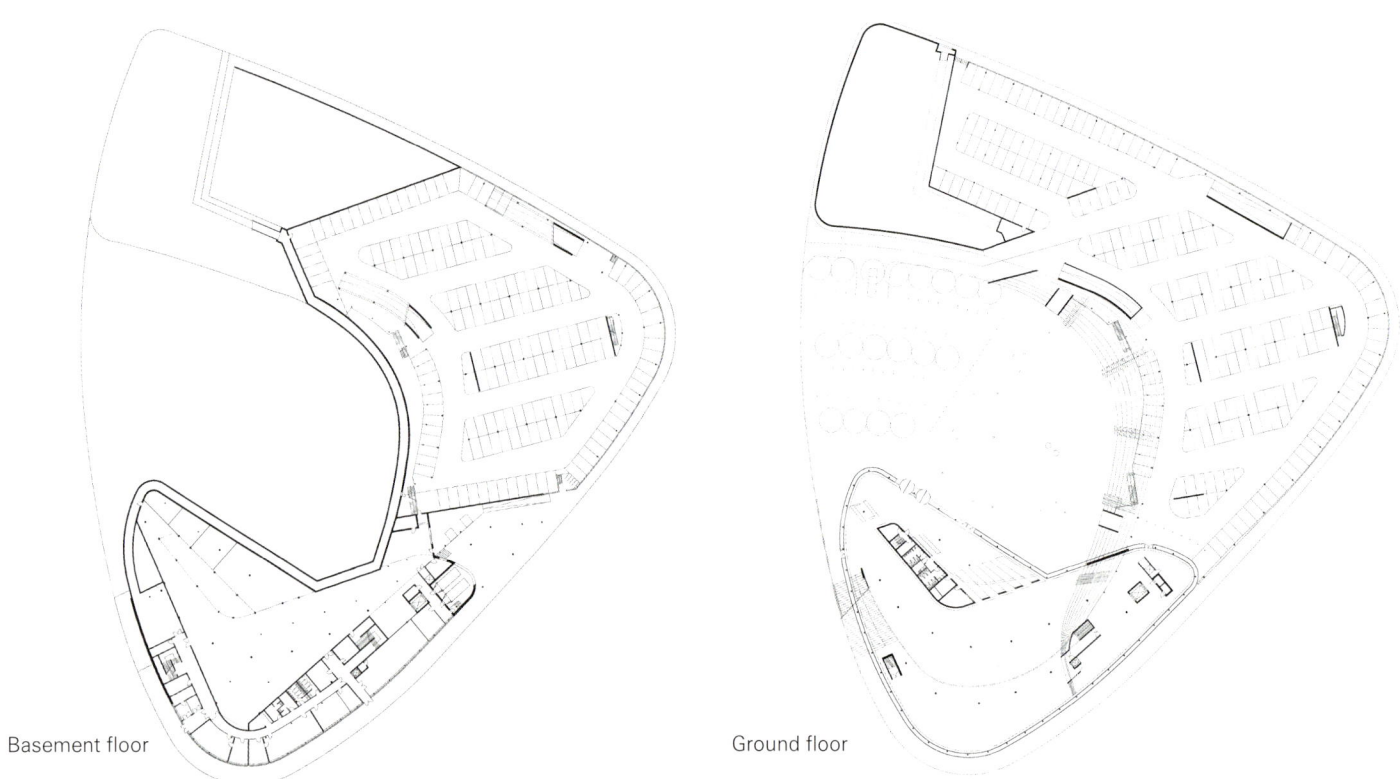

Basement floor

Ground floor

© Roland Halbe / ARTUR

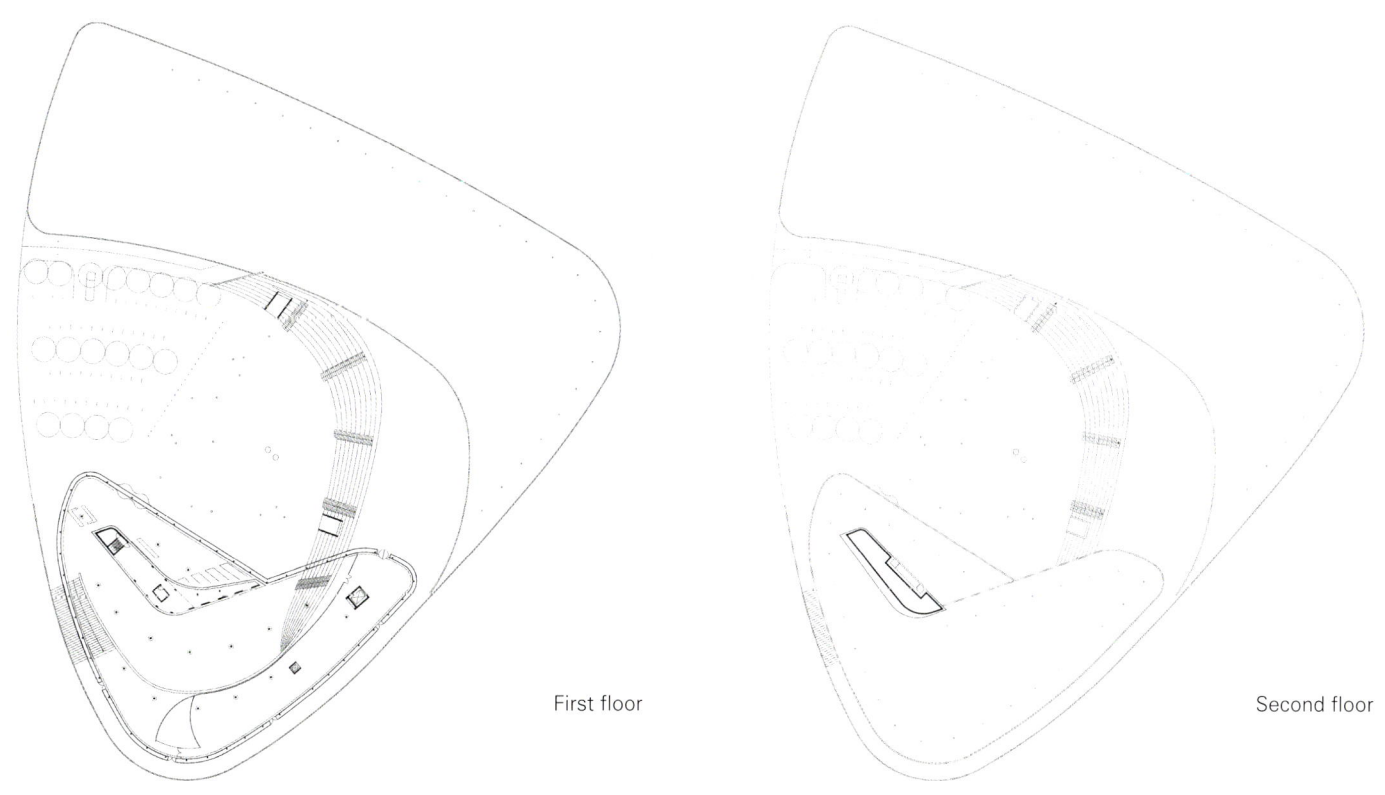

First floor   Second floor

© Wulf & Partner

South-west elevation

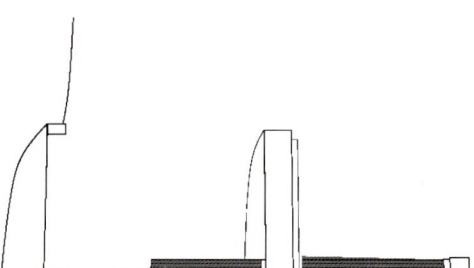

South-east elevation

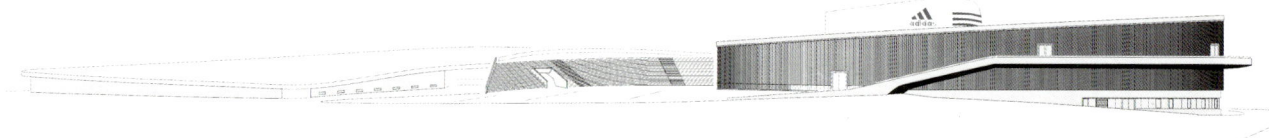

The momentary nature of sporting events was addressed
in the design concept, and appears as Corporate Design
in the car park in just the same way as it does in the factory outlet, the forecourt and the open air areas.

© Wulf & Partner

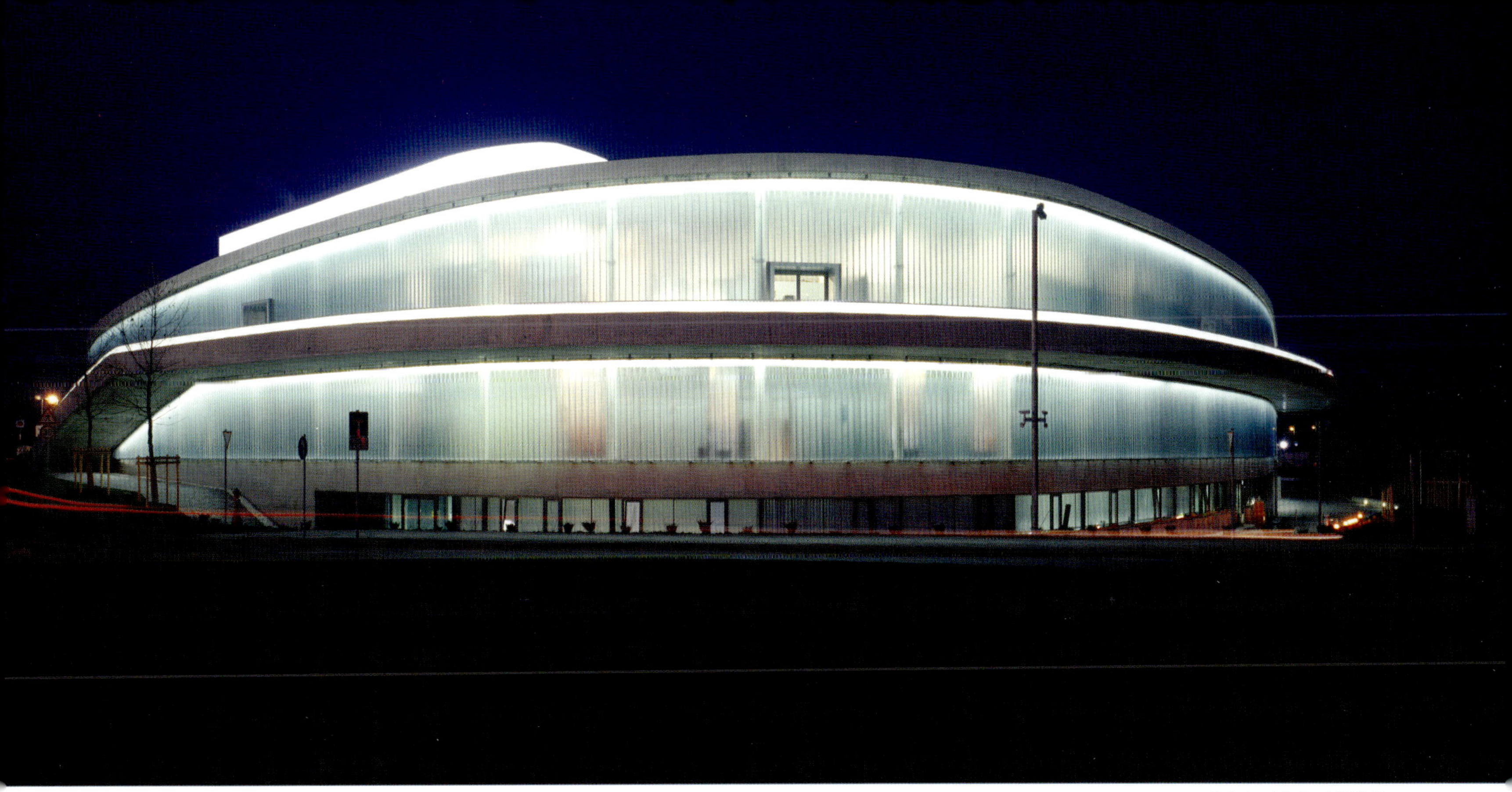

© Roland Halbe / ARTUR

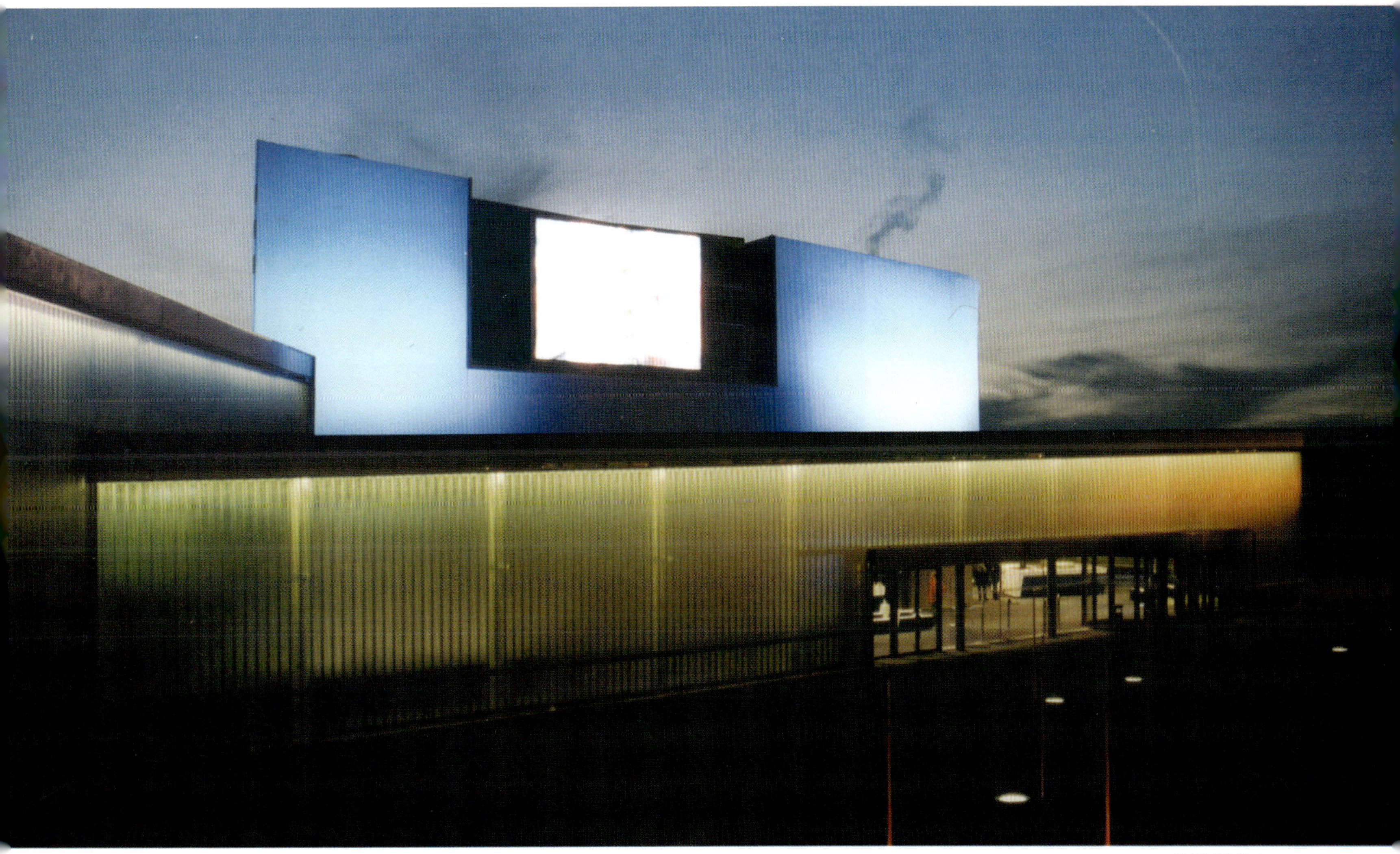

© Wulf & Partner

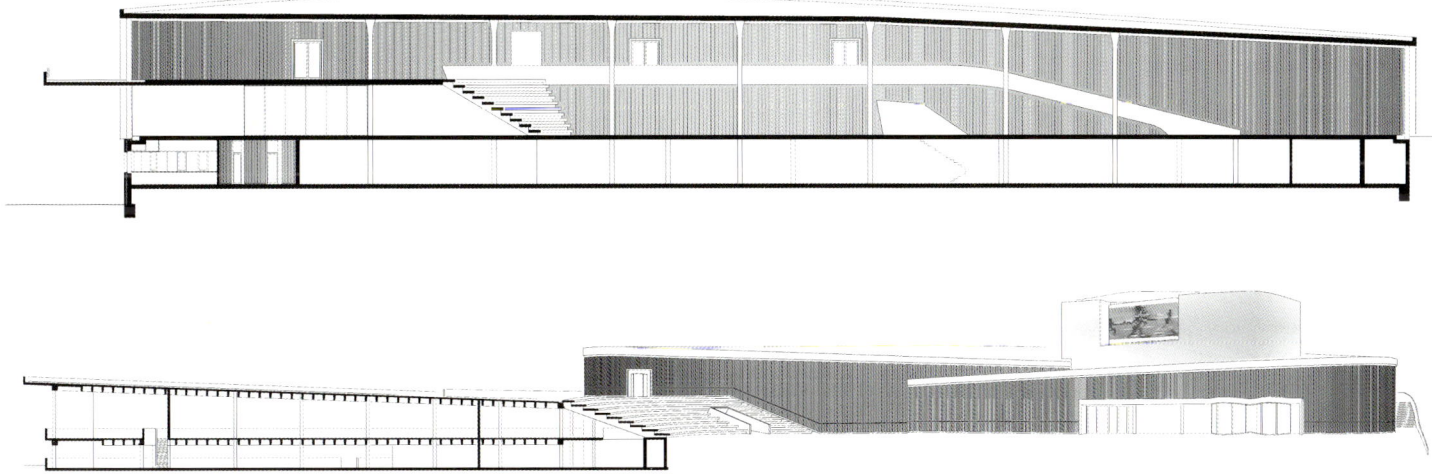

© Roland Halbe / ARTUR

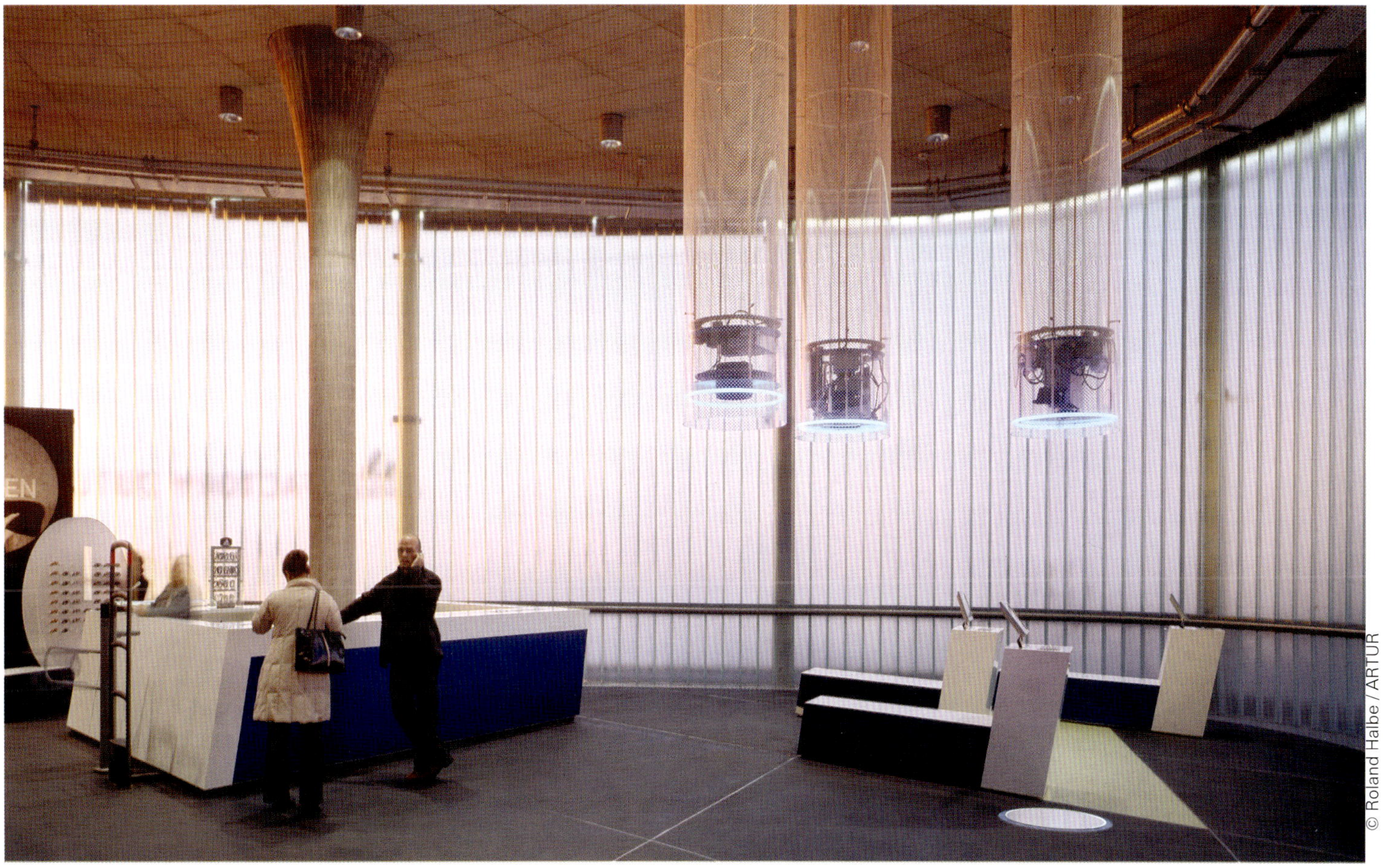

© Roland Halbe / ARTUR

© Wulf & Partner

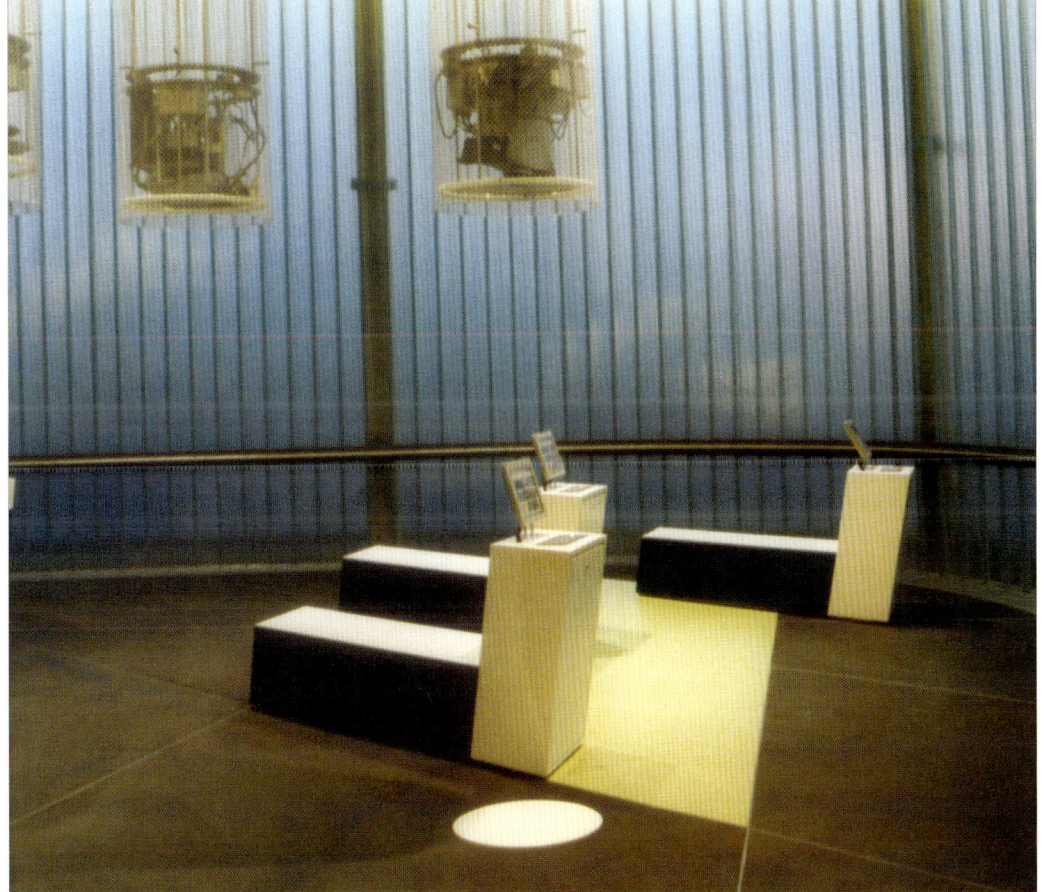

Various media are brought into play to convey an impression of a thoroughly sporting dynamic, thus complementing the architectural concept. The tower is bright with pulsating light, visual and acoustic media devices are installed in the foyer, and these also support the interior dynamics as light objects. Special furniture like the bar, Internet access points and checkout counters are designed as dynamically distorted blocks.

Randy Brown AIA

Madame Suren

Omaha, USA

Photographs: Farshid Assassi

A women's boutique provided the perfect opportunity for the design office to challenge the typical retail store convention in which, generally, the walls, ceilings, floors and furniture are all separate elements. The program specified three main targets: 1. To present the merchandise as though each item were a piece of art. 2. To shroud the existing structural column of the building. 3. To enhance the perception of display fixtures as architectural details. The proposal of the Randy Brown design team for the interior of the 1,100 sqft retail space developed from experiments with the folding and cutting of a piece of paper, thereby notably simplifying the design language. This continuous surface bends and folds in a variety of ways to fulfill a variety of functions, displaying merchandise of different characteristics and simultaneously creating concealed "negative" spaces, to carry the ductwork for the mechanical,

electrical and structural systems. After the existing space was pruned down to its basic structural constituents and painted white, this "folded object" was introduced there as a "foreign body". The overall layout of the space accentuates the long narrow bay by separating the store into an open area and an enclosed area.

The subtle magic ambience is a result of the lightness and transparency of the design, which transmits the illusion that the merchandise is floating, levitating in the light. The enclosed space houses the check-out desk, restrooms and a stairway leading to a mezzanine above. As a type of retail space, a women's boutique requires certain qualities that invite creative and playful design approach and is an ideal ground for experimentation. In this case, the result was the outcome of using a conceptual design methodology to explore space and light.

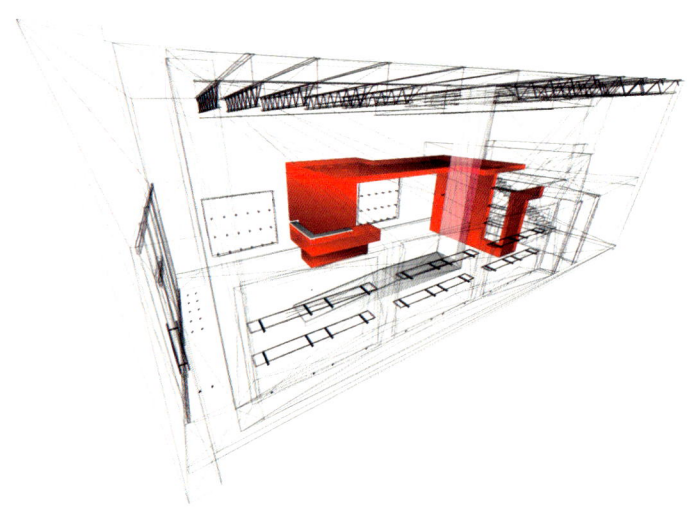

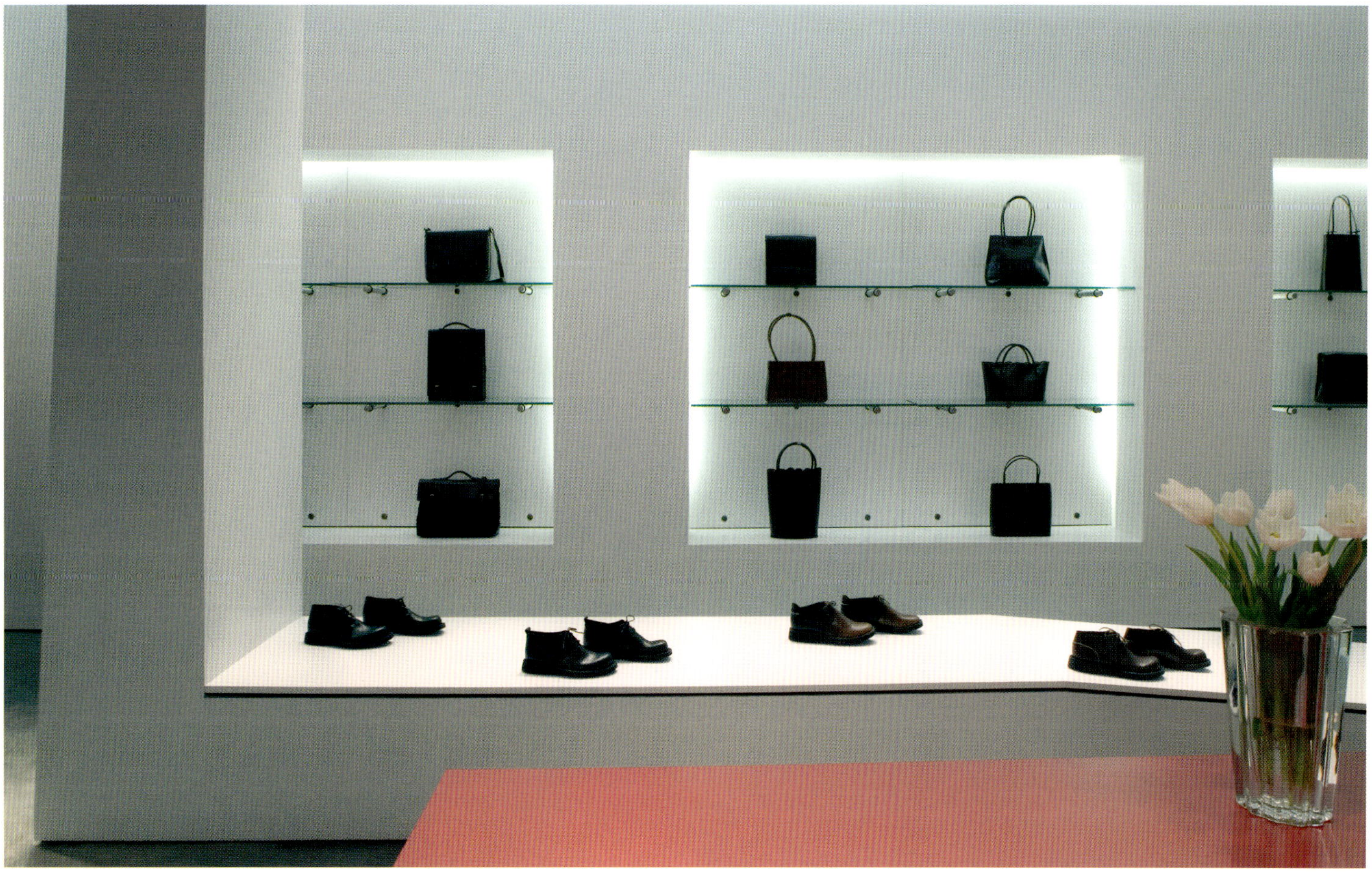

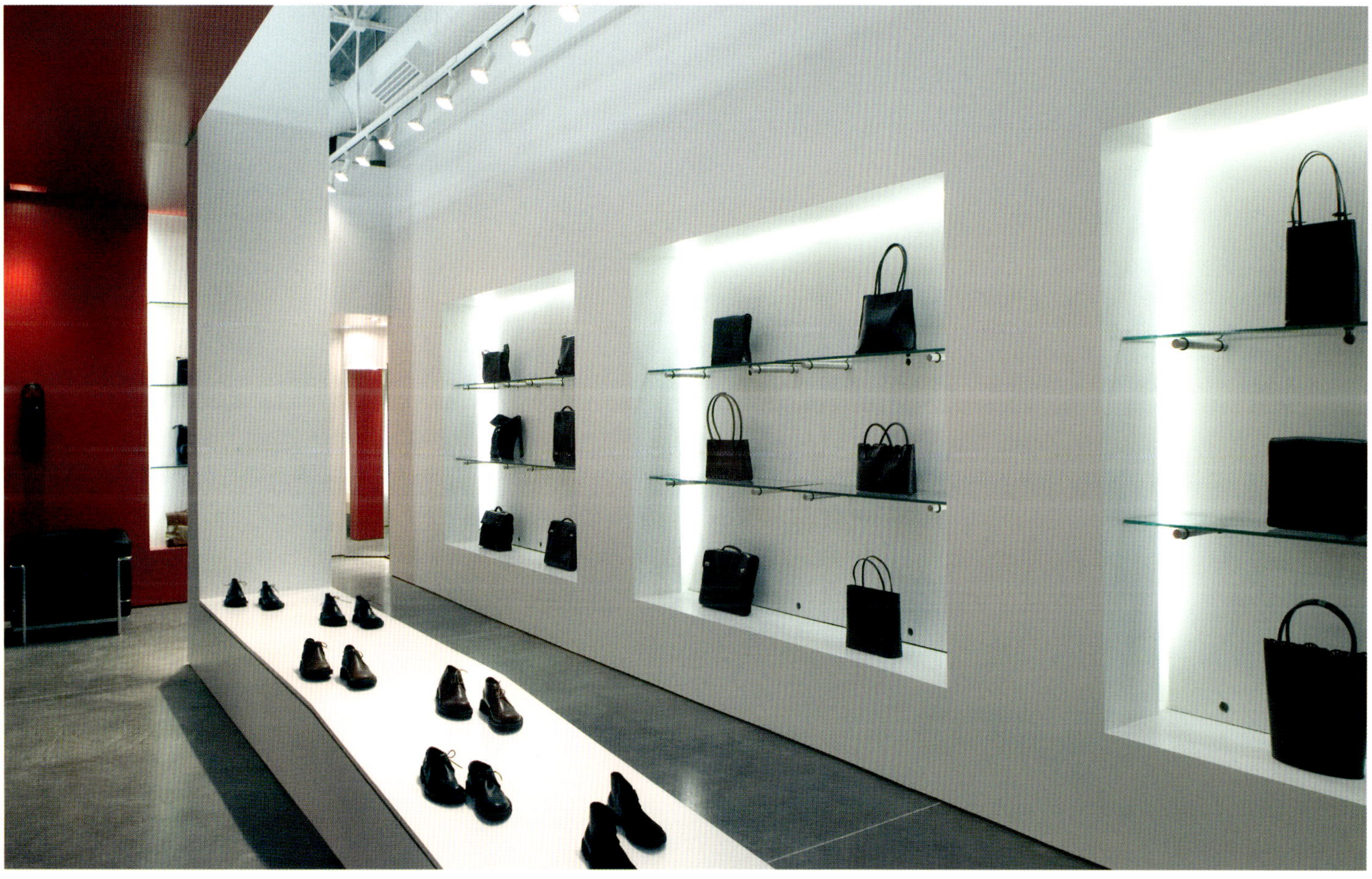

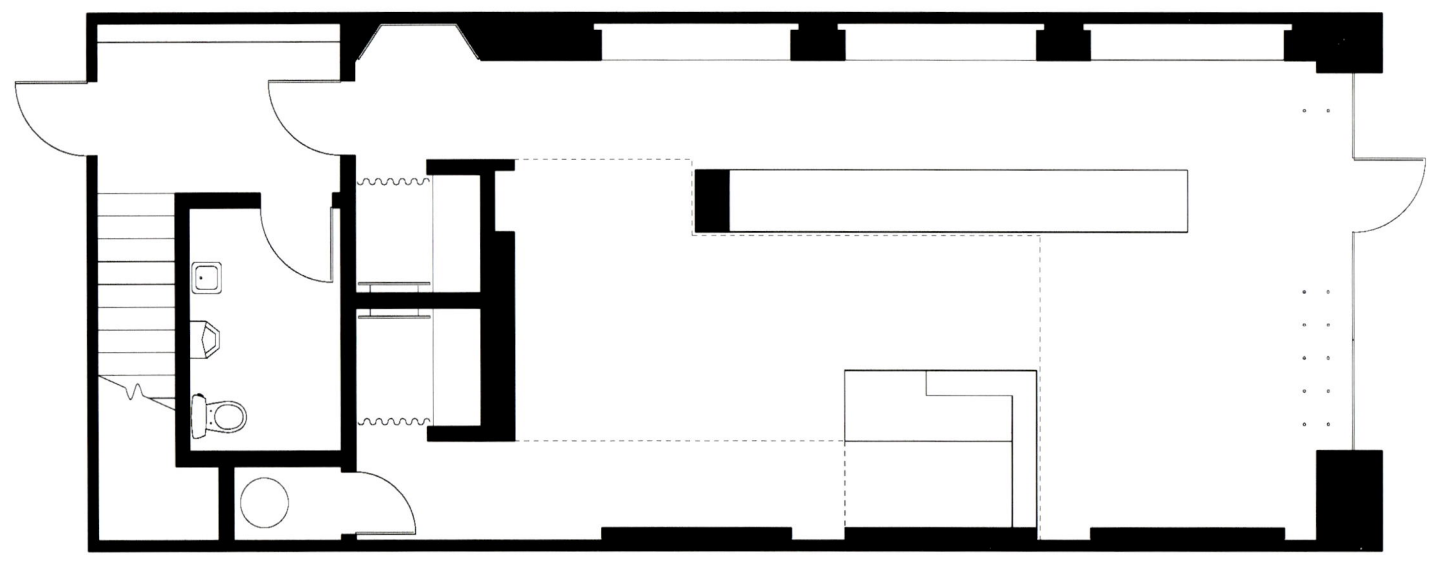

Jun Aoki + Eric Carlson

Louis Vuitton

Tokyo, Japan

Photographs: Daici Ano,N. Naka

Tokyo's tree-lined Omotesando Avenue is quickly gaining world renown as a leading street for flagship stores of luxury brands. The commission to design Louis Vuitton's new store, set on a privileged site on the avenue, was won in an international competition; and the doors were opened on the first day of business to over 1400 eager customers.

Inspired by the company's beginnings in the late 1800's as a luggage manufacturer, the designers struck upon the idea of creating a structure composed of an immense stack of randomly piled "trunks".

The delicately shimmering façade was created using a combination of finely woven metal mesh, steel panels polished to a mirror-like sheen and glass etched with a striped pattern. The overall effect deliberately mimics a fine moiré.

Originally used in the manufacture of industrial conveyer belts, this fine metal mesh is also used in the interior. In three varying densities, it has been painted cream and red and is found draped along walls, windows and stairwell voids, recreating in the interior the building's exterior moiré-like aspect. The dual skin system used on the façade is used for the dividing walls inside the store; here, though, lighting has been inserted between the two layers.

The façade's implied stacked trunks also continue in the volumes of the interior, where each space has been treated as its own independent unit, rather than designing each floor in a uniform manner. Custom-designed retail fixtures designed by Louis Vuitton's architecture department fill the spaces, just as they do in the company's Paris headquarters, thus granting a trademark look to an otherwise entirely original design scheme.

A dramatic multipurpose hall on the top floor displays a markedly different design scheme. With luxurious white velvet ceilings and cream-colored terrazzo flooring, the only identifiable element linking it to the rest of the store is the subtle inclusion along the windows of the same fine metal weave found throughout the building.

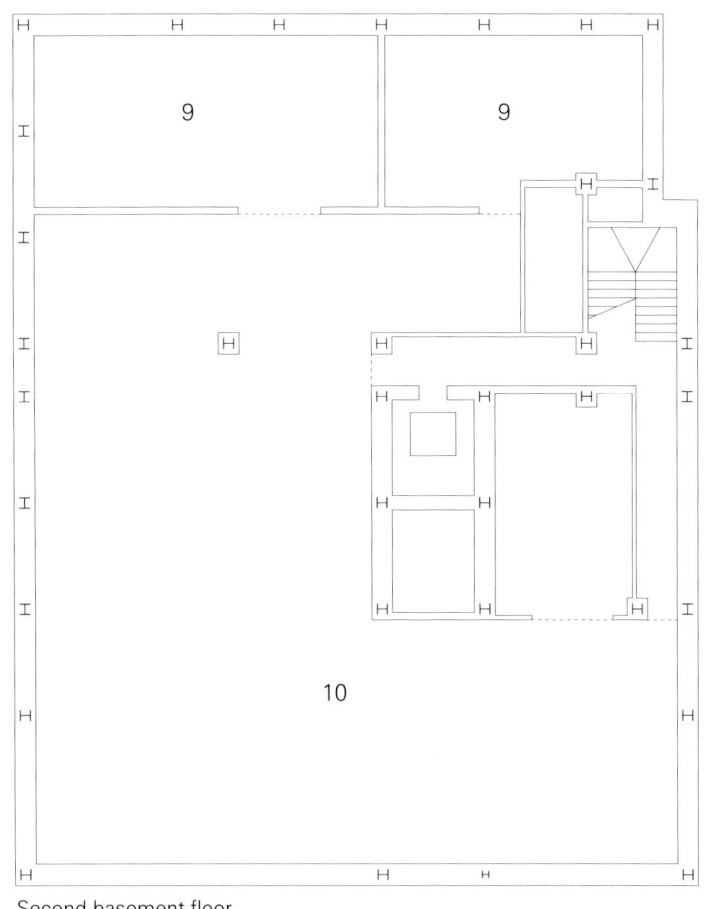

Second basement floor

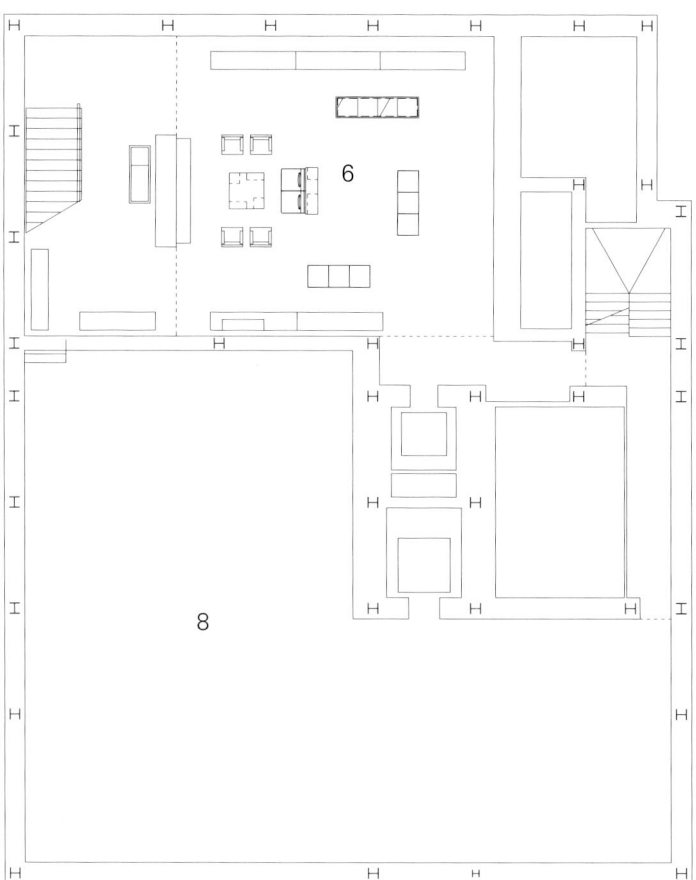

First basement floor

Ground floor plan

First floor plan

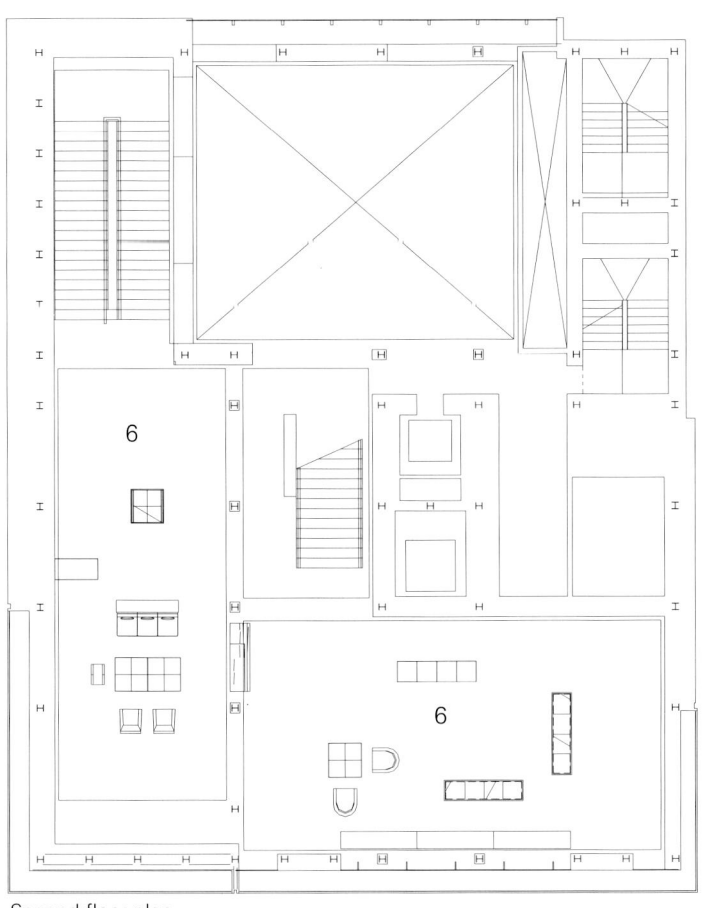

Second floor plan

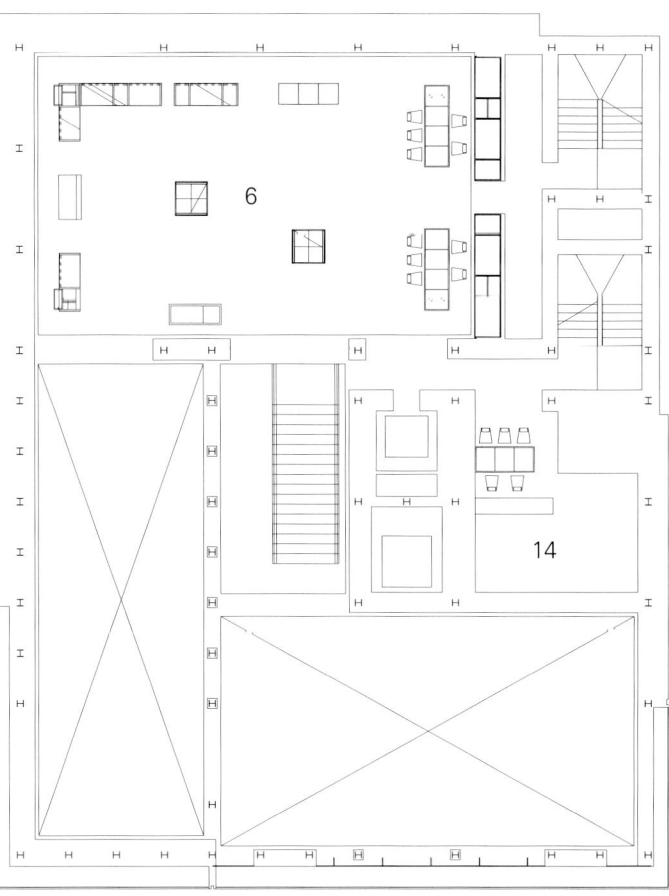

Third floor plan

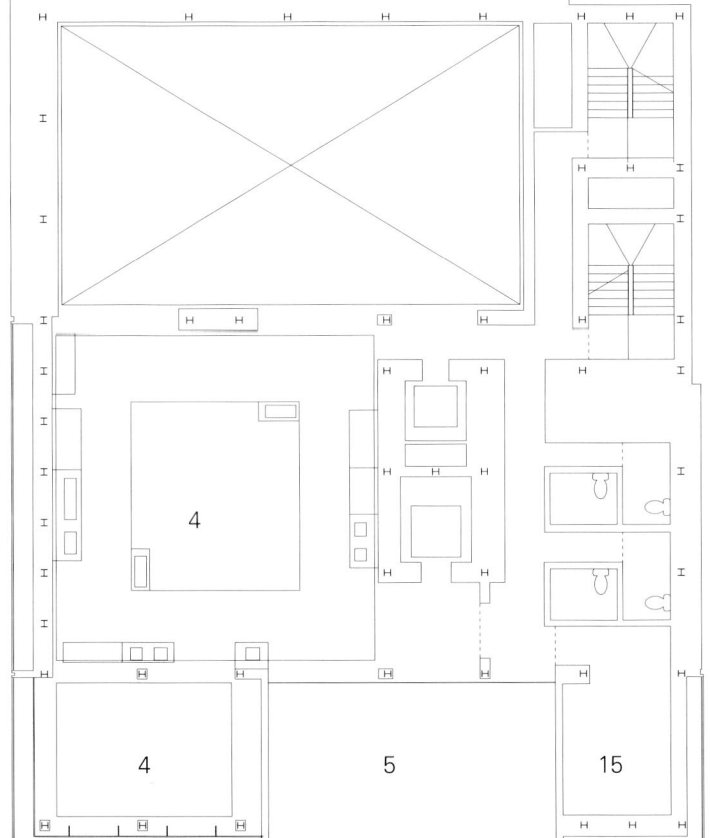

Fourth floor plan

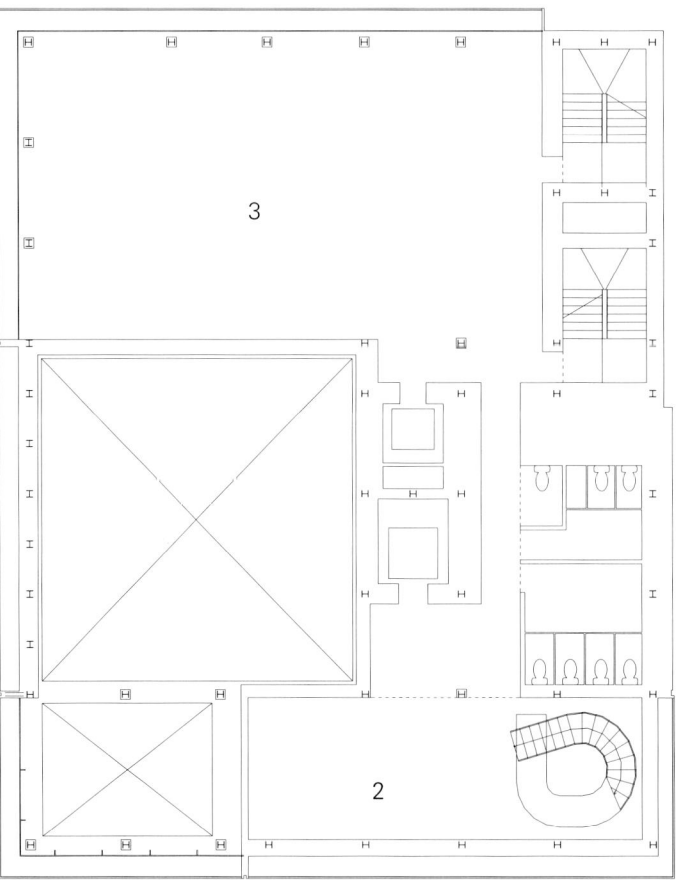

Fifth floor plan

127

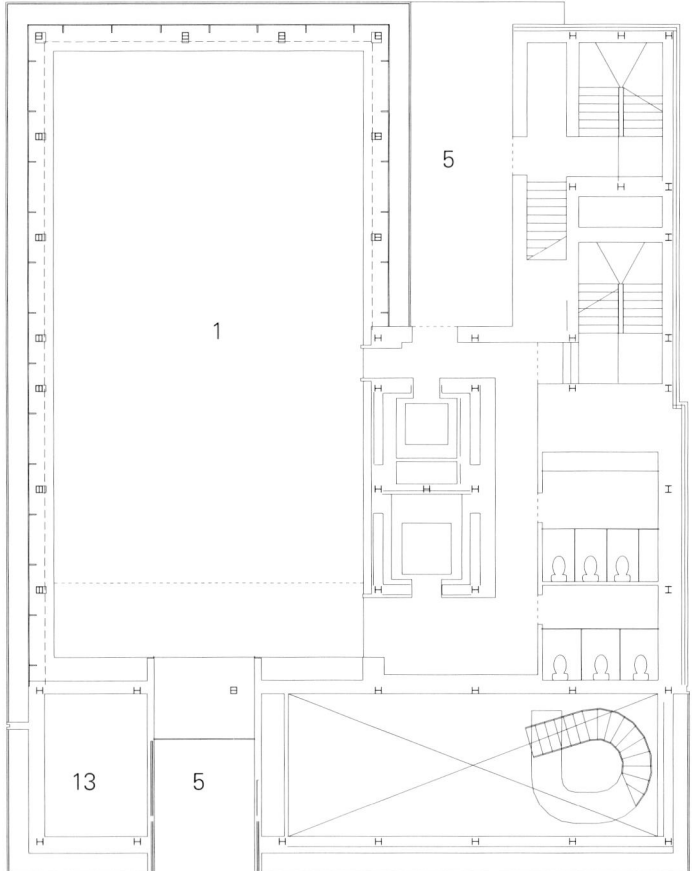

Sixth floor plan

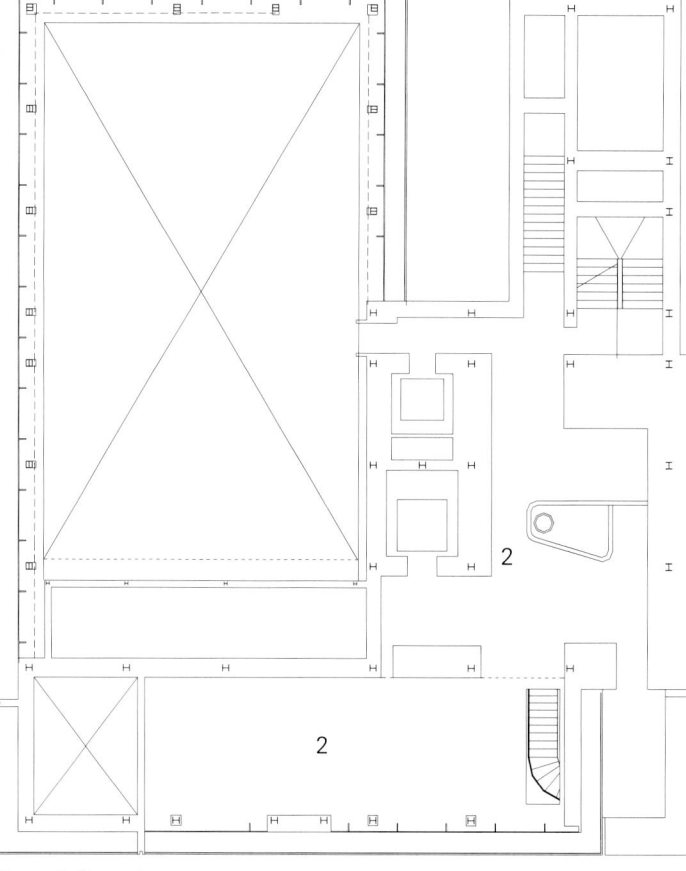

Seventh floor plan

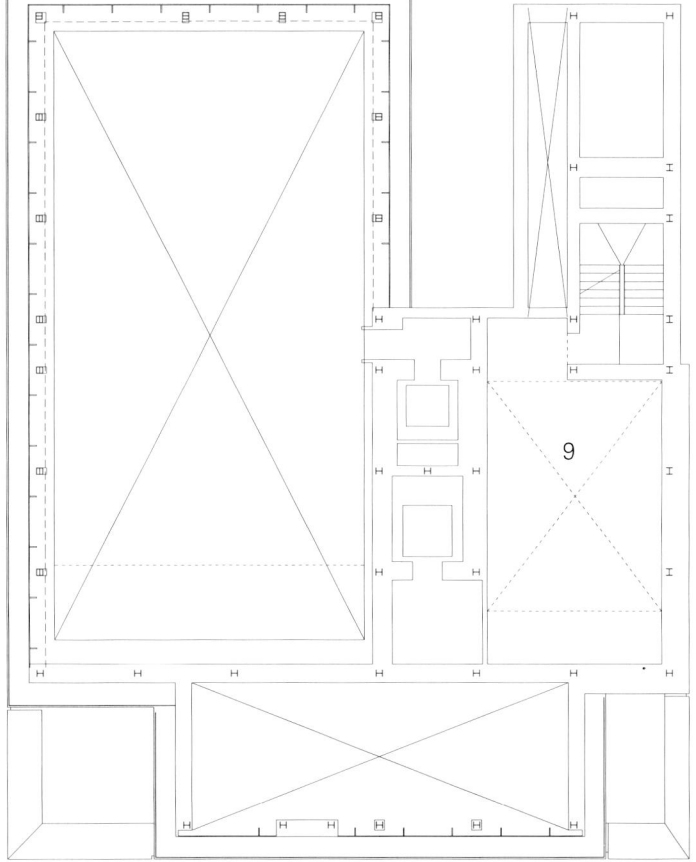

Eighth floor plan

1. Louis Vuitton Hall
2. Celux (Member's salon)
3. Office
4. Louis Vuitton Salon
5. Terrace
6. Retail (Shop)
7. Entrance
8. Beauty salon
9. Machine room
10. Parking
11. Car Entrance
12. Sub entrance hall
13. Storage
14. Repair room
15. Pantry

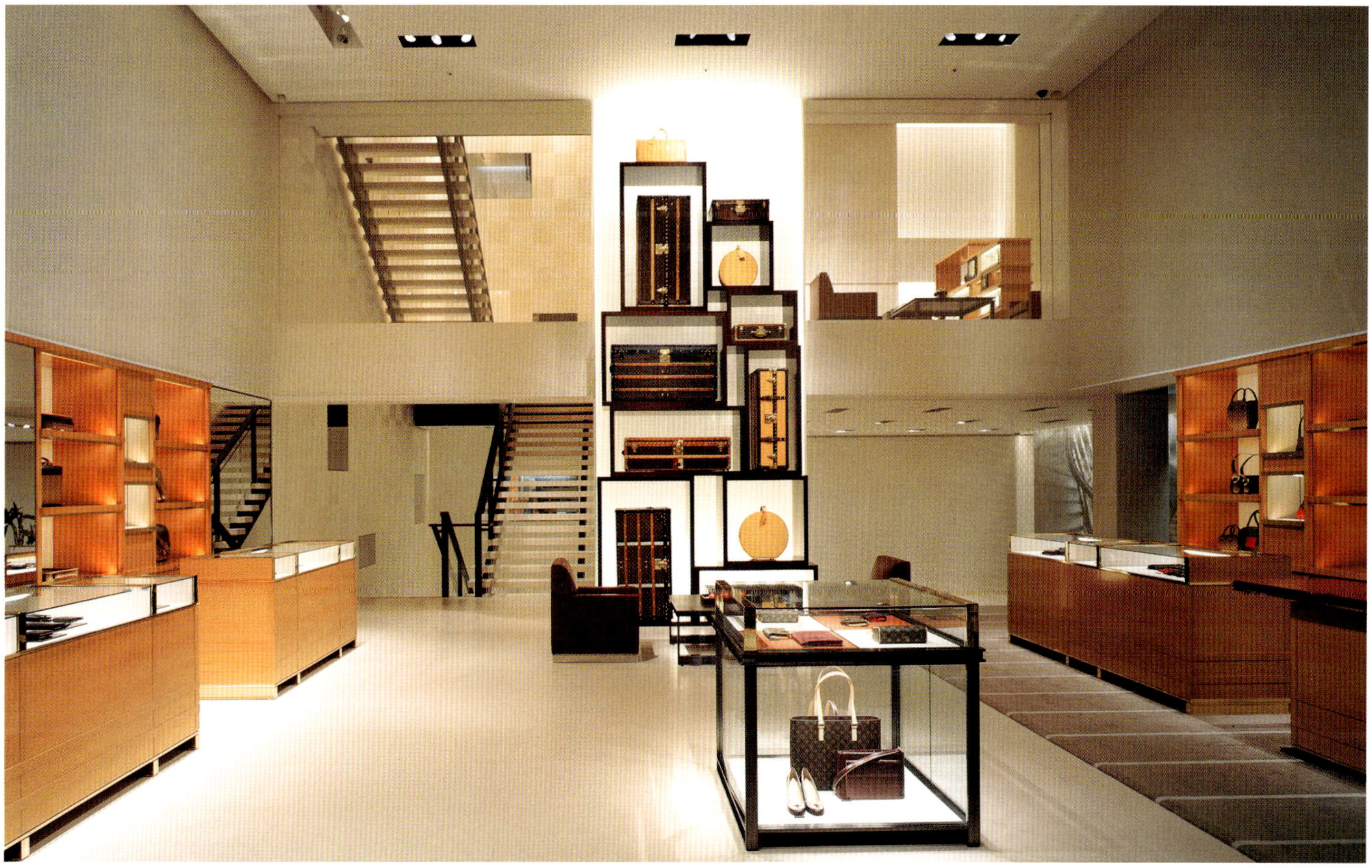

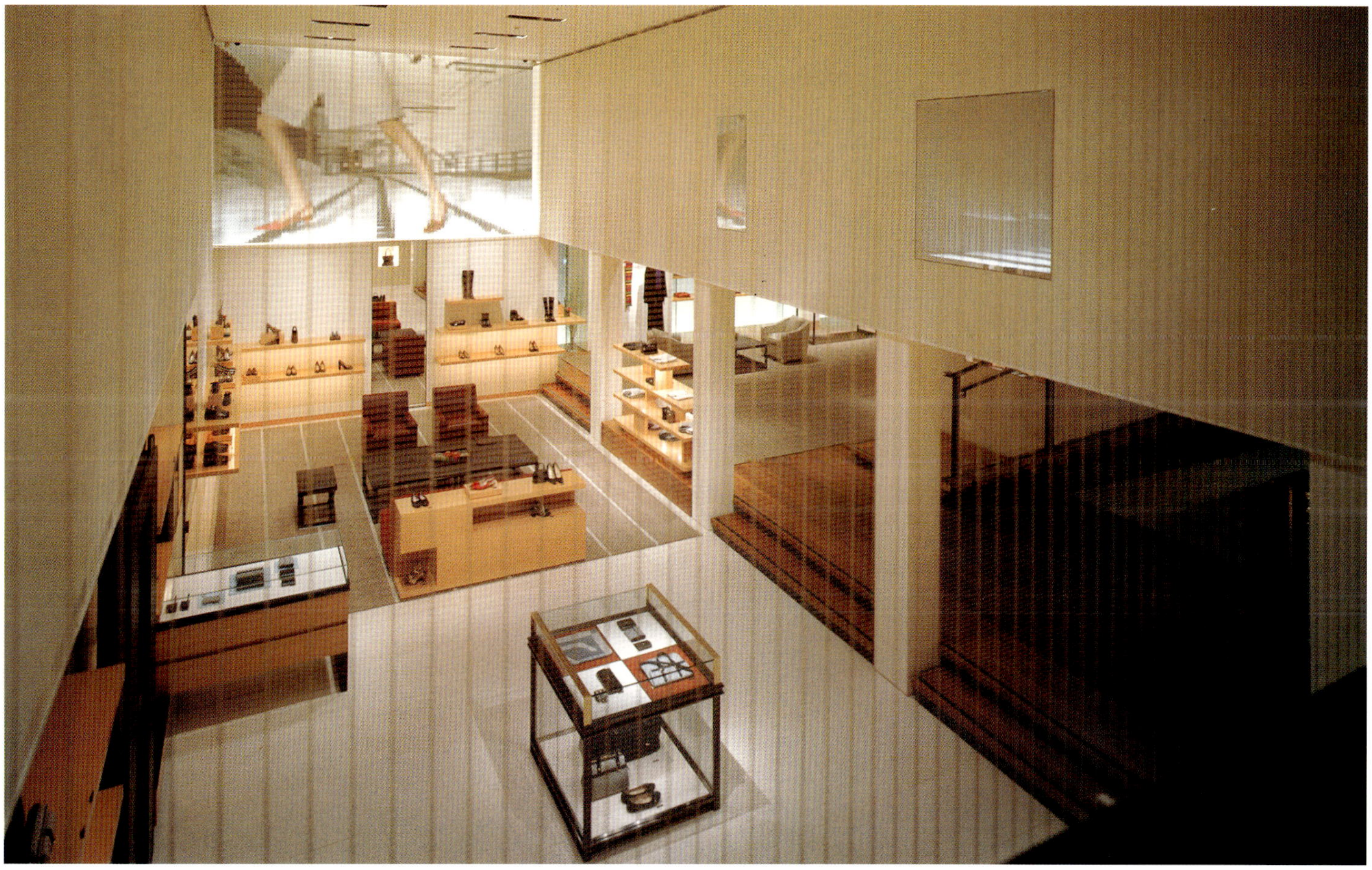

The building is designed as a collection of "trunks" of different sizes, proportions and lighting conditions, an allusion to the fact that Louis Vuitton began as a manufacturer of trunks. The trunks, each of which is basically a two-story box, are piled up and set slightly out of alignment both in plan and section. The void housing the stairwell is also treated as its own upright trunk.

1. Louis Vuitton Hall
2. Celux (Member's salon)
3. Office
4. Louis Vuitton Salon
5. Terrace
6. Retail (Shop)
7. Entrance
8. Beauty salon
9. Machine room
10. Parking

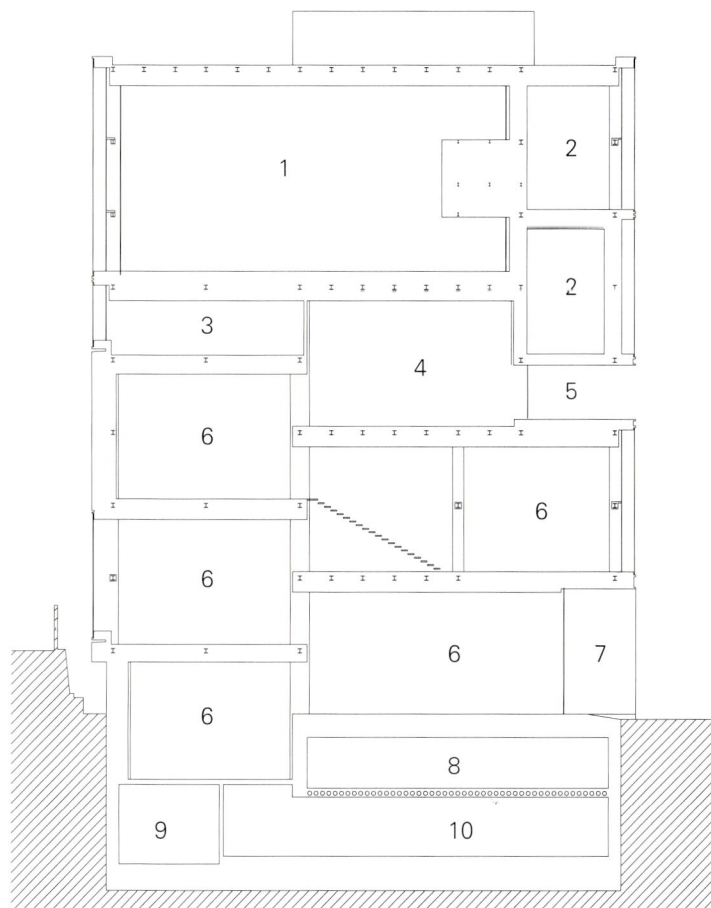

North elevation

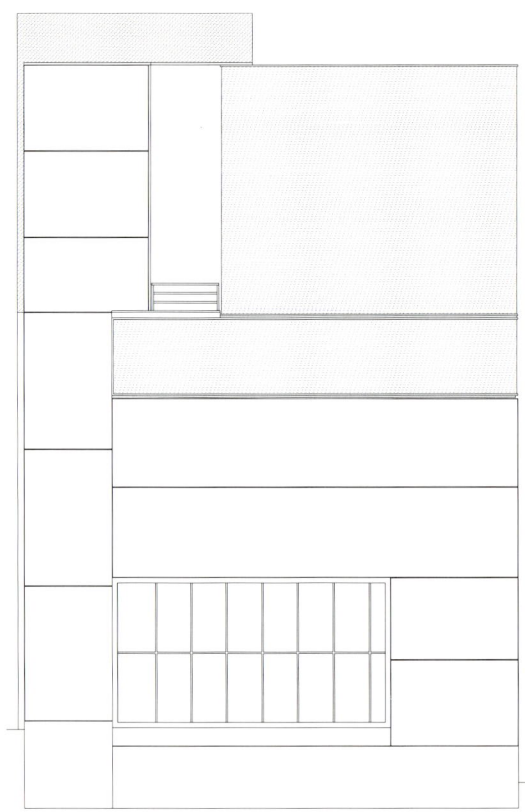

South elevation

A layer of glass panels etched with vertical stripes comprises the first layer of the façade's double skin. Over this are three kinds of light metal mesh, each with a different weave, and two kinds of stainless steel panels (polished and gilded) in rose and gold tones. The overall effect intentionally mimics the watery shimmer of moiré.

East elevation

West elevation

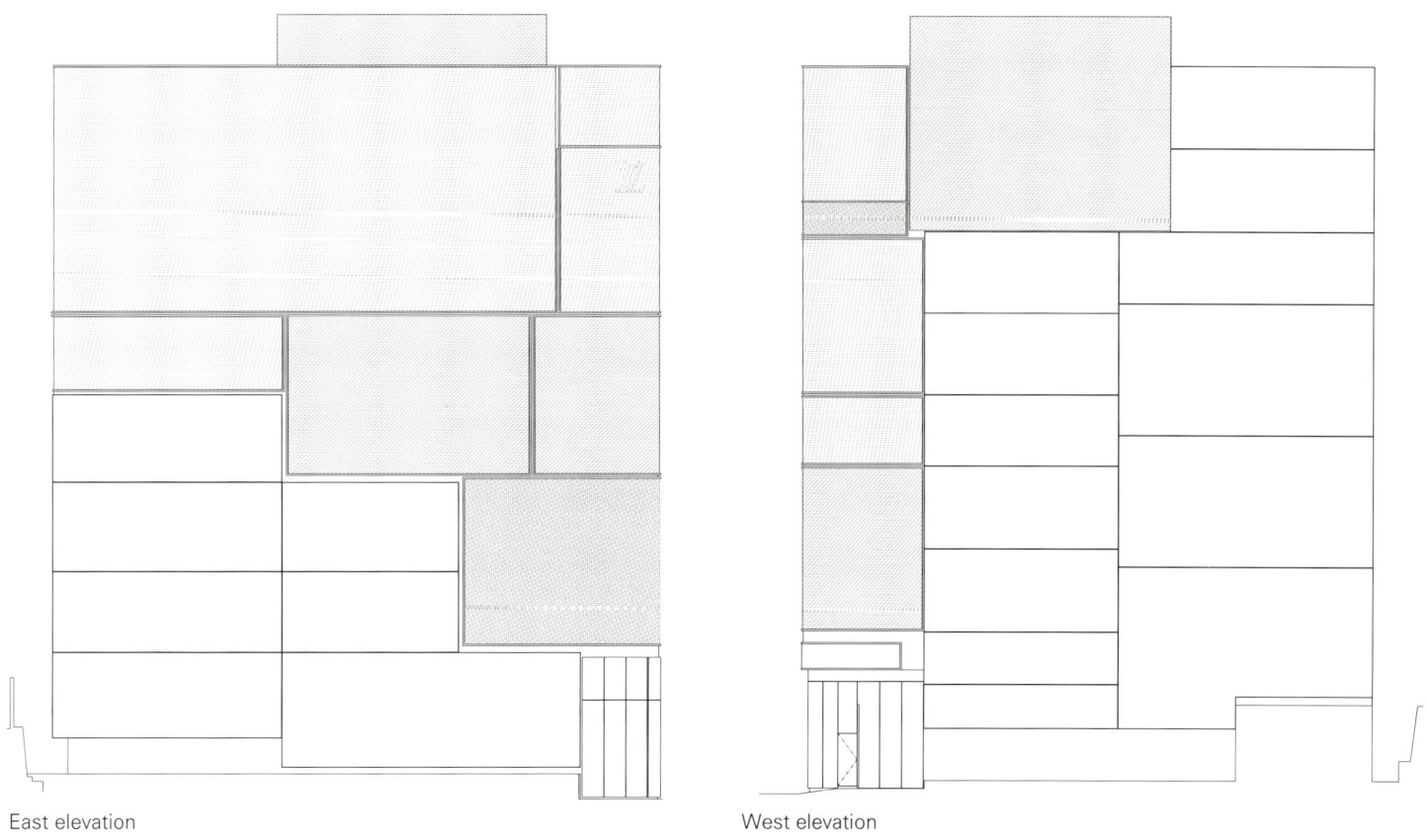

Javier Maroto & Álvaro Soto

La Oreja de Plata II

Madrid, Spain

Photographs: Juan Merinero

The jeweler's store La Oreja de Plata II, for the designer Chus Burés, occupies two floors, with the Calle Jorge Juan entry level measuring just 7 sqm in area, and a lower space of approximately 40 sqm. The architects decided to make the entrance floor a void from which one descends a transparent staircase, so that the space would be revealed slowly. In fact, the architects imagined that the whole entrance would be experienced as if inside a shop window that customers would not leave until they had gone down to the lower floor. In this movement, visitors are accompanied by display cabinets and glass boxes suspended from the ceiling onto which light is projected. The jewels and the objects are thus exposed to view, casting evocative shades on the glass supports.

On the lower floor there is a rectangular room ("a Mediterranean space", as Chus Burés called it) that is gently lit from above, reminiscent of the way light falls on the clear walls of a southern courtyard. The floor is of dark wooden planks without a skirting board, and creaks under the feet of the customers. The architects have created a radical and totally interior space because most of the work was done in the basement. They were interested in the idea of projecting the variable brightness of the natural and artificial light that passes through each cabinet. They converted the small street level entrance space into a skylight that illuminates the lower level of the shop and contains an almost transparent staircase.

Access to the shop is through a tiny floor that acts as a shop window. The boundaries between the shop window and the staircases leading to the basement are blurred, creating a bright space in which the elements on display float freely.

Elevation of a back-lit suspended cabinet

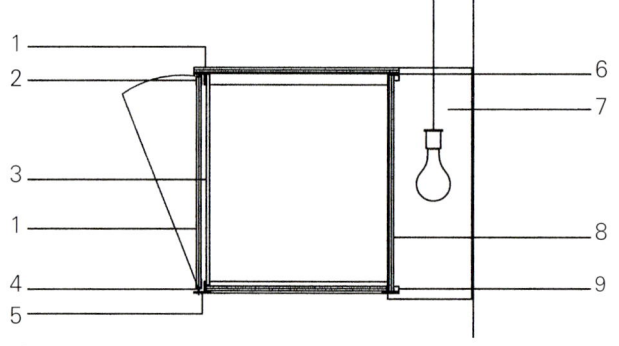

Section of a back-lit suspended cabinet

1. 4x4 mm STADIP transparent butyral
2. 15x10 mm U profile
3. 6 mm diameter bar
4. Bolts
5. e=2 mm T profile
6. 20x20 mm L profile
7. e=3mm painted plate RAL 9006
8. 4x4 mm STADIP white butyral
9. 10x10 mm bowtell

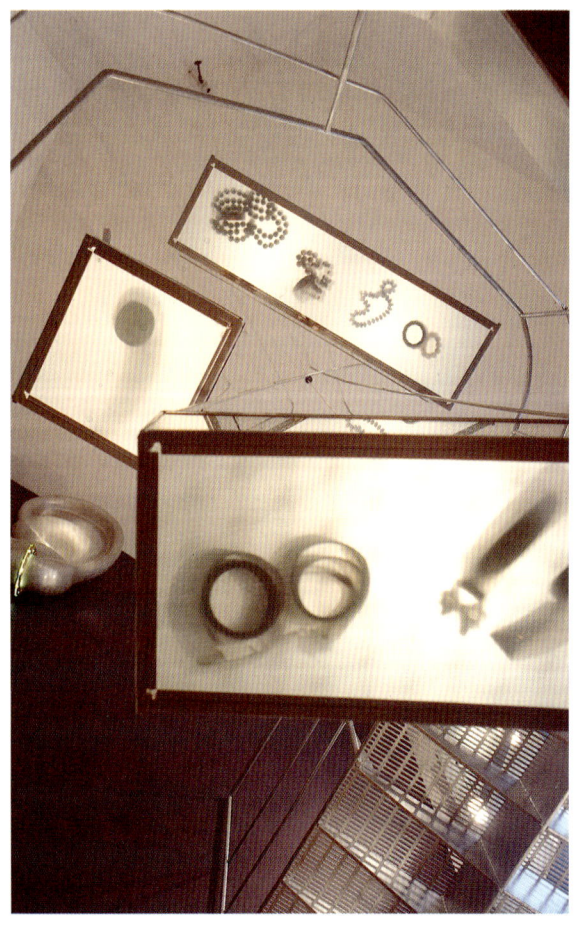

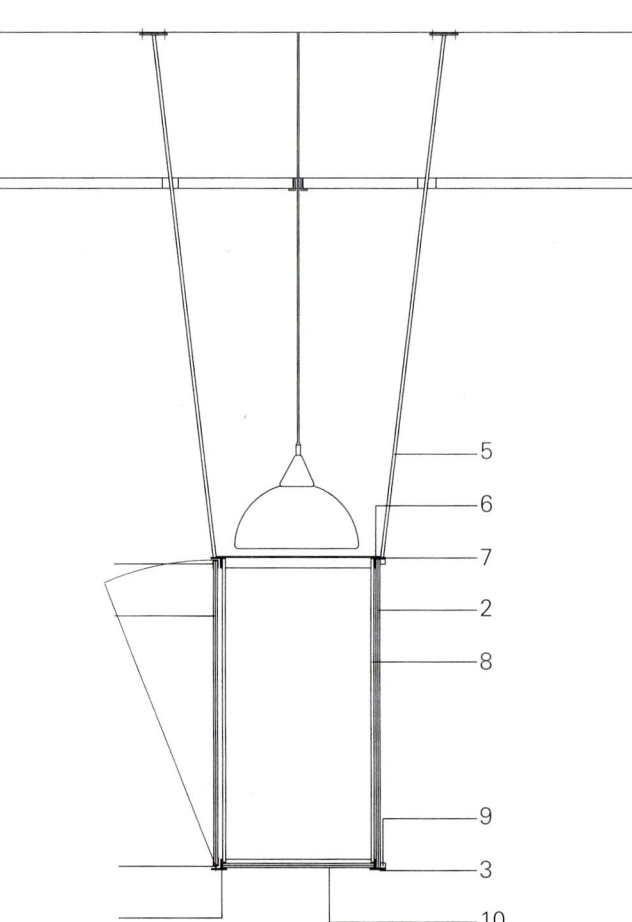

Section of a suspended cabinet

1. 15x10 mm U profile
2. 4x4 mm STADIP transparent butyral
3. Bolts
4. e=3 mm T profile
5. e=6mm bars
6. e=1mm perforated plate
7. 20x20 mm L profile
8. 6 mm bolts
9. 10x10 mm bowtell
10. 4x4 mm STADIP White butyral

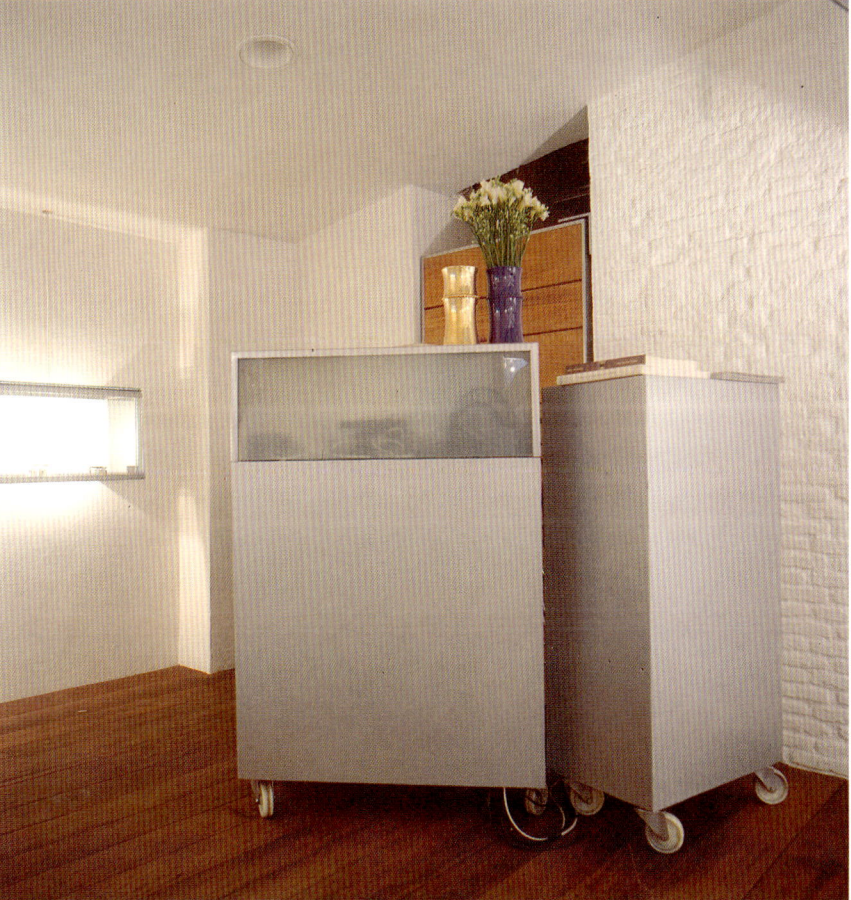

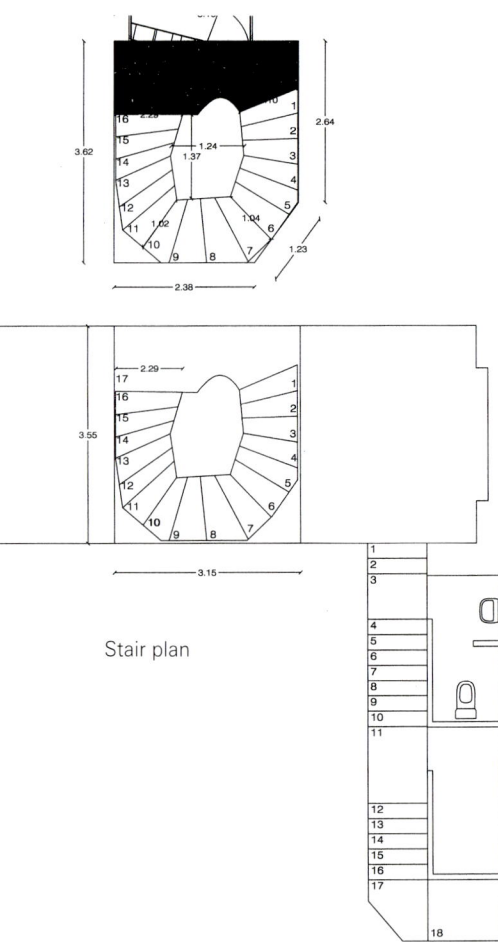

Stair plan

Artificial lighting is projected through the cabinets, transforming them into lamps. They are variable in shape, location and brightness.

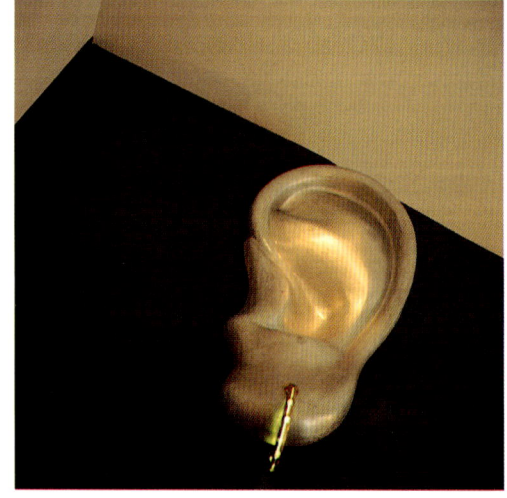

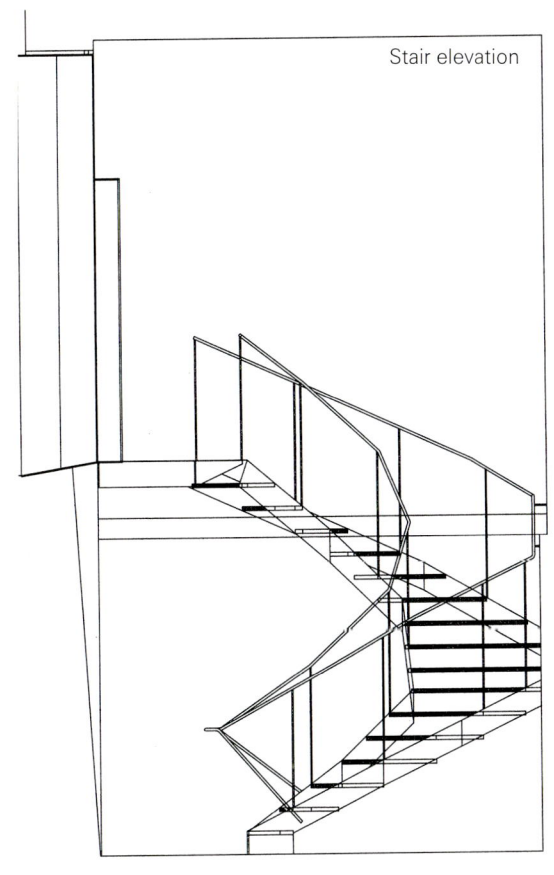

Stair elevation

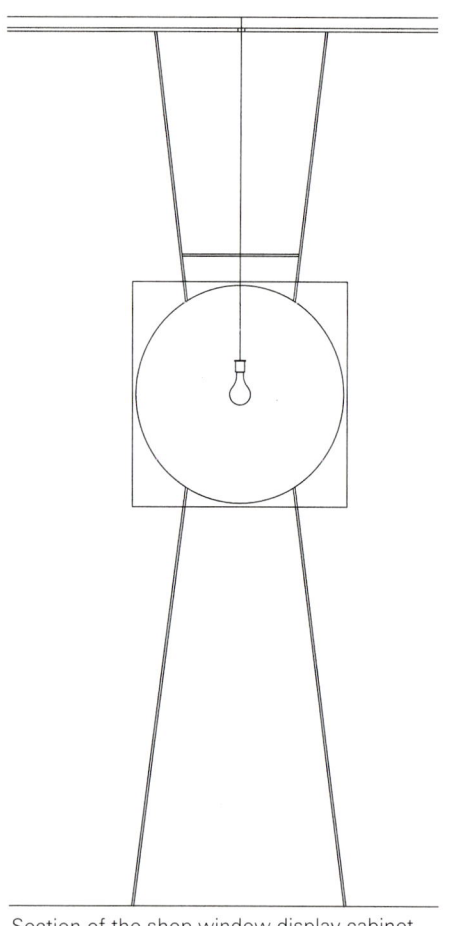

Section of the shop window display cabinet

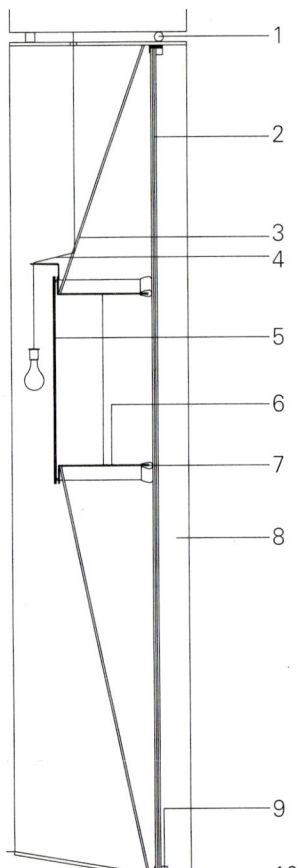

1. Neoprene profile
2. 6x5x6 mm STADIP
3. e=6 mm bars
   (welded to the shop
   window frame)
4. e=3 mm bar
5. 3x3 mm STADIP
   white butyral
6. e=3 mm plate
7. Neoprene profile
   supported by glass
8. e=10 mm frame
   polished and varnished
   steel
9. 20x20 mm bowtell
10. 40x20 mm L profile

Sergio Calatroni

Copy Center

Shizuoka, Japan

Photographs: Sergio Calatroni

The 66 sqm premises located in a shopping mall have become a focus of attention, an advertisement and the representative image of this copy service company. The scheme is integrated in mall elements, thus creating a sensation of greater space. The premises function as a shop window presenting the work that goes on inside it.

The scheme is developed through a startling interplay of lights, textures and colors that attract the attention of potential customers. The architect used transparent and reflective materials such as glass, metal, mirrors and colored Plexiglas. Most of the furniture is painted in opaque gold.

The purity of forms and the simplicity of the walls collaborate with the materials to enhance the intensity of the colors, which form an integral part of the design. The architect thus uses the interplay of light and color as a major element of the design.

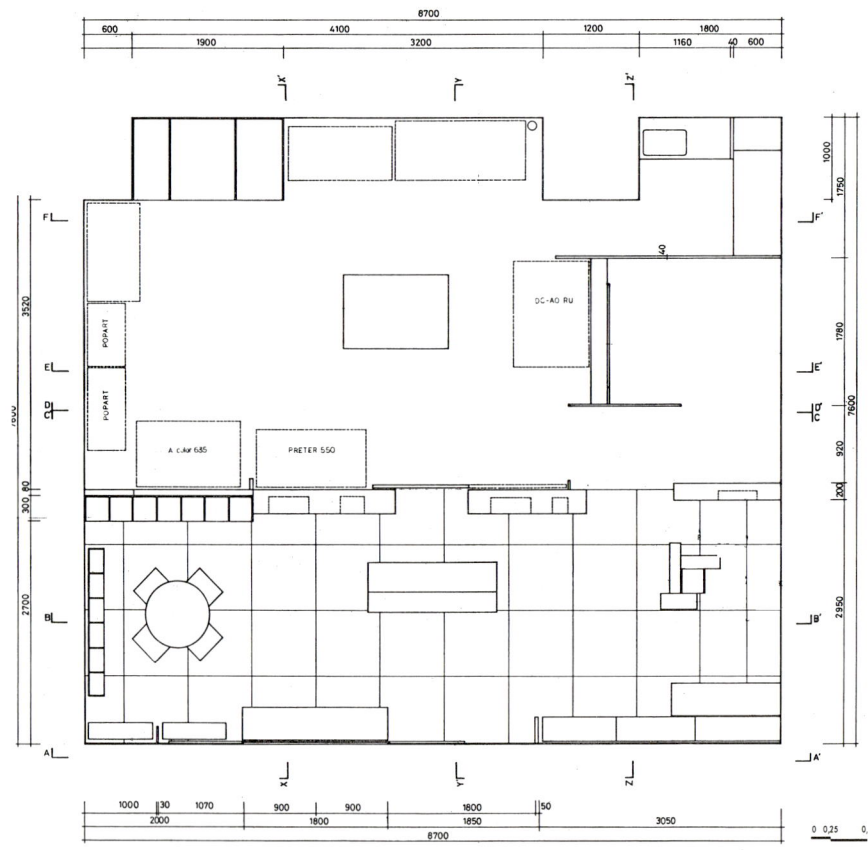

Ground floor plan

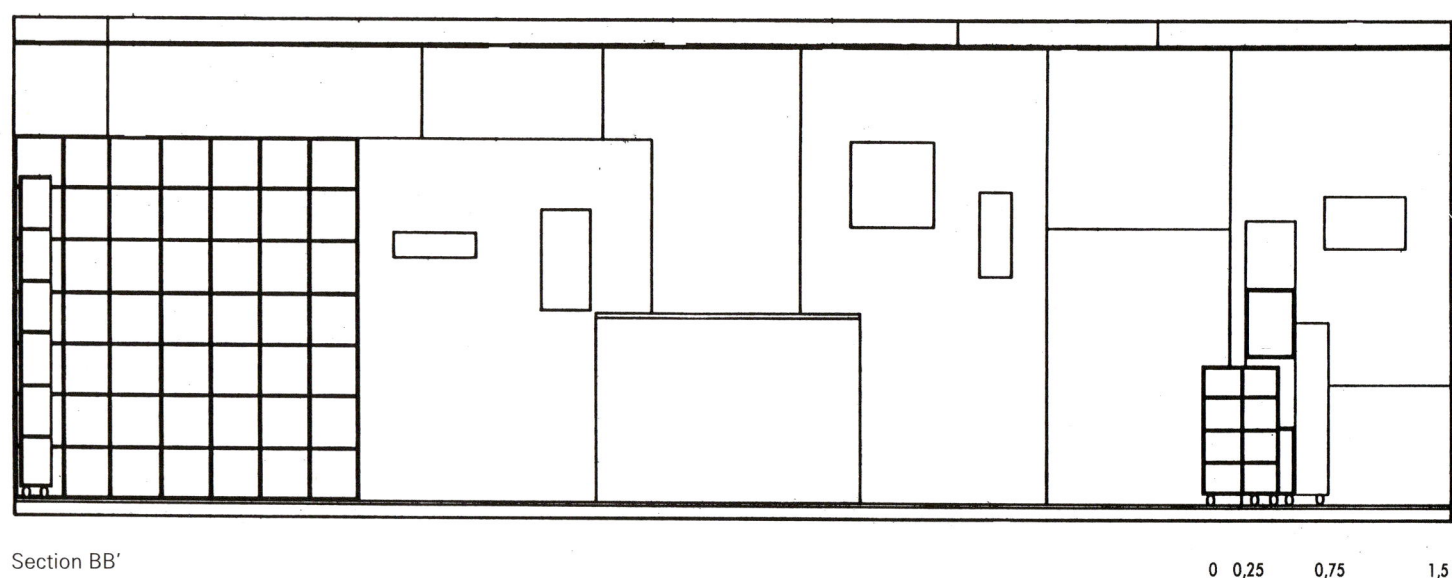

Section BB'

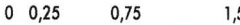
0   0,25   0,75   1,5

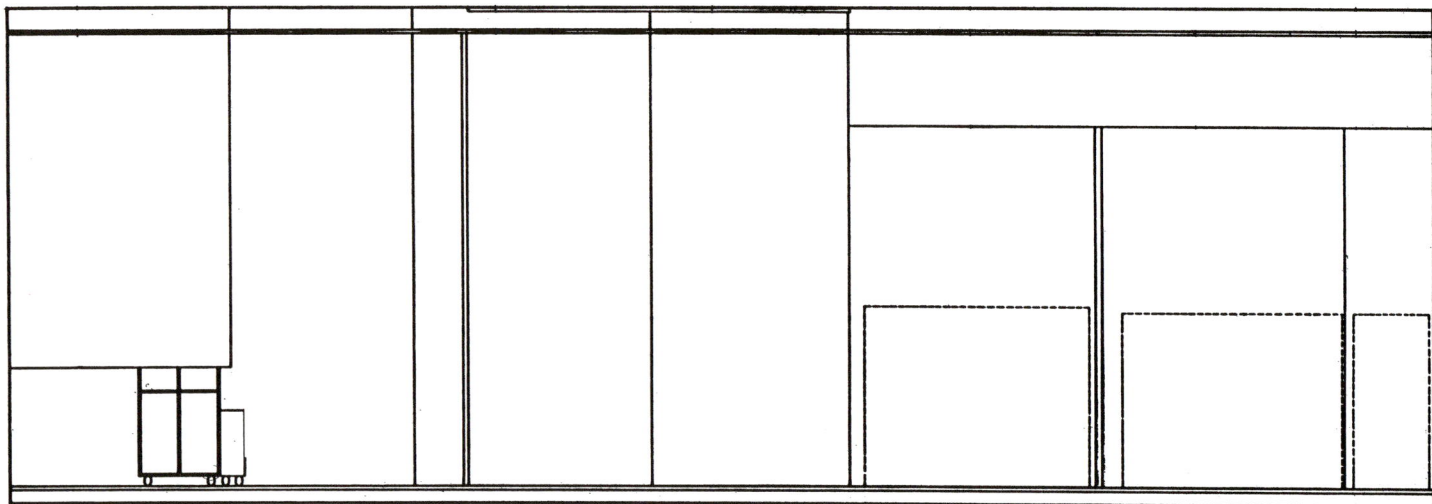

Section CC'

148

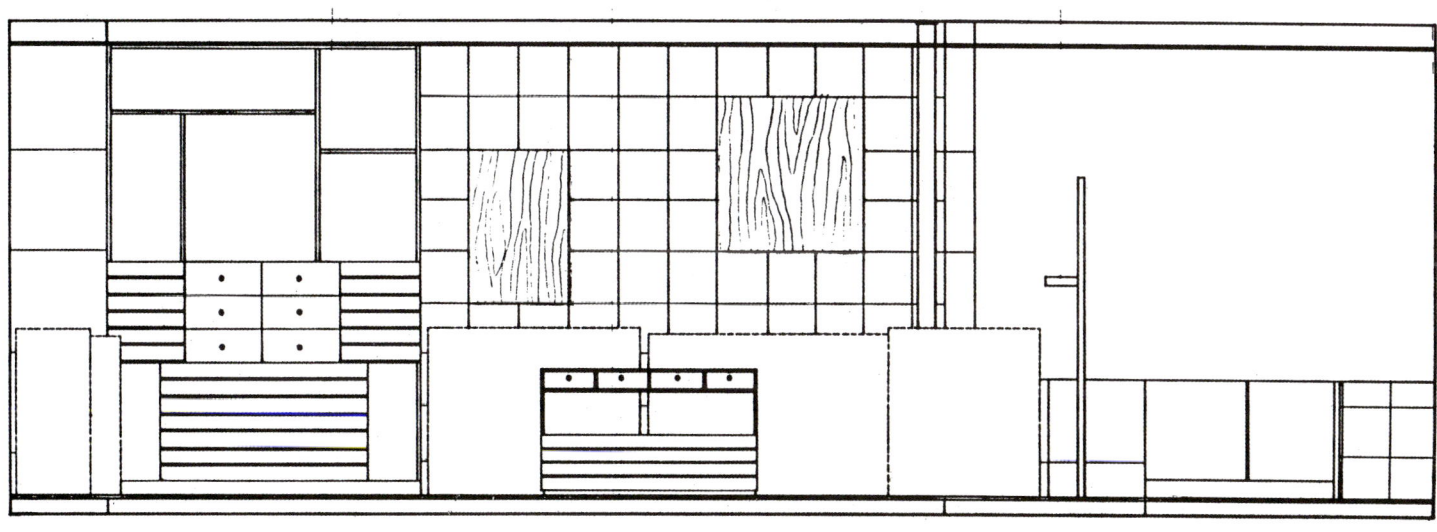

Section EE'

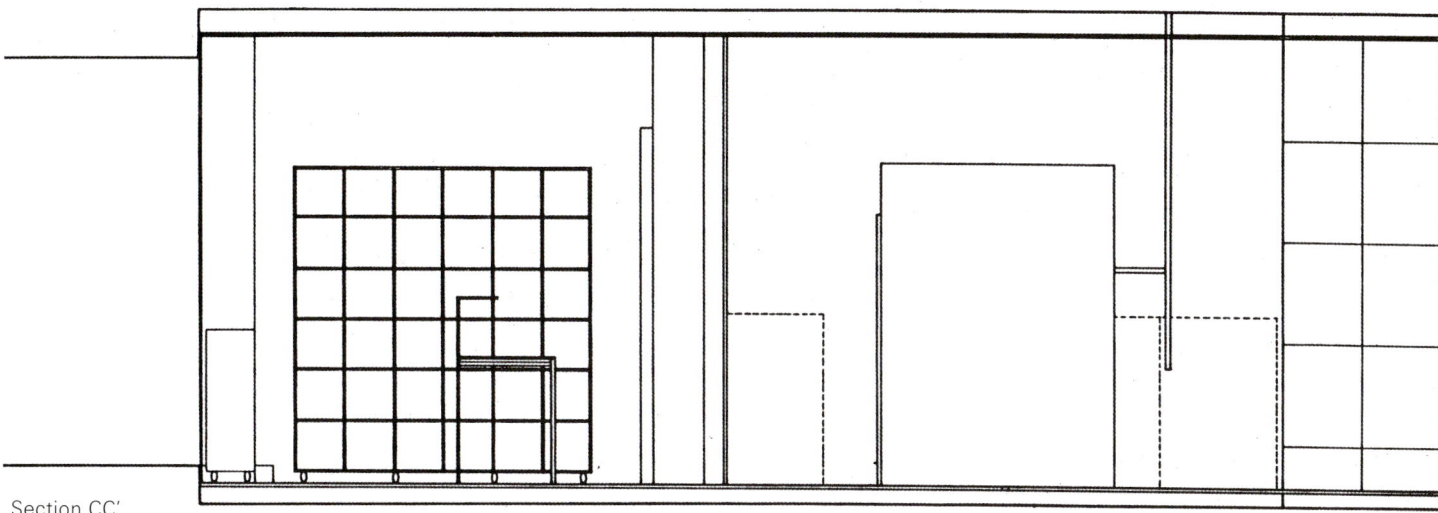

Section CC'

Patrick Genard

Sephora

Barcelona, Spain

Photographs: Jordi Miralles

This project involved the remodeling for commercial use of the interior of the premises located in Avinguda de la Llum, in "El Triangle" shopping centre of Barcelona. The premises are located in a double space. One part is in a space known as Avinguda de la Llum (the basement), and the other occupies part of the building of "El Triangle" shopping centre (the ground floor and mezzanine). The premises are on three levels with double access on the ground floor: direct street access from Carrer Pelai, and access from the common areas of the shopping centre. Ground floor access to the premises is through a double height hall that communicates with the basement by means of a double escalator and a lift for the disabled. The basement, which occupies the whole length of Avinguda de la Llum, will be for commercial use. At the sides of this space are the complementary areas such as: wardrobes, toilets for employees and the public, services and staff rooms.

Sephora is signalled from the entrance by a colonnade that is reflected to infinity, leading toward the vault of mirrors, a magnificent showcase that constitutes its architectural identity. A red carpet is an element of orientation and decoration, distributing the main corridors of the store. The floor of black and white marble and the black furniture confirm the sober and luxurious expression of the interior architecture.

From the street to the product, everything has been conceived to give the customers autonomy and rapid orientation, so that they can linger at will or seek guidance. The store is spatially distributed according to three different universes, three beauty trades: perfumery, make-up and beauty care.

The scheme takes the aesthetic concept of Sephora to an extreme: materials, furniture, design and scenery reflect the black and white chromatics of the other stores of the chain, whilst highlighting the architectural identity of Avinguda de la Llum.

One enters the store through a row of black and white grooved columns, reflected to infinity by mirror panels dotted with elliptical windows that allow one to see perfumes and monitors. The sides of the corridor and of the ceiling are also lined with mirrors that reflect the colonnade to infinity, upwards and downwards.

FUMS I DE COLORETS.   S'ABRIGUEN AMB L'AMISTAT I ES DISTAPLA AMB LA PASSIO

EL PETÓ

153

The general lighting of the store is provided by 16 rows of suspended lights per vault and lines of fluorescent tubes that directly illuminate the curved drop ceiling of the side galleries. In this area the perfumes are displayed on shelving units of black painted veneer and glass with integrated lighting.

Lazzarini Pickering Architetti

Fendi

Paris, France

Photographs: Matteo Piazza

This Rome-based architectural practice was engaged by Fendi to develop the new international image of its boutiques worldwide. The display elements in this shop create architecture rather than merely fill a space. These elements (shelves, tables and horizontal and vertical hanging fascias) have been proportionately scaled according to the dimensions of the space. The shelves measure up to 10 meters long, the tables up to 7, and the hanging fascias may be up to 20 meters in length. The entire boutique revolves around the staircase, which is crossed by metal elements that mark its progress upward in various directions. A series of display units were custom-designed for the project; as a whole, these bear a clearly defined geometry, yet they are differentiated by the use of materials, such as dark wood, wax-finished iron, prism mirror and glass tops. The space and position of each boutique will require a different architectural configuration of these display elements. This means that the many Fendi Boutiques around the world are instantly recognizable, while being inherently different, making each a unique spatial and shopping experience and also open to incorporating local architectural traditions and materials. The configuration of the shelves, fascias and tables encourages an informal display arrangement and movement through the store. Coats are hung or laid out in an apparently casual but sculptural way. The use of traditional and humble, low-tech materials offers the possibility of trying out new finishes. Rough rendered surfaces are finished with a varnish normally used to protect metal surfaces; the crude iron is first treated with a nitrate solvent to make it virtually stainless and is then finished in wax.

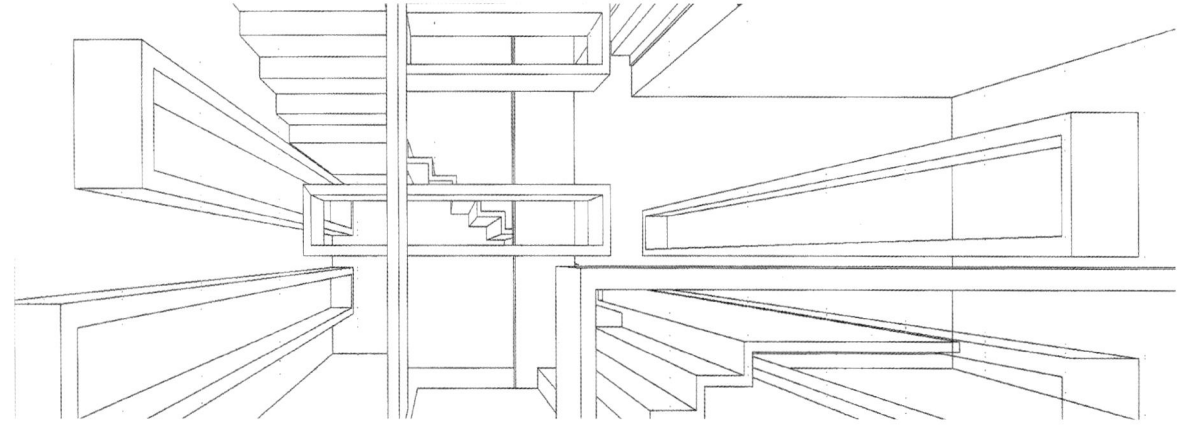

The entire boutique revolves around the staircase, which is crossed by metal elements that mark its progress upward in various directions. A series of display units were custom-designed for the project; as a whole, these bear a clearly defined geometry, yet they are differentiated by the use of materials, such as dark wood, wax-finished iron, prism mirror and glass tops.

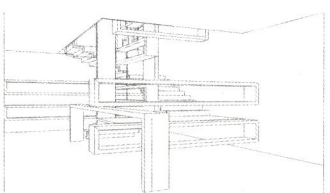

Ground floor plan

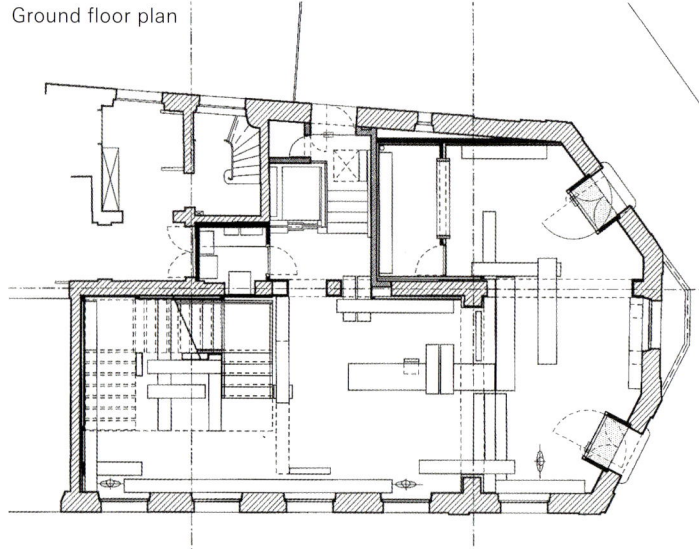

First floor plan

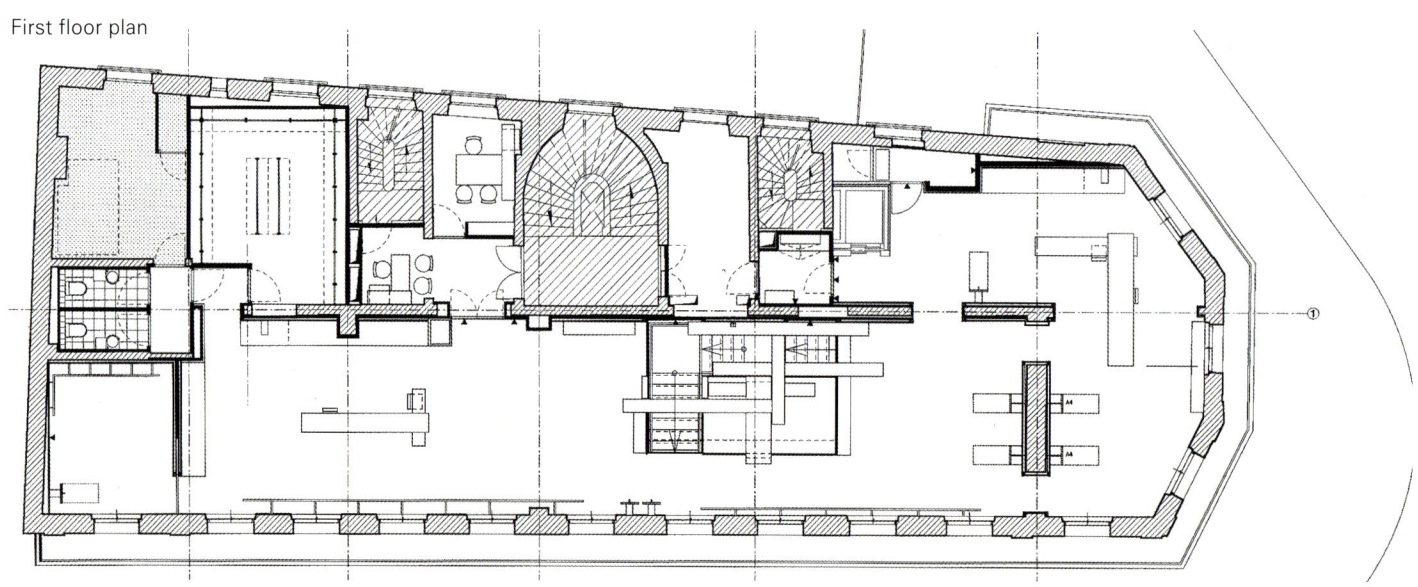

Second floor plan

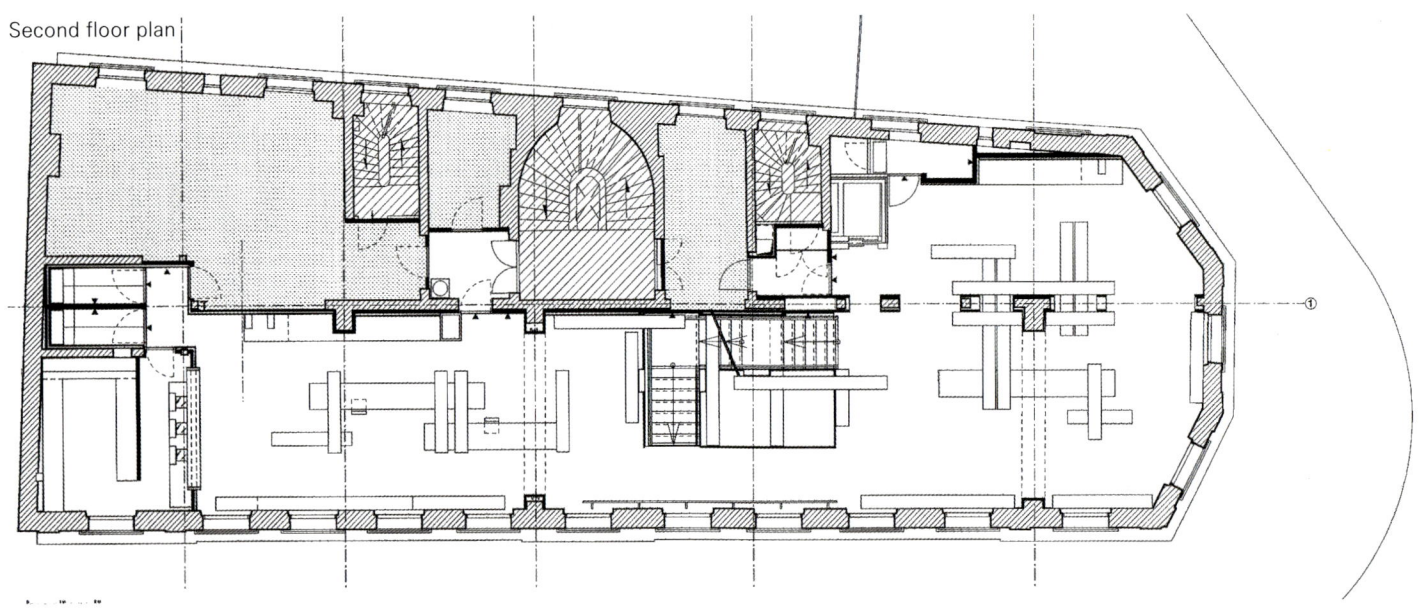

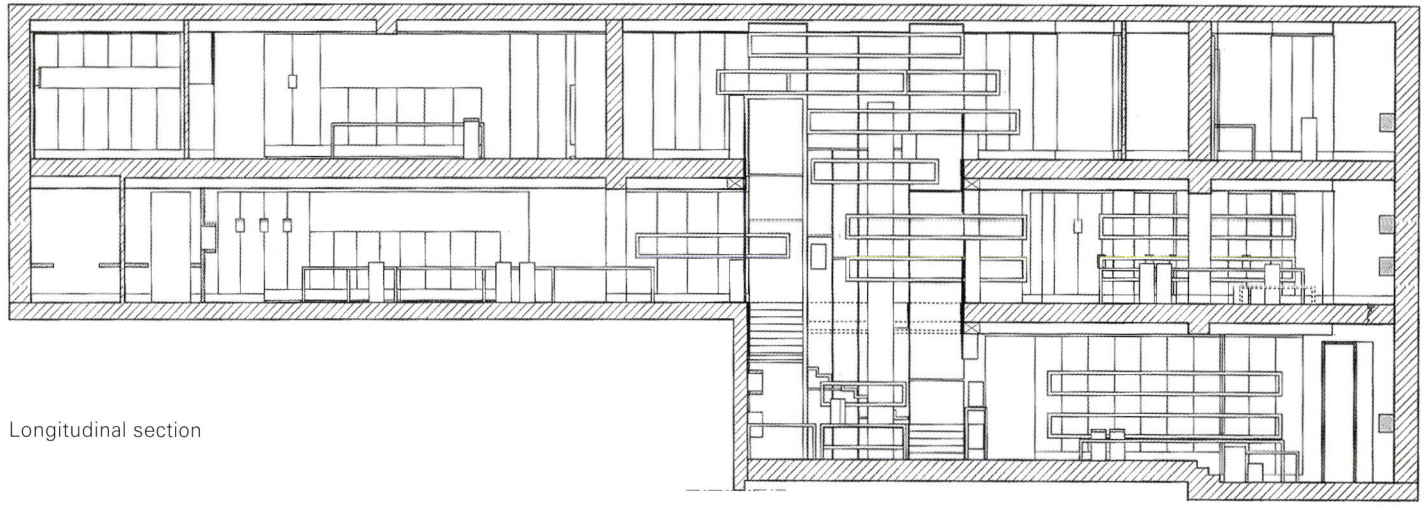

Longitudinal section

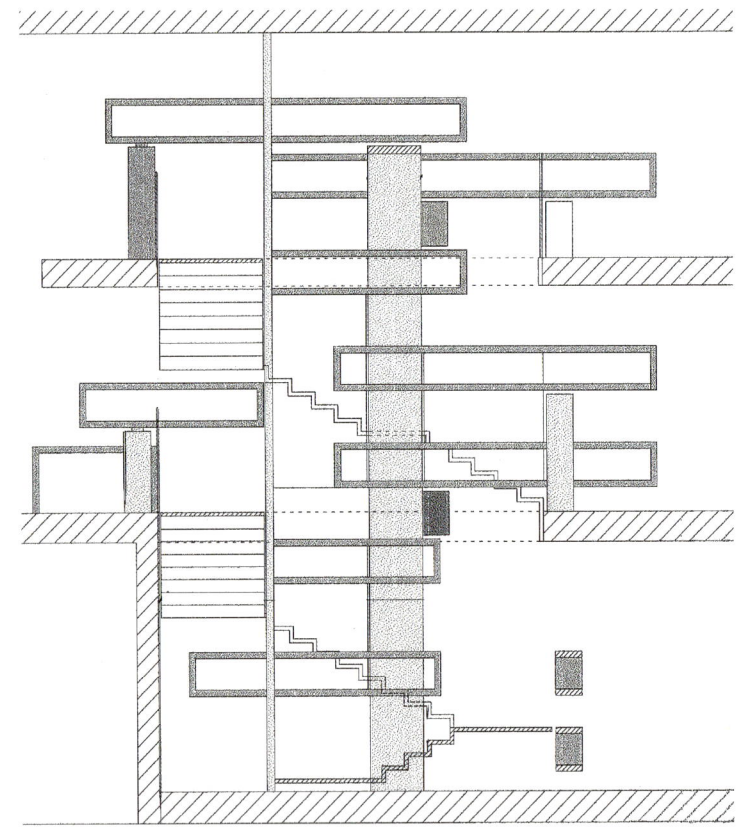

Cross sections

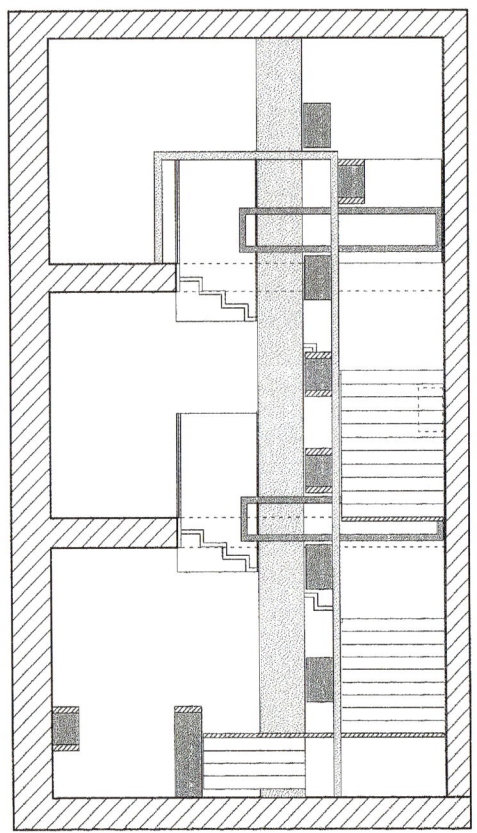

The use of traditional and humble, low-tech materials fits in with the idea of keeping the style informal and also provides the possibility of trying out new finishes. Rough rendered surfaces have been finished with a varnish normally used to protect metal surfaces; the crude iron is first treated with a nitrate solvent to make it virtually stainless and is then finished in wax.

J. Greco & J. Smolenicky

Zelo Hairdresser

Zurich, Switzerland

Photographs: Christian Kerez

A vibrantly coloured interior glows from behind a mellow grey sandstone facade. This relationship of colours between town and shop is a central element in the design. Visual charm, and the effect of advertising which is linked with it, is the real essence of the project. Its colourfulness is intended to achieve an effect which is similar to that of the enormous illuminated hoardings which cast a spell over the town at night.

In this instance, however, the advertising has not been pasted on. The room itself is an advertisement; and in fact the kind of advertisement which was created by spatial means. Inside the room there is an artificial tension. So much of what composes our daily spatial reality is absent. Everything that could compete with the effect of colour has been extracted from this reality. Apart from the necessary seating there is no reference to human proportions. In this room there are no shapes, no materials which would allow volume perception. There are no details. The result is the sensation of a two-dimensional room as in a hyper-realistically-reconstructed comic, or as if one had entered the synthetic world of a video clip. All that remains of everyday reality is a wafer-thin surface. The room consists of colour and light. The diminution of spatial reality is not intended to be abstract but rather elementary in order to be able to reach the essential power of the colour in spite of its diminution; the project is not an installation but continues to be committed to everyday use.

The main intention was to set the direct expression of the colourfulness against surroundings dominated by shades of grey.

The shop is designed as a direct expression of colour in contrast to the dark and grey surroundings. The elements used daily have been reduced to a minimum expression in order to create a neutral interior to highlight the powerful use of colour.

Except for the necessary chairs, nothing suggests the functional nature of the elements of which the shop is made up or relates them to human proportions.

Roger Hirsch

IS Industries Stationery Store

New York, USA   *Photographs: Patrik Rytikangas*

For the Industries Stationery Store project, the architects have created a flexible and stimulating space, a window that captures the attention of pedestrians and attracts them into the interior of the store, without detracting from the product on display. All this with a budget of just $25,000 and in only three months from the conception of the design to completion of the work. The interior structure was stripped of all extra elements, respecting only the old brick walls and the irregular wooden floor. The main display elements are made from natural maple wood, unpolished aluminum and untreated wooden boards. The placement of these elements emphasizes the long, narrow shape of the space and enhances the products on display.

A maple wood counter measuring amost 5.5 meters, in the form of a long box supported on aluminum legs with a square section, seems to float above the floor. Inside it conceals all the store's services, such as the computer (of which only the monitor is visible), the cash register and the space for storing bags and gift-wrapping. This counter also acts as a display, and its exaggerated length induces customers to travel along the long, narrow space.

The system of steel shelves running along the brick wall is suspended from the ceiling and rests on the floor, leaving two display surfaces, one at counter level and another at eye level. Papers and envelopes hang from a steel band that runs along the rear of the shelf. The papers and envelopes on display are attached to the shelf by small magnets, and can thus be easily replaced. This display system is illuminated by a strip of halogen lamps inserted in the front rail of the upper shelf. The electric cables of the shelves and the counter are hidden inside tubular aluminum structures. The front display area that acts as a shop window houses a sculptural system consisting of a stack of wooden boards crossed by two floor-to-ceiling steel bars. At the opposite end of the store a 2.74 x 3.04 m fabric screen conceals 2.4 m fluorescent tubes, creating the effect of a box of light and giving clarity and brightness to the area furthest from the street.

The colorful and lively shop window creates a strong impact in the environment. The products on display act as decorative elements, attracting the attention of passers-by.

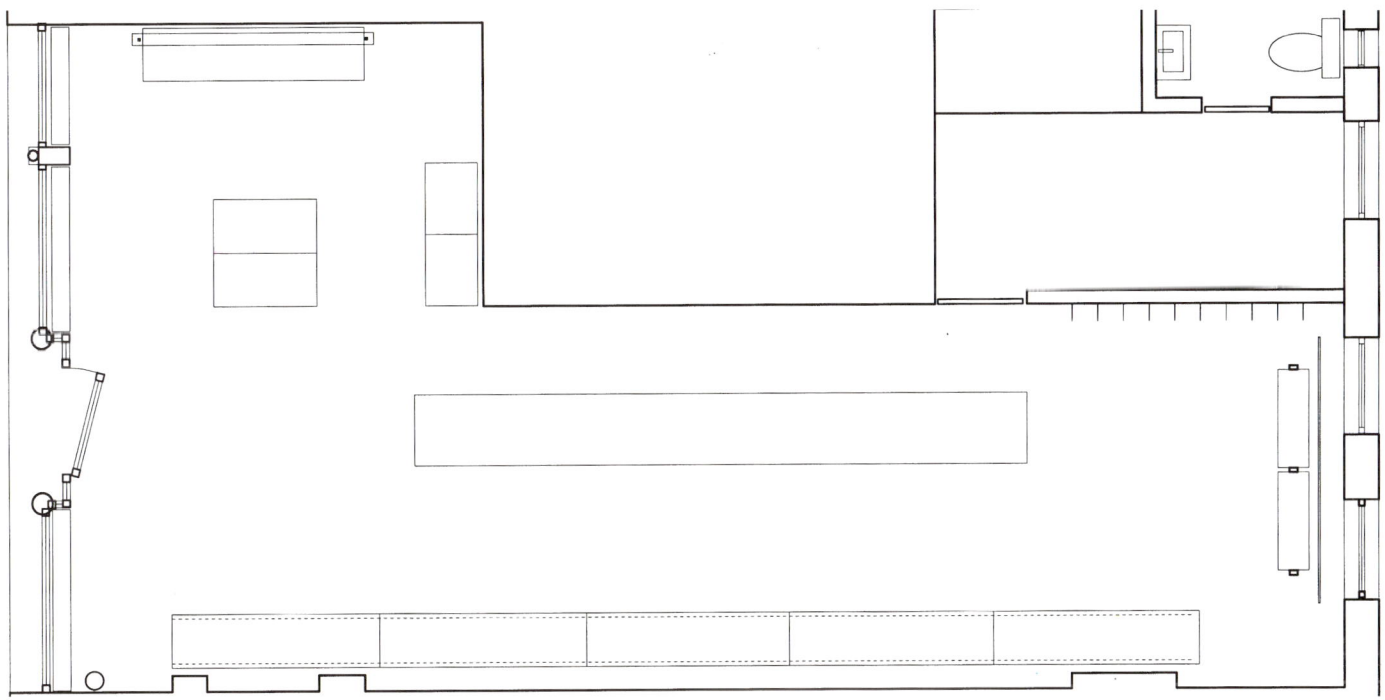

Ground floor plan

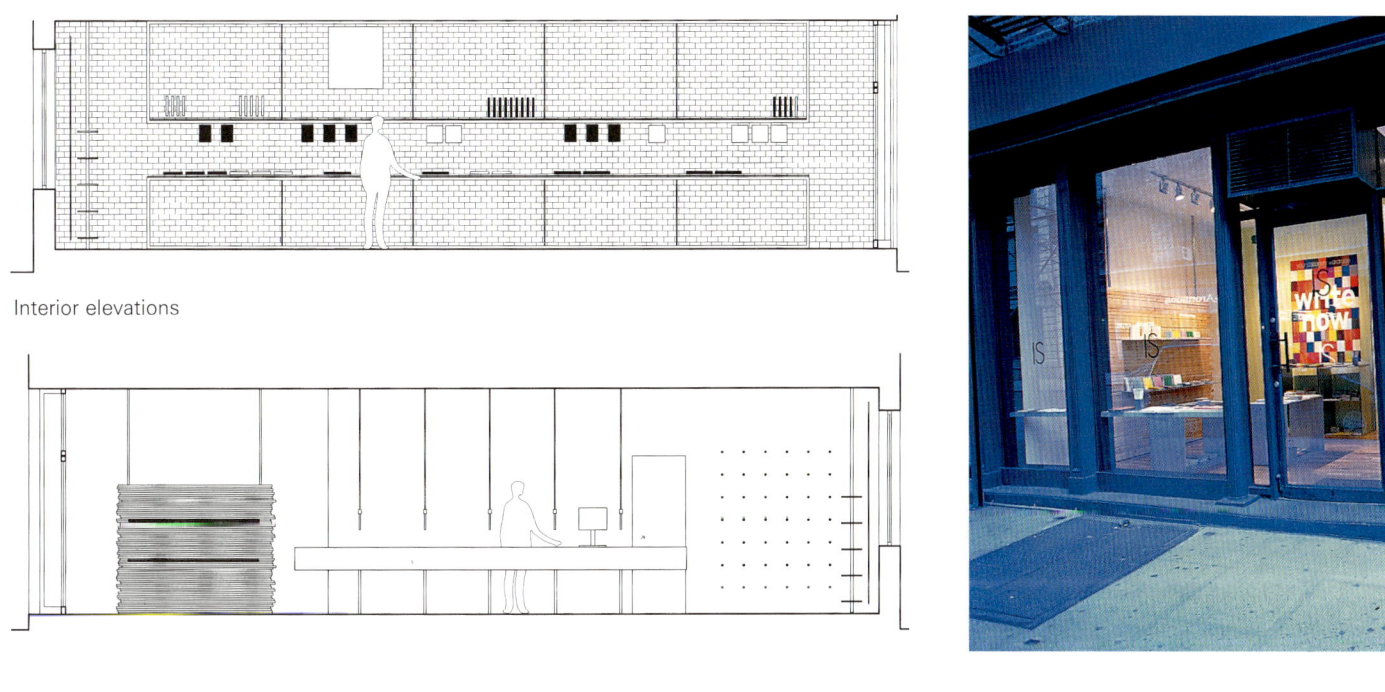

Interior elevations

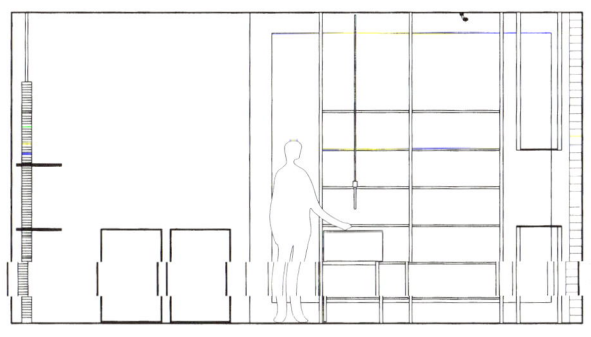

Aluminum shelves can be placed between the boards, since the weight of the wood keeps them in place. Easily movable aluminum boxes, open at the sides, occupy the entrance area in front of the stacked wooden boards.

The highly geometric display elements and counter reinforce the linear nature of the space and invite customers to move along the circulation space.

your stationery wardrobe

write now is

ADD+ (Manuel Bailo, Rosa Rull)

Sita Murt Boutique (Avinyó Street)

Barcelona, Spain *Photographs:Giovanni Zanzi*

The project for the shop Sita Murt began when, during an initial visit to the site (a small, ground floor space), a stairway leading to a basement with a barrel vault ceiling was discovered. The wish to incorporate this space into the overall design scheme led to the idea of punching openings into the vaulted ceiling to bring air and light into the basement's darkest recesses.

From the start, the construction process was presented as an exercise in metal. First was the pick-up drill work and the creation of a number of holes in varying diameters done with an orderly repetition of precise, 20-centimeter socket punches, the end result being a series of flowery button-holes. Next came the placing of structural light fittings made of curved sheet metal. Via their anchorage system to the vault of the ceiling, the light fixtures help redistribute the load that these very same openings had destabilized. Finally, a network of curved and bent metal tubes was suspended from the ceilings, weaving their way throughout the space, turning the light openings into buttonholes.

Given its concentrated structural capacity, construction in metal enables both a reduction in width and thickness of the elements used and an increase in their amount of available length for support.

The anchorage for the eight-millimeter curved sheet metal structural caps supports the ceramic vault covering the basement, thus enabling their perforation. Being higher than is strictly necessary, these structural sheet metal elements also serve as lighting fixtures and display cases.

The two sections of curved and bent metal tubes (of three and ten centimeters in diameter) which sew the space together from top to bottom with the minimum number of auxiliary pieces, serve to support the stairway as well as provide hangers on which clothes can be displayed.

The dimensions of both the ground floor and the basement, and the way they have been treated as two different containers, suggested the use of a single color in each space. The design scheme thereby plays up the contrast created between the two levels through the interplay of openings.

AVINYO STREET

For the choice of color on the ground floor and façade, a preliminary study of the range of colors seen in the new shops which have sprung up recently on Calle Avinyó (viewed as a representative sample of those that have opened throughout Barcelona's old city) was conducted. Among the spectrum of bright colors available, that corresponding to the address of number 18 was chosen.

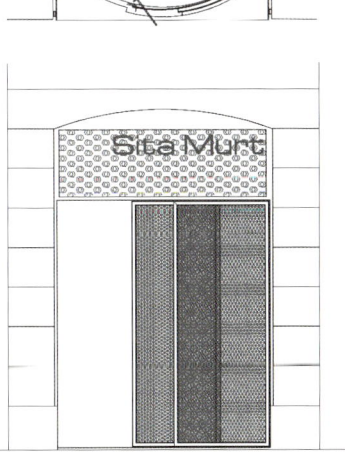

1 Entrance
2 Counter
3 Changing rooms
4 WC
5 Store
6 Stars leading to the basement
7 Stars leading to the mezzanine

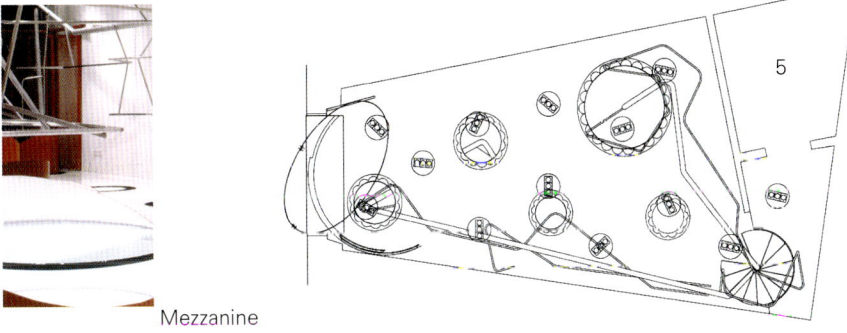

Mezzanine

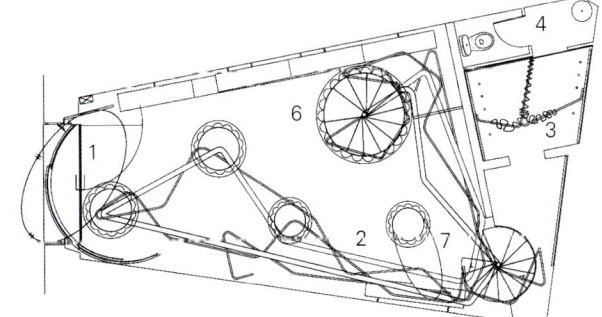

Ground floor

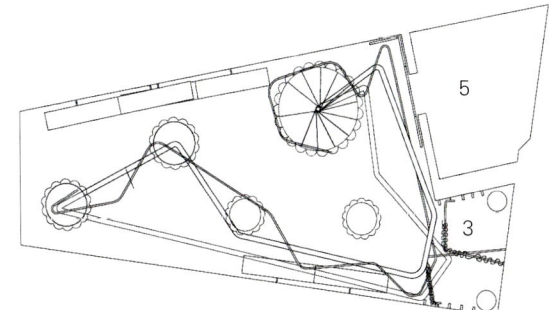

Basement

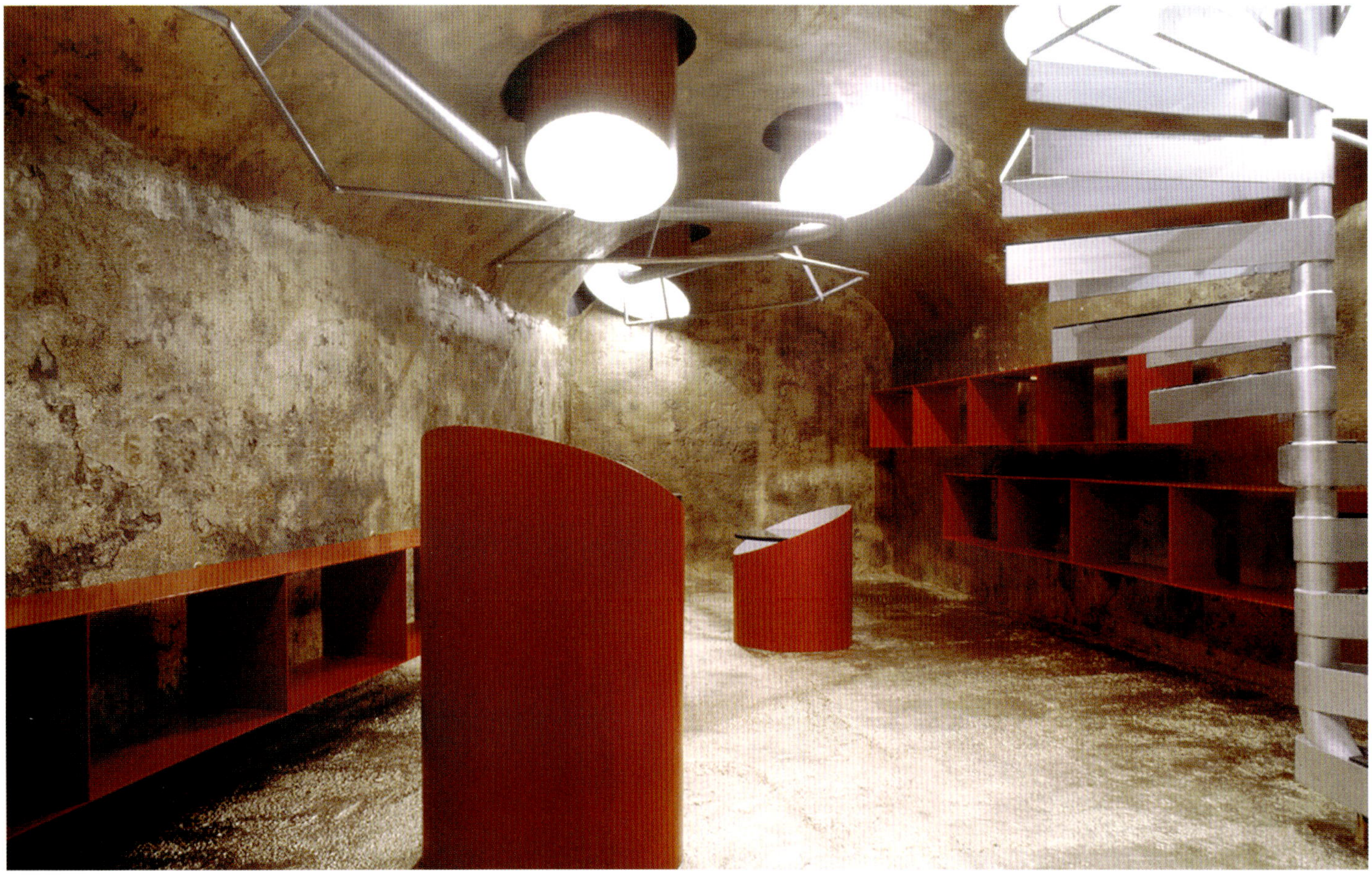

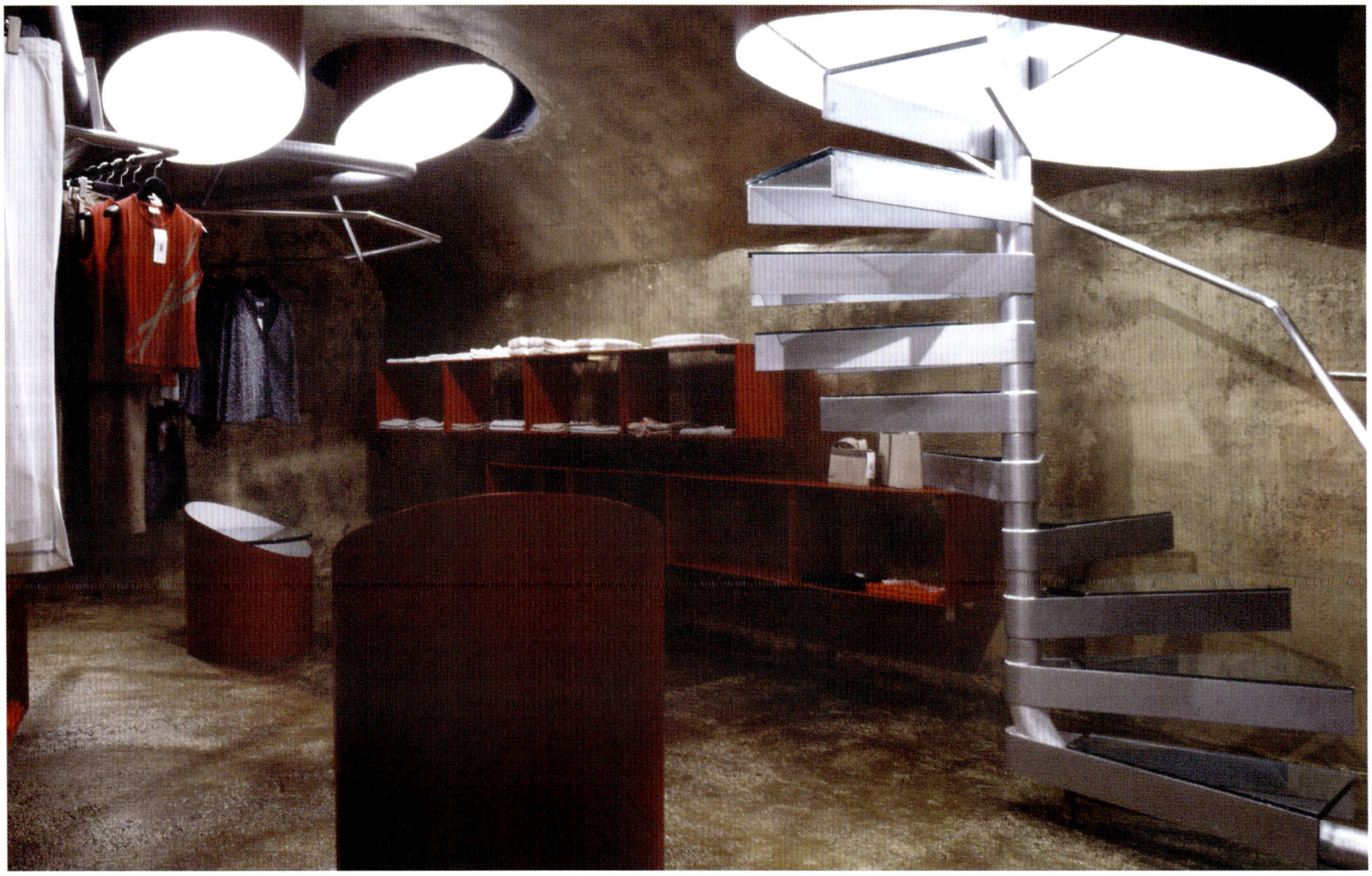

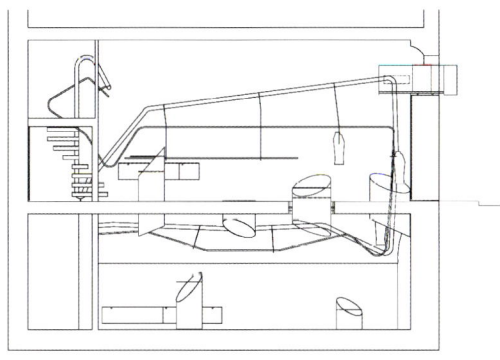

Longitudinal section of light fixture

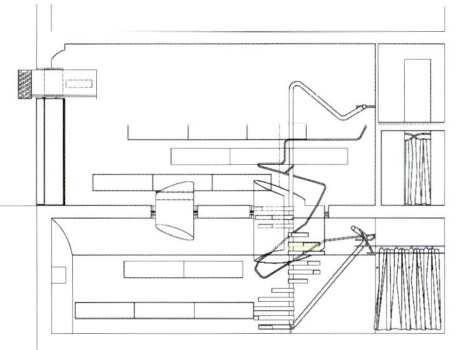

Longitudinal section through the stairs to the basement

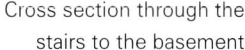

Cross section through the stairs to the basement

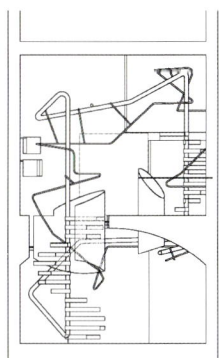

The color for the basement was chosen with a view to putting the rustic texture of the walls to use, bringing out its qualities by giving it a sheen.

Detail of one of the skylights

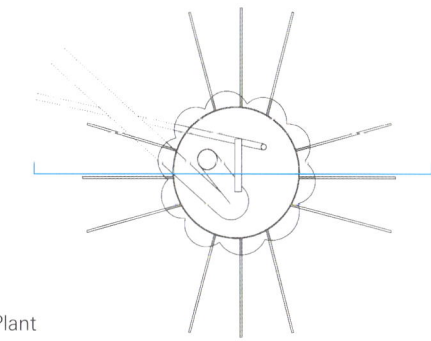

Plant

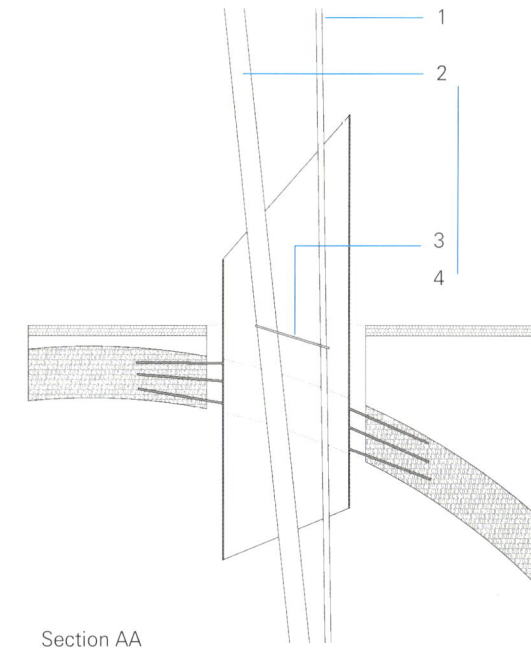

Section AA

1. Hanger
2. Support tube
3. Bracket
4. Vault

Unfolding of the vault retaining shee

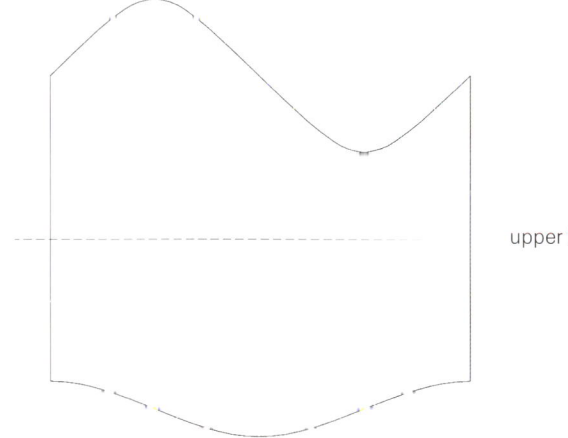

upper floor level

Muti Randolph

Galeria Melissa

Sao Paulo, Brazil

Photographs: Romulo Fialdini

Plastic.o.rama made in Brazil, is a project that arose under the auspices of Melissa, a major plastics producer that recently celebrated its 25th birthday.

Famous for the "Hawaianas" rubber sandals that have invaded the world, Melissa has become an effective worldwide representative of Made in Brazil, Melissa creates fashion accessories in plastic, especially footwear. The enterprise has commissioned renowned personalities in the worlds of fashion and design (Fernando & Umberto Campana and Karim Rashid, among others), to generate a colorful, fantastic world of plastic, a sort of ethical Disneyland for design accessory fans.

The setting for the collection, Galeria Melissa, is also a hymn to plastics. Muti Randolph has utilized plastics in all possible expressive ways. (...) The footwear in bright colors is contained in transparent bubbles that emerge from something similar to shiny horns-of-plenty. The unusual display system features clusters of these elements that descend from the ceiling or wrap themselves around bases rising from the floor, moulded in shiny white plastic.

There are also biological connotations: the display fixtures look disturbingly like large spermatozoa. The sinuous pattern of the stripes, an effective op reference, produces psychedelic sensations. The recessed volume, off-axis with respect to the street, leaves a polygonal plaza underlined by a bright yellow base and a sky blue tympanum. This space can be used for outdoor events. The perspective device gives the façade the role of a flag (striped) visible from a distance.

Not just a boutique but also an exhibition space, Galeria Melissa hosts seasonal art installations in its plastic garden. In the spring of 2005 (our autumn) the green stems brandished large colored buds. Because the very evident aim is to astonish, the setting changes with each season, including new furnishings created by the imaginative Muti Randolph, making Galeria Melissa a space in a continuous state of mutation.

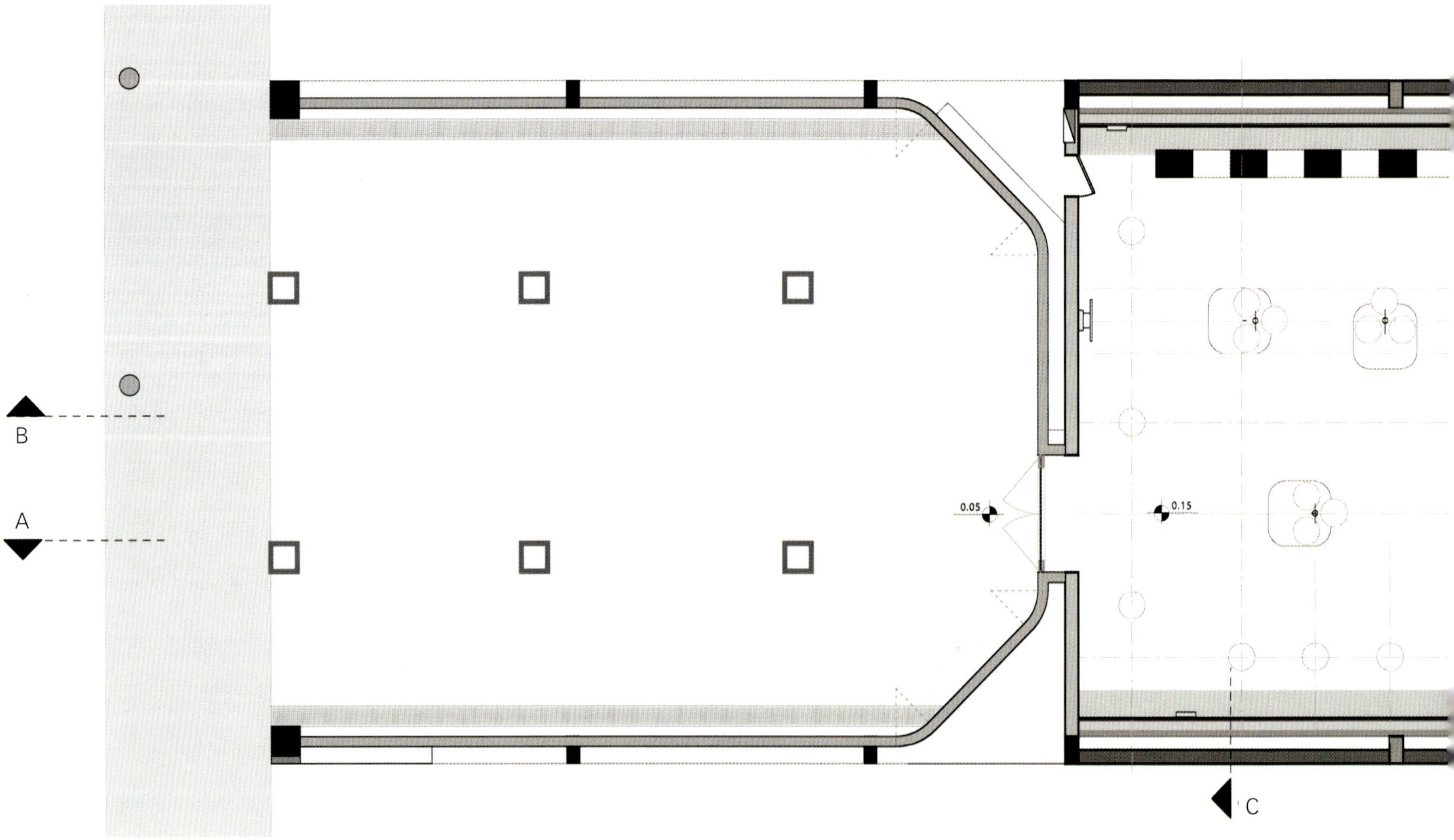

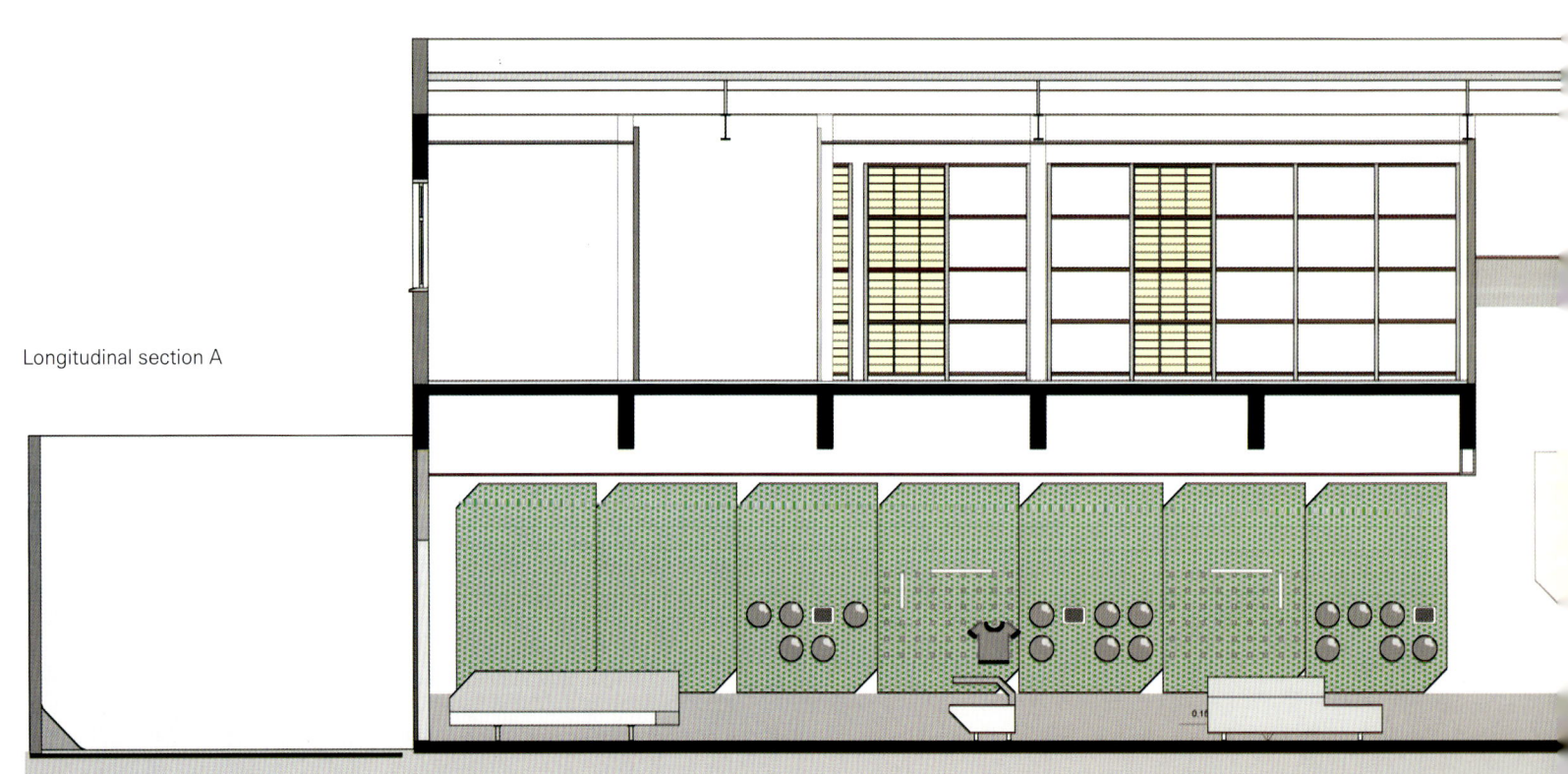

B

A

C

0.05

0.15

Longitudinal section A

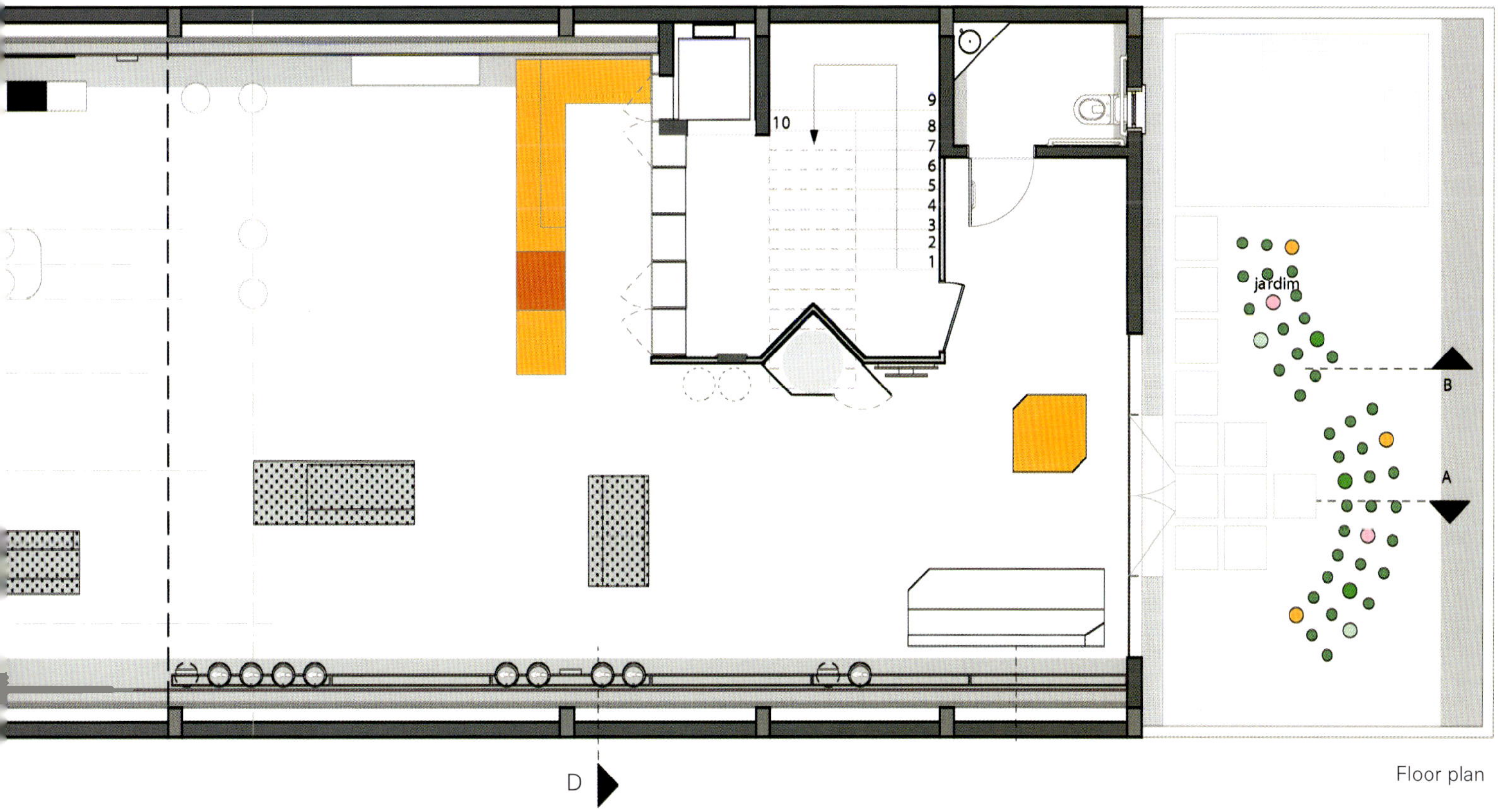

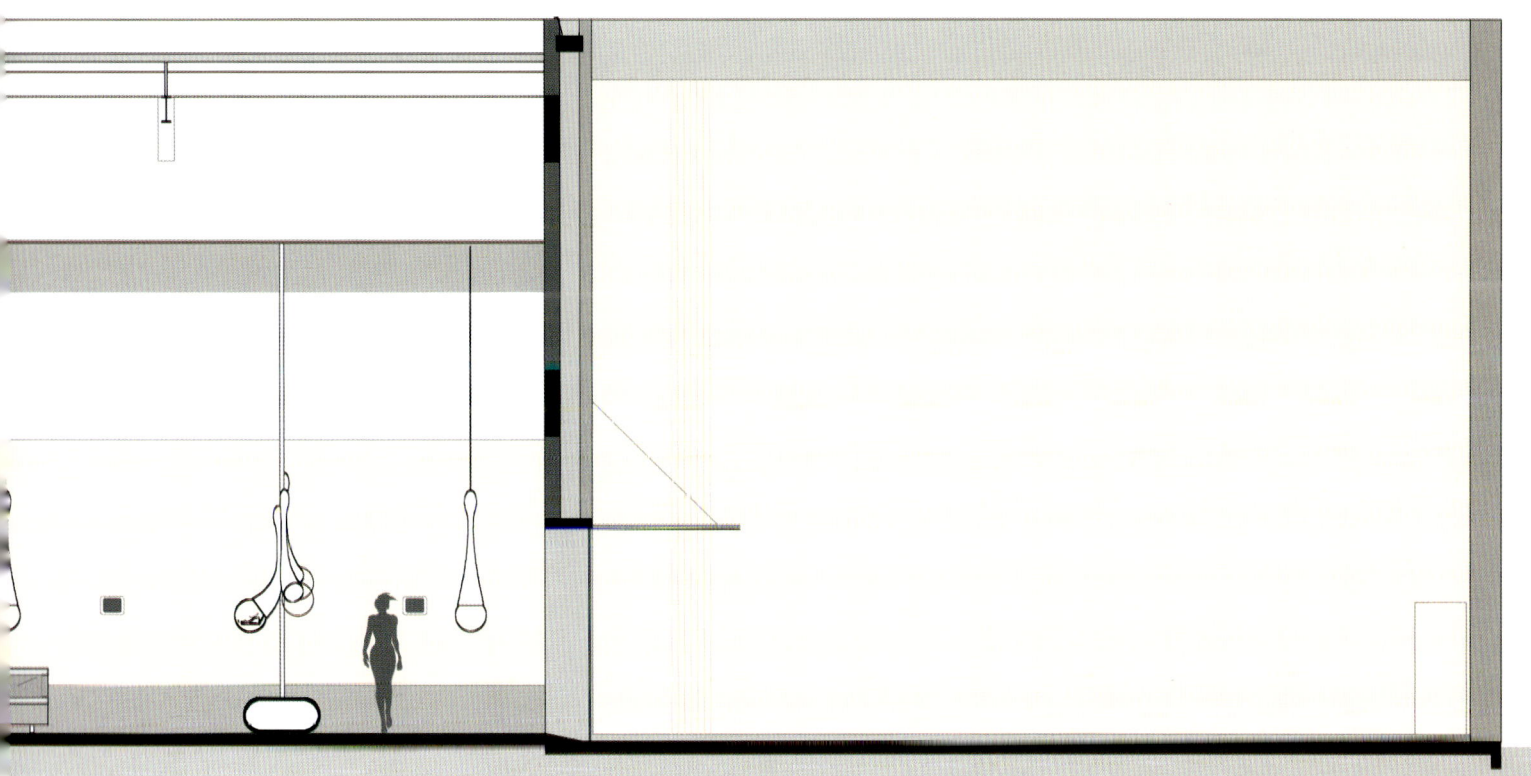

jardim

9
8
7
6
5
4
3
2
1

10

D ▶

B

A

Floor plan

Cross section D

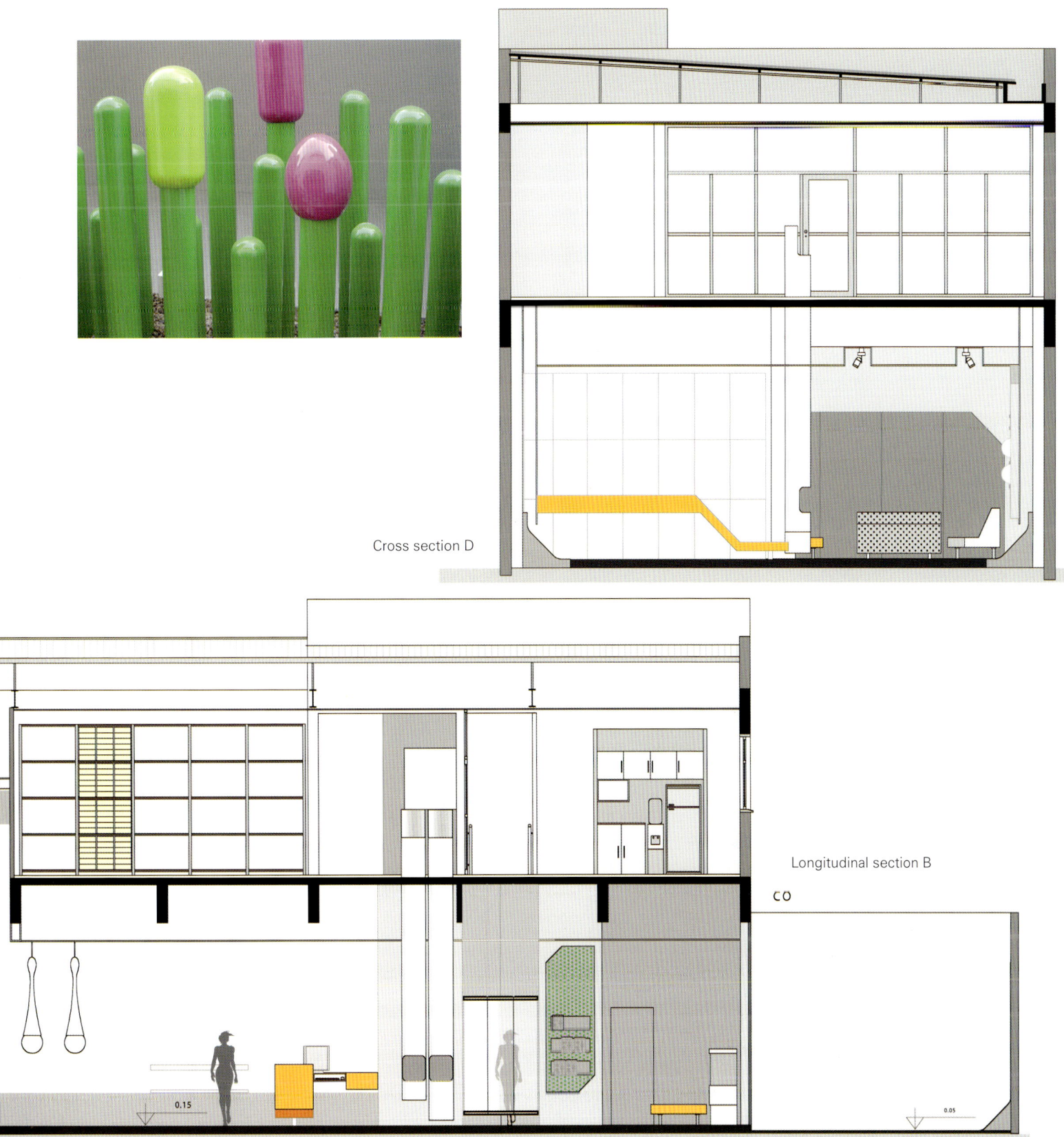

Cross section D

Longitudinal section B

CO

0.15

0.05

The sinuous pattern of the stripes, an effective op reference, produces psychedelic sensations. The recessed volume, off-axis with respect to the street, leaves a polygonal plaza underlined by a bright yellow base and a sky blue tympanum. This space can be used for outdoor events. The perspective device gives the façade the role of a flag (striped) visible from a distance.

Rem Koolhaas-OMA

Prada LA

Los Angeles, USA

Photographs: Prada, Phil Meech, OMA, Lydia Gould

The new Prada Epicenter is located at 343 North Rodeo Drive in Beverly Hills and comprises a total of 24,000 square feet with 14,750 square feet of retail space on three floors.

The entire width of 50 feet along Rodeo Drive opens up to the street without a traditional storefront or glass enclosure and invites the public to enter the building. Climatic separation is achieved through an environmentally responsive air-curtain system that profits from Los Angeles' pleasant weather. At night, an aluminum panel rises from the ground and hermetically seals the building. Large display cones are embedded into the ground to reveal merchandise without physically obstructing the open street front. Inside the store, a large wooden stair forms a 'hill'-counterpart to the 'wave' in the New York store - that supports an aluminum box floating above the entrance. A roof structure spanning the entire third floor admits daylight to the 'scenario-space', where the merchandise is arranged on an open, flexible floor plan. Roller tables and media gates form part of an airport-like display installation that draws reference to today's omnipresent security procedures. The character of the space is further defined by a

mural of wallpaper that - like the one in the New York store - allows for simple but radical change of the environment. A soft curtain provides a flexible enclosure and privacy for VIP and personal shopping.

Technology is integrated in the Beverly Hills Epicenter in an unobtrusive, functional way: plasma screens built into furniture or hanging between garments and merchandise, connect the store to actual events in the world outside; the dressing rooms throughout the store are equipped with 'magic mirrors': A plasma screen built into the large mirror allowing customers to see themselves both from the front and the back at the same time. A time delay captures and replays movements.

The elevator features a series of small LCD screens integrated into the cabin that scan virtual imagery while the elevator travels through the shaft.

After a first generation of aura and service-oriented applications, prototyped and tested in the New York Epicenter, Prada prepares for further development of a service network across all Epicenter stores. Applications of RFID (RadioFrequency Identification) systems are being further developed and will be integrated in the company.

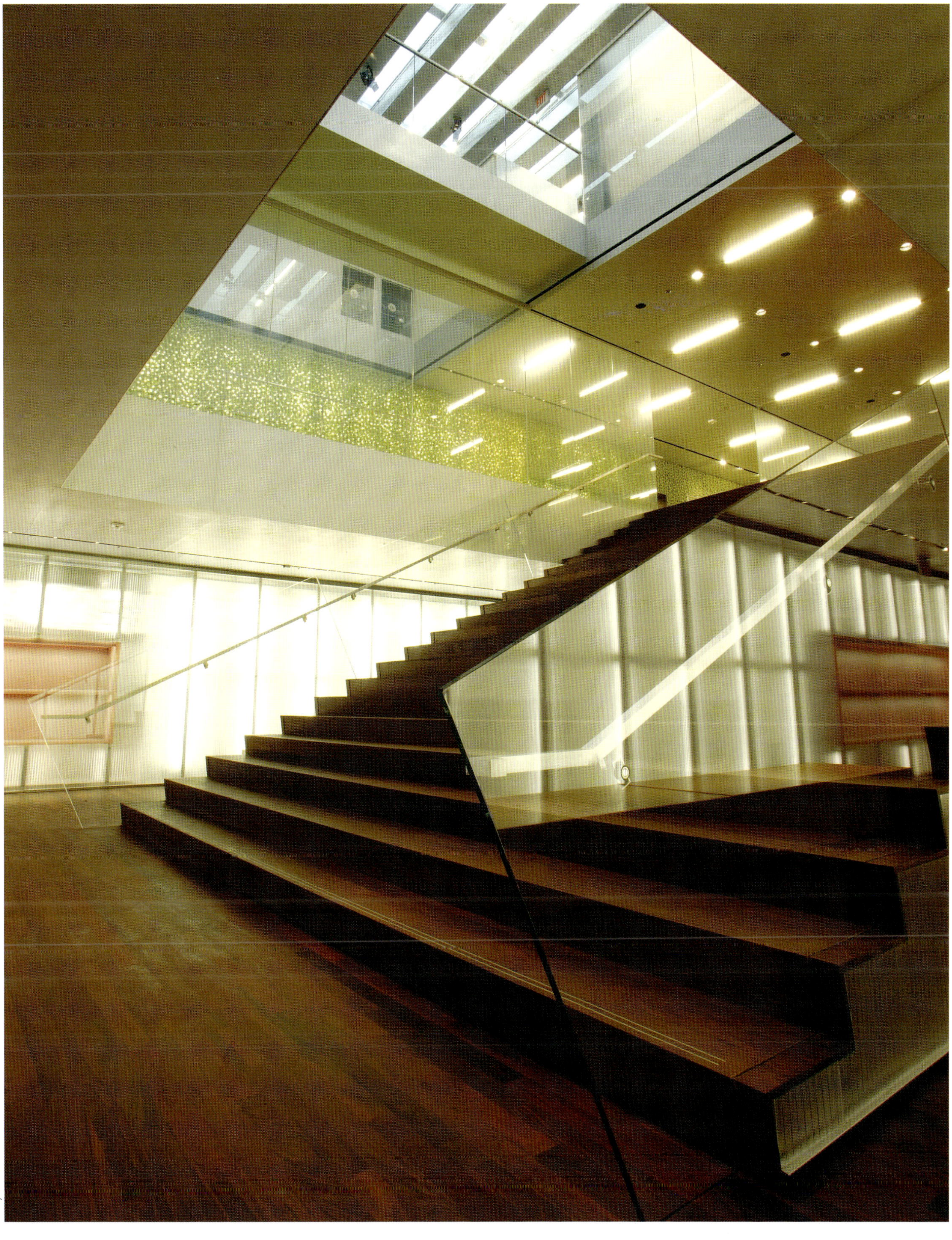

© Lydia Gould

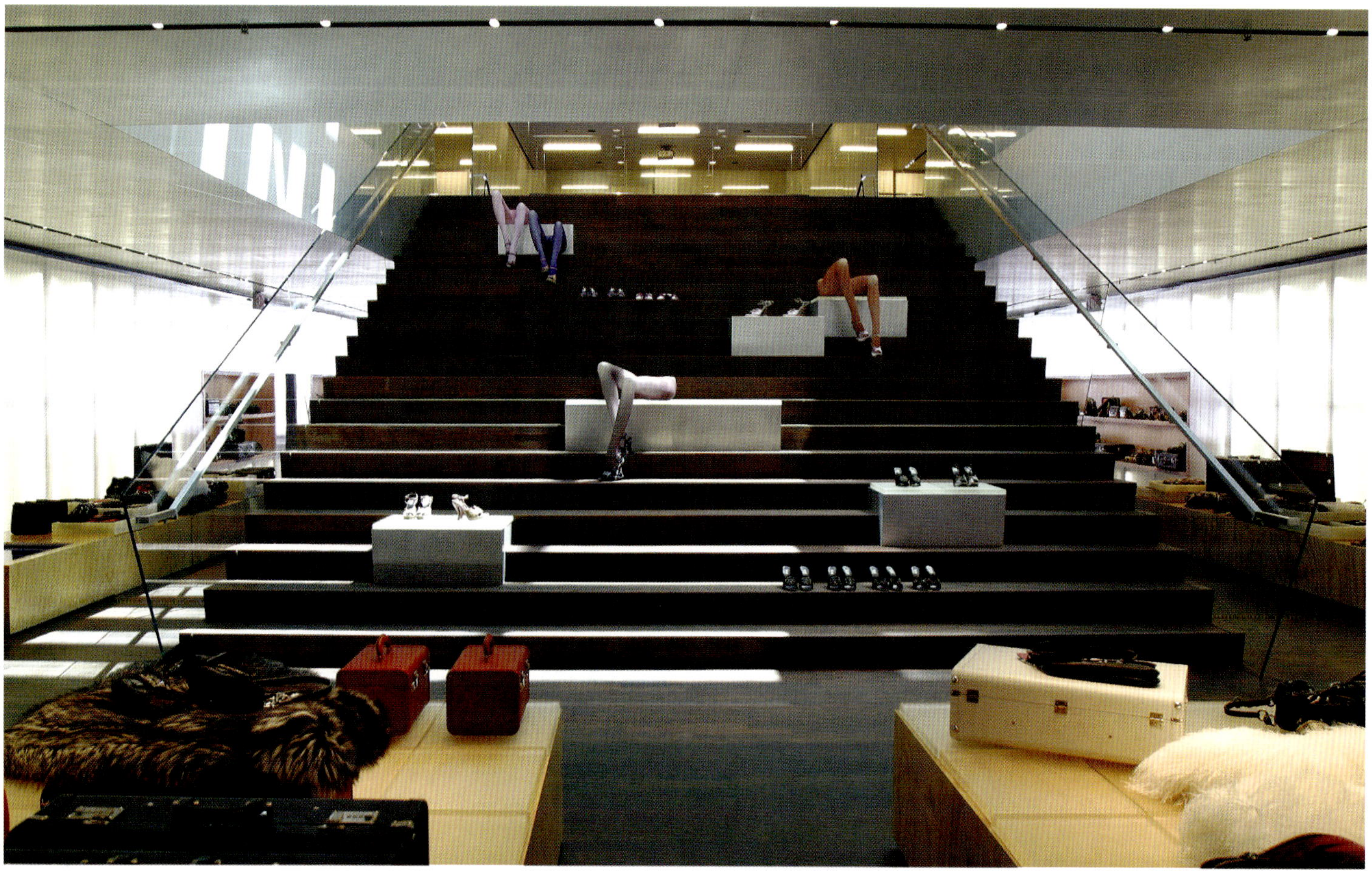

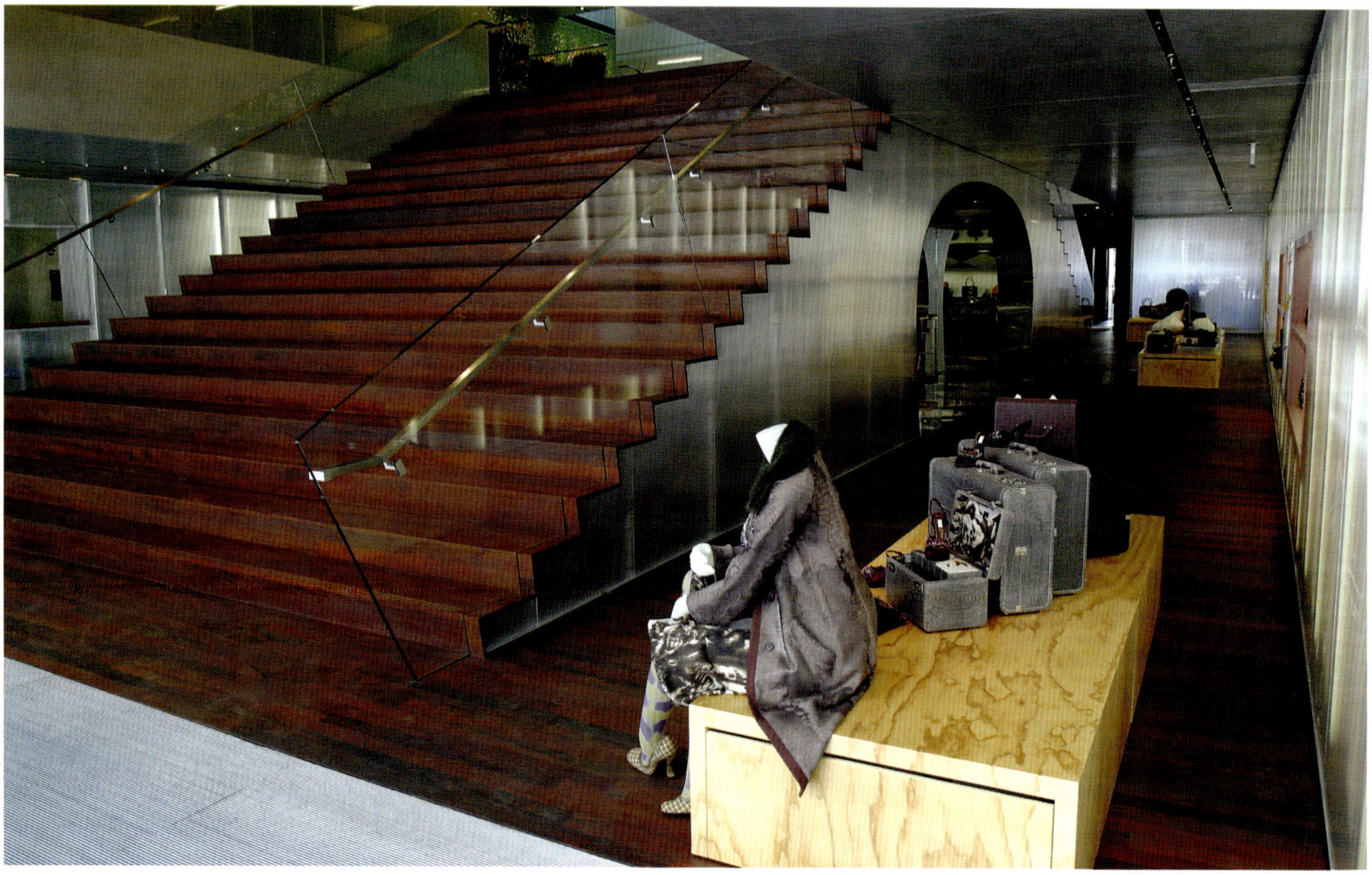

▦ Hangers	▦ Viewing room		
▦ Shelf display	▦ Cash\ Packing		
Table layout	■ Storage		
░ Dressing room	▯ Mirror		

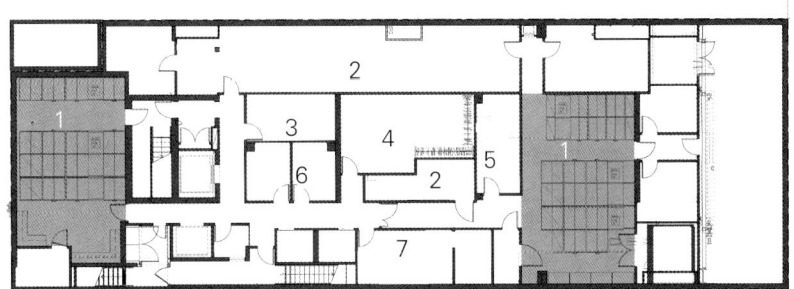

Basement

1. Storage
2. Mechanical
3. Snack area
4. Tailor
5. Communication
6. Staff dressing
7. Offices

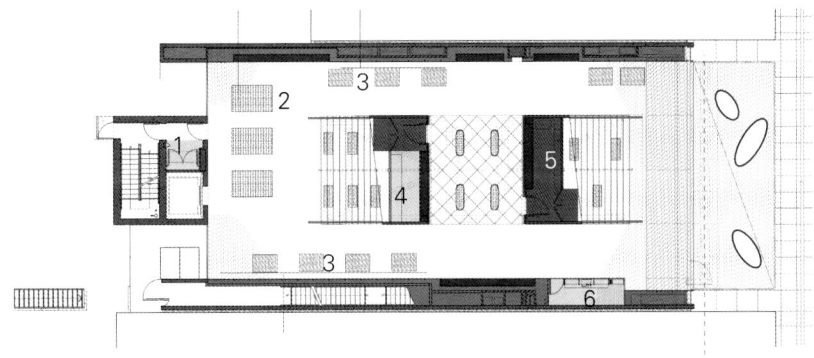

Ground floor

1. Fold away desk
2. Local storage
   in furniture
3. Optional: Hangbars
4. Cash/ Wrap
5. Intranet
6. Reception cash /Wrap

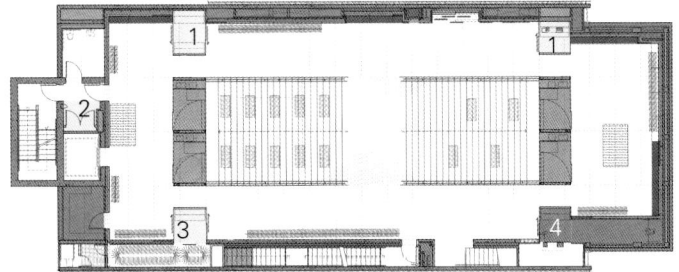

Second floor

1. Cash
2. Fold away desk
3. Wrap with intranet
4. Technical room

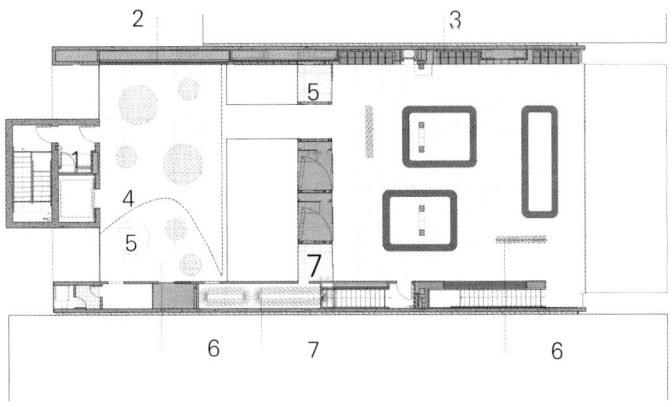

Third floor

1. Fold away desk
2. Cosmetics
3. Pull-out storage
4. Vip curtain options:
   either entire back of
   store or portion indicated
5. Personnal shopper´s
   and assistant desk with
   integrated cash
6. Floor sockets
   for hangbars

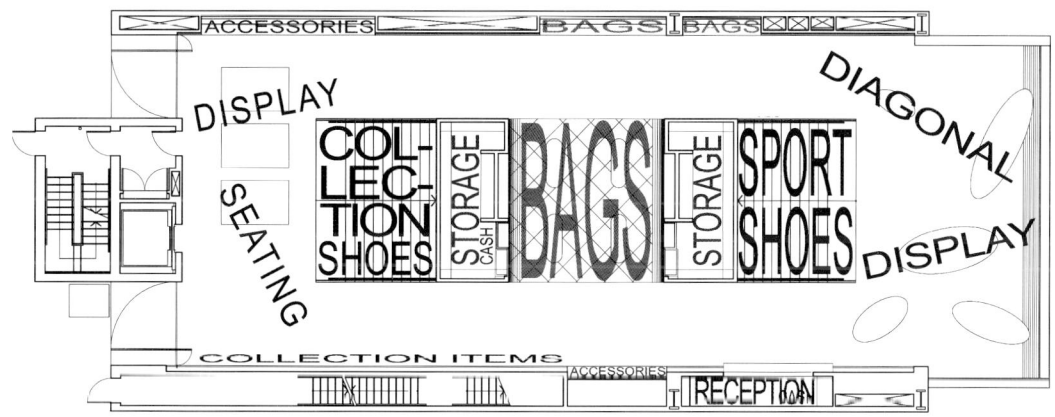

Ground floor plan

Accesories
Collection Items

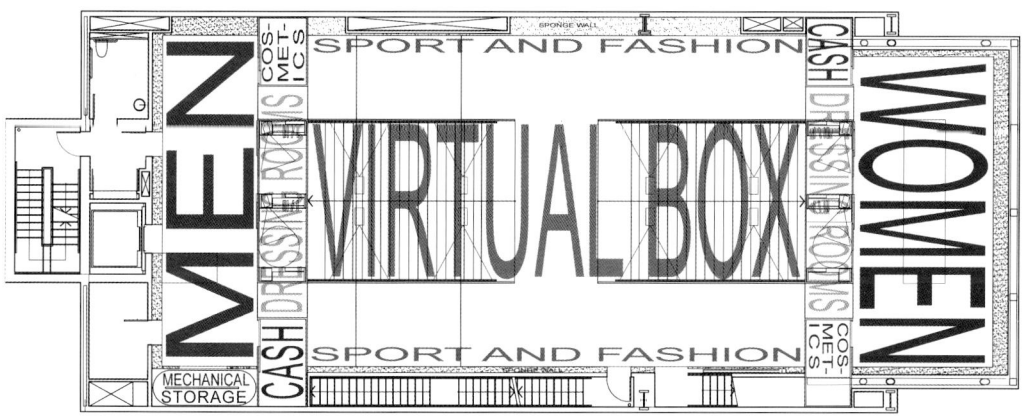

First floor plan

Fashion men/ women
Sports men/ women

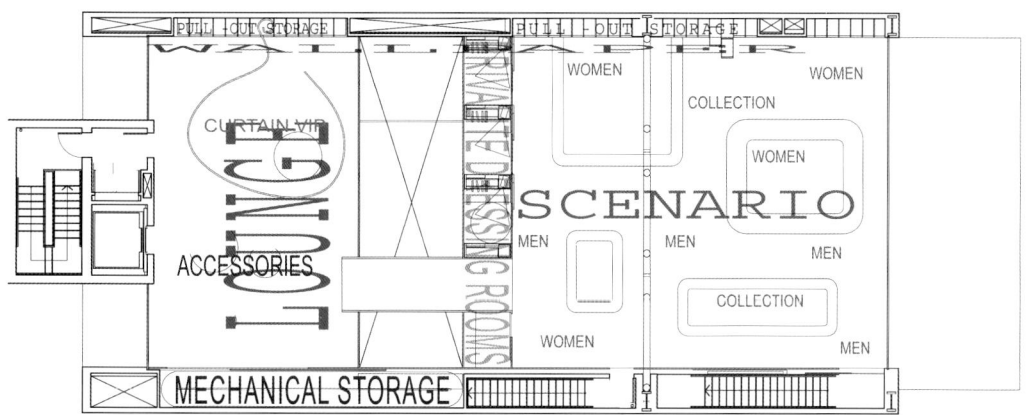

Second floor plan

Collection men / women
Lounge / VIP

The stair is framed with laminated glass fading from translucent to transparent, seemingly shrinking or enlarging the store's size in response to the presence of customers. In the mirrored alcove beneath the stair-hill, the black and white marble floor and the vitrines make reference to the first Prada store from 1913 in Milan.

© Phil Meech

© Phil Meech

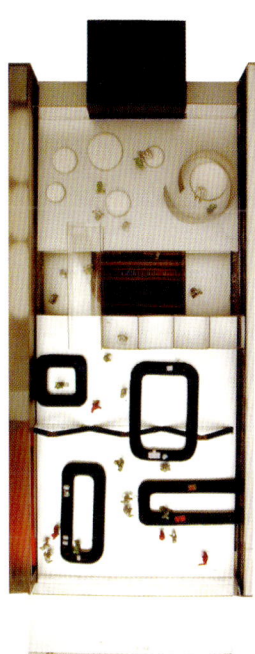

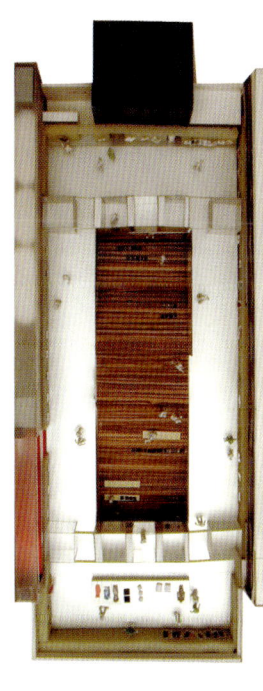

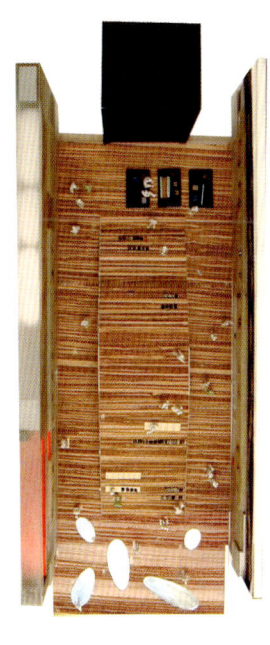

The aluminum box in the first floor is lined with a new material specifically developed for Prada: Half matter, half air, the 'sponge' provides a porous artificial background for the merchandise and further expands Prada's physical identity in its stores.

© Lydia Gould

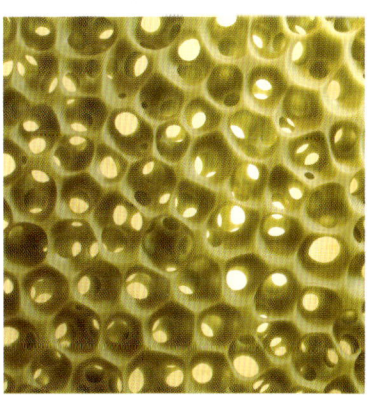

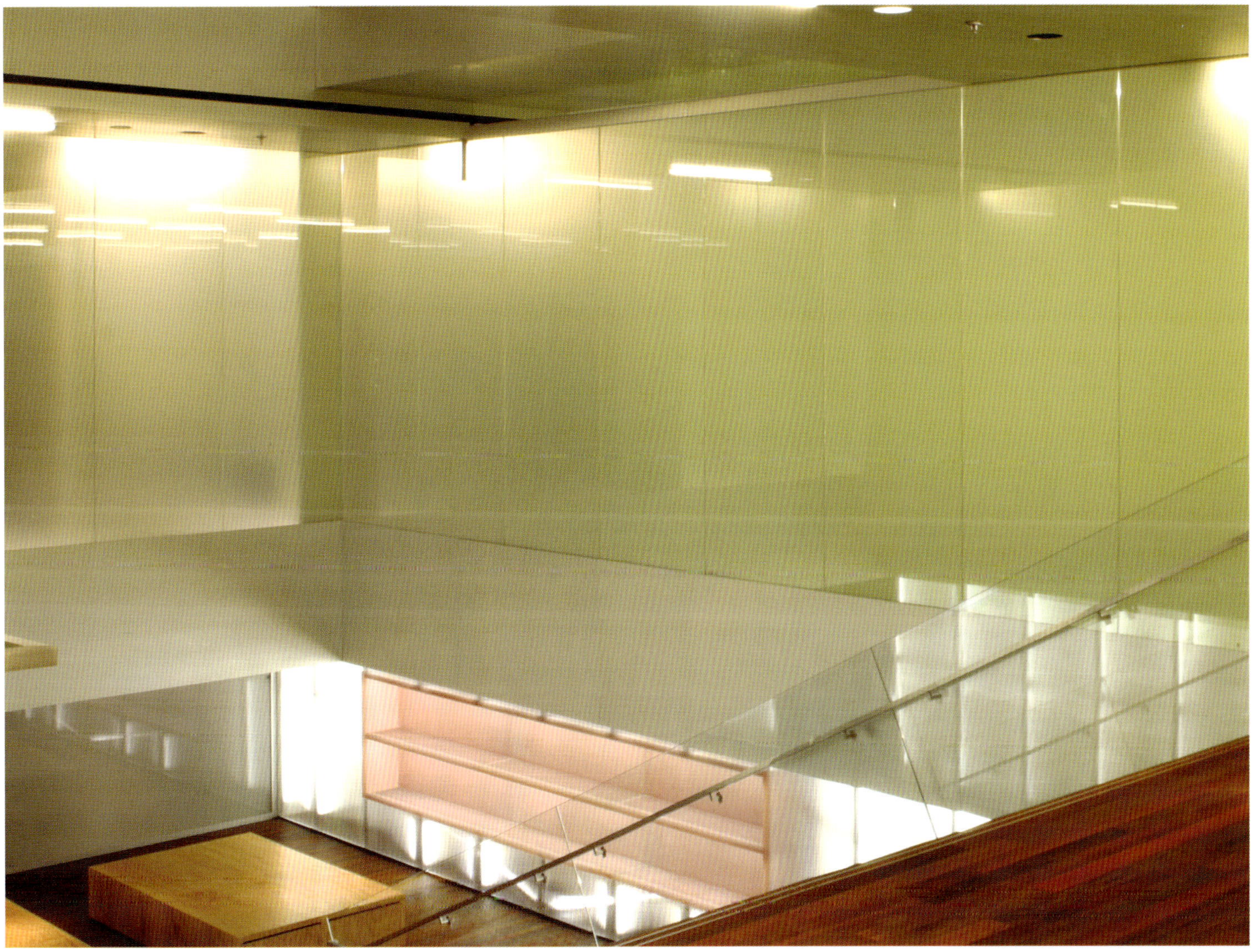

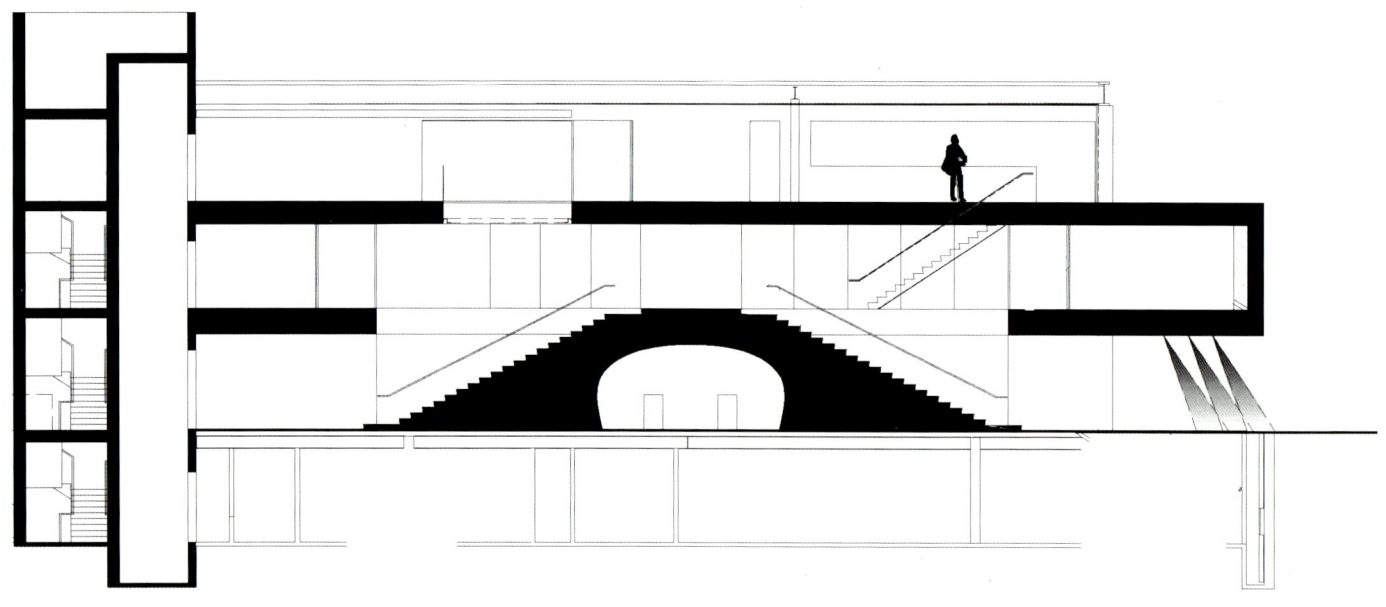

© Lydia Gould

Keiichiro Sako (SKSK Architects)

Kid's Republic

Beijing, China

Photographs: Minoru Iwasaki

KID'S REPUBLIC is a children's bookshop in Beijing, consisting of an event room on the first floor and a bookstore for children on the second floor. The event room on the first floor is a rainbow space, made of 12 connected rings of different widths, each one a different color of the rainbow. The difference between the consecutive rings leaves a series of gaps along the floor, the walls and the ceiling, which are used to house lighting and sound systems, or display cases. The resulting steps in the floor make suitable seating when the space is being used as an auditorium, for the performance of activities like story telling sessions and animation shows. The floor is fully carpeted and children can sit or lie on it freely.

The children can follow the stairs up to the second floor, to enter into a world of picture books. A rainbow-colored ribbon starts from the hall and goes up along the stairs to the bookstore. This 100-meter-long colored ribbon traces a random path through the bookshop, retracing its way and finally becoming the armrest of the stairs that lead back to the first floor.

The front covers of picture books have bright, rich colors. Compared to bookstores selling professional books, the collection of many picture books produces a cheerful space. No orderly bookshelves are found here; children can sit in their favorite places and read the picture books at their pleasure. The colored ribbon emerges from the stairs, curls and, twists through the store, becoming a bookshelf, part of the ceiling, a table, a gate, or a checkout counter or the armrest of the stairs.

Holes of different sizes pierce the surrounding bookshelves, providing windows to pass internal and external information, but also reading bubbles for the children. The image of children sitting and reading there decorates the outer façade of the store and reminds people outside of the delightful shop they are standing next to. Interior design generally classifies the floor, wall, ceiling and furniture. It is an easy way to sort out articles and establish a certain order in the adult world. The design here cancels all of these. Sensible children don't need these. There is no separation for them between reading and playing.

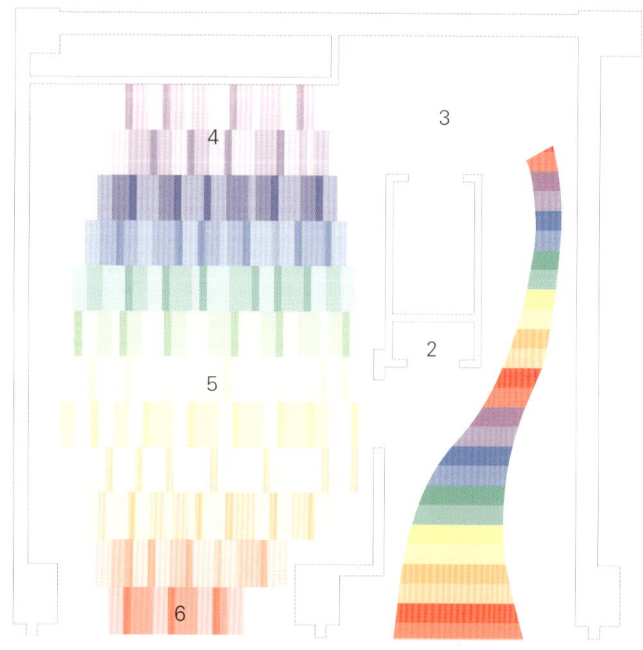

Ground floor plan
1. Entrance
2. Showcase
3. Stock room
4. Stage
5. Event space
6. Display

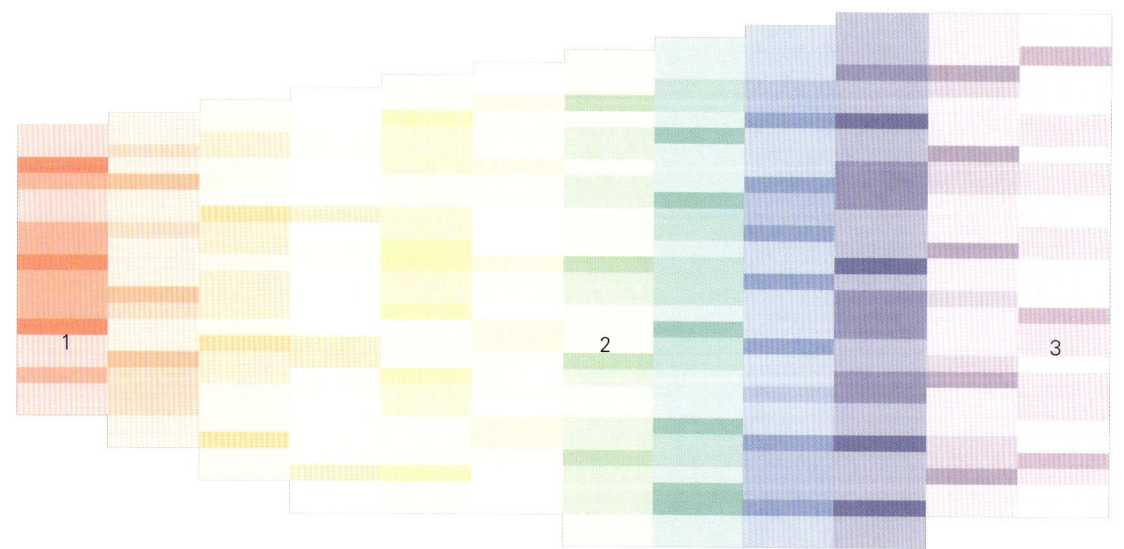

Ground floor event space
south elevation
1. Display
2. Event space
3. Stage

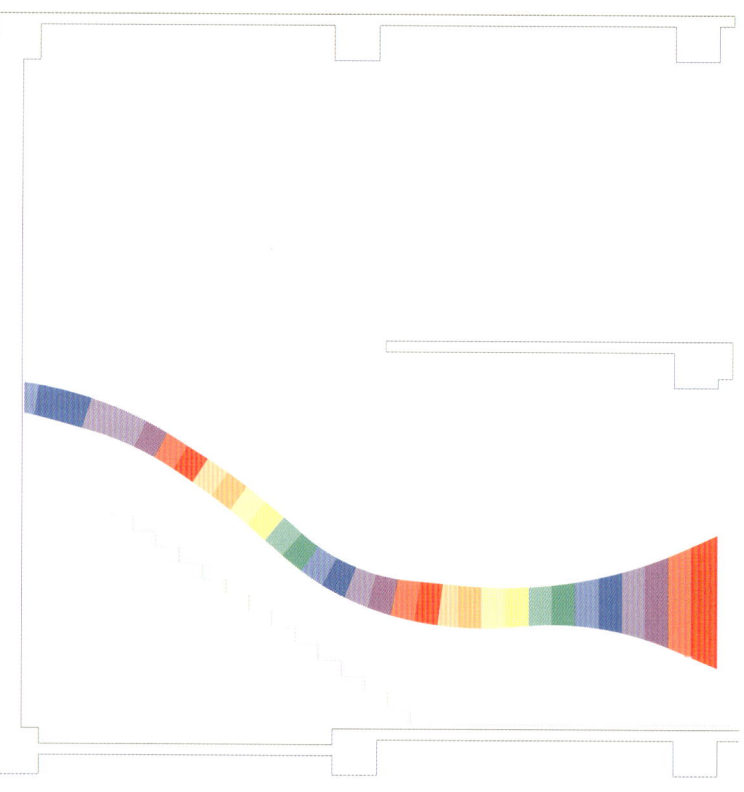

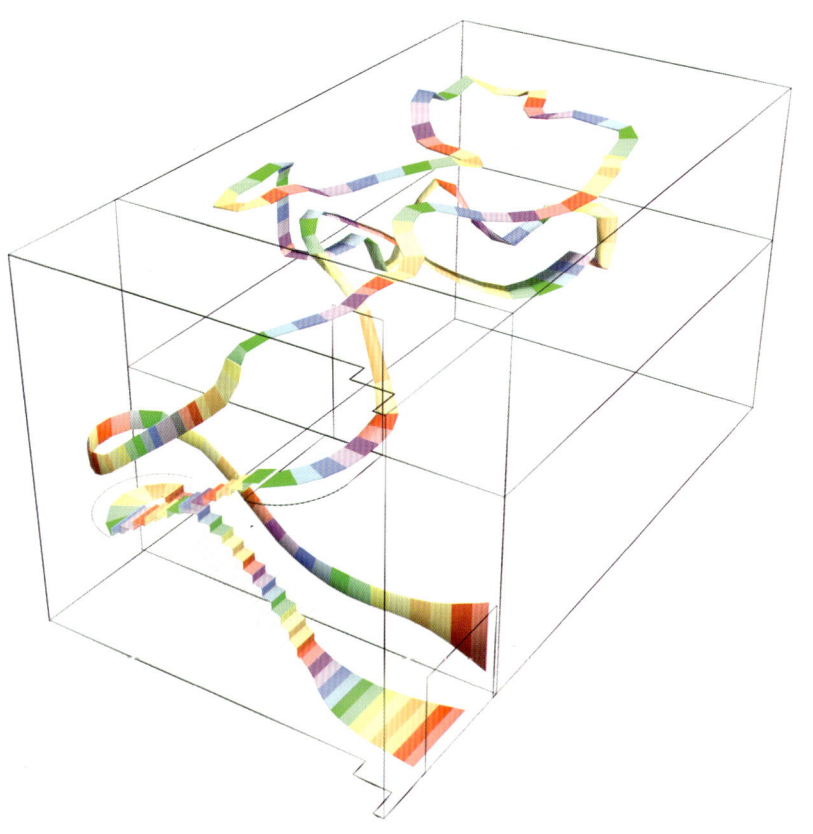

The children can follow the stairs up to the second floor, to enter into a world of picture books. A rainbow-colored ribbon starts from the hall and goes up along the stairs to the bookstore. This 100-meter-long colored ribbon traces a random path through the bookshop, retracing its way and finally becoming the armrest of the stairs that lead back to the first floor.

First floor plan
1. Entrance
2. Counter
3. Book shop
4. Book shelf
5. Staff room

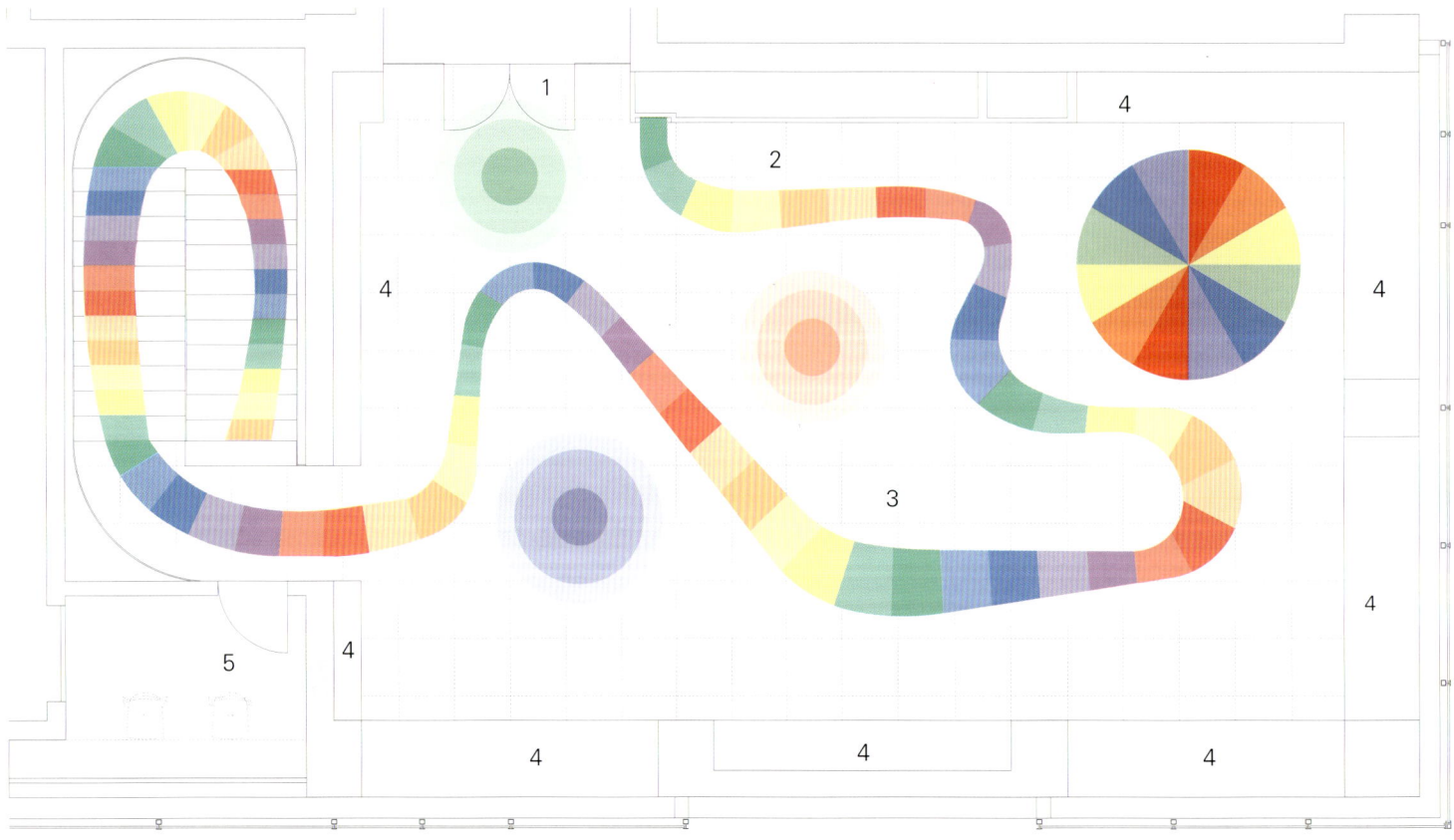

x architekten

Jewelry Mayrhofer

Linz, Austria

Photographs: Max Nirnberger.

This small jeweler's shop possesses a total usable surface area of 55 sq m., and a volume of only 277 cubic meters. It is superbly located on the main square of Linz, in upper Austria. The building is among the items listed in the town's architectural heritage, which seriously condition the possibilities of any exterior transformations. The existing building consisted of a traditional structure of stone pillars and a mixed construction of various sorts of masonry, including brickwork vaults between beams at different levels. In order to transform this space into a meaningful experience for the senses, the idea arose to base the design on the soft inner surface of a jewel case, the geometry of which exists in response to the objects placed inside it. To achieve this, the underlying shell was completely clad in a skin of fiberglass-hardened plasterwork attached to a wooden supporting frame. The resulting surfaces were entirely upholstered in a soft velvet

sheath. The resulting composition of sensitive and gently rounded forms establishes an apparently simplified, but in fact geometrically complicated continuum that unifies the floor, the walls and the ceiling. The introduction of an independent volume into the historical context implied necessarily leaving behind the customary references for this type of re-form project. All the surfaces were carefully leveled, filled, and stuffed, to give the room's homogenous skin the required smooth evenness. To avoid over-stressing the softness of the "jewel-case" theme, all the supplementary furniture in the shop is un-upholstered. The lacquered cabinets have concealed hinges and fixtures, maintaining a restrained overall attitude that enhances the wonder of the refined handmade artifacts on display. Even the halogen spotlights are built-in flush with the furniture surfaces, contributing a sharp-edged luminous contrast to the predominantly soft character that qualifies this commercial venture.

www.xarchitekten.com

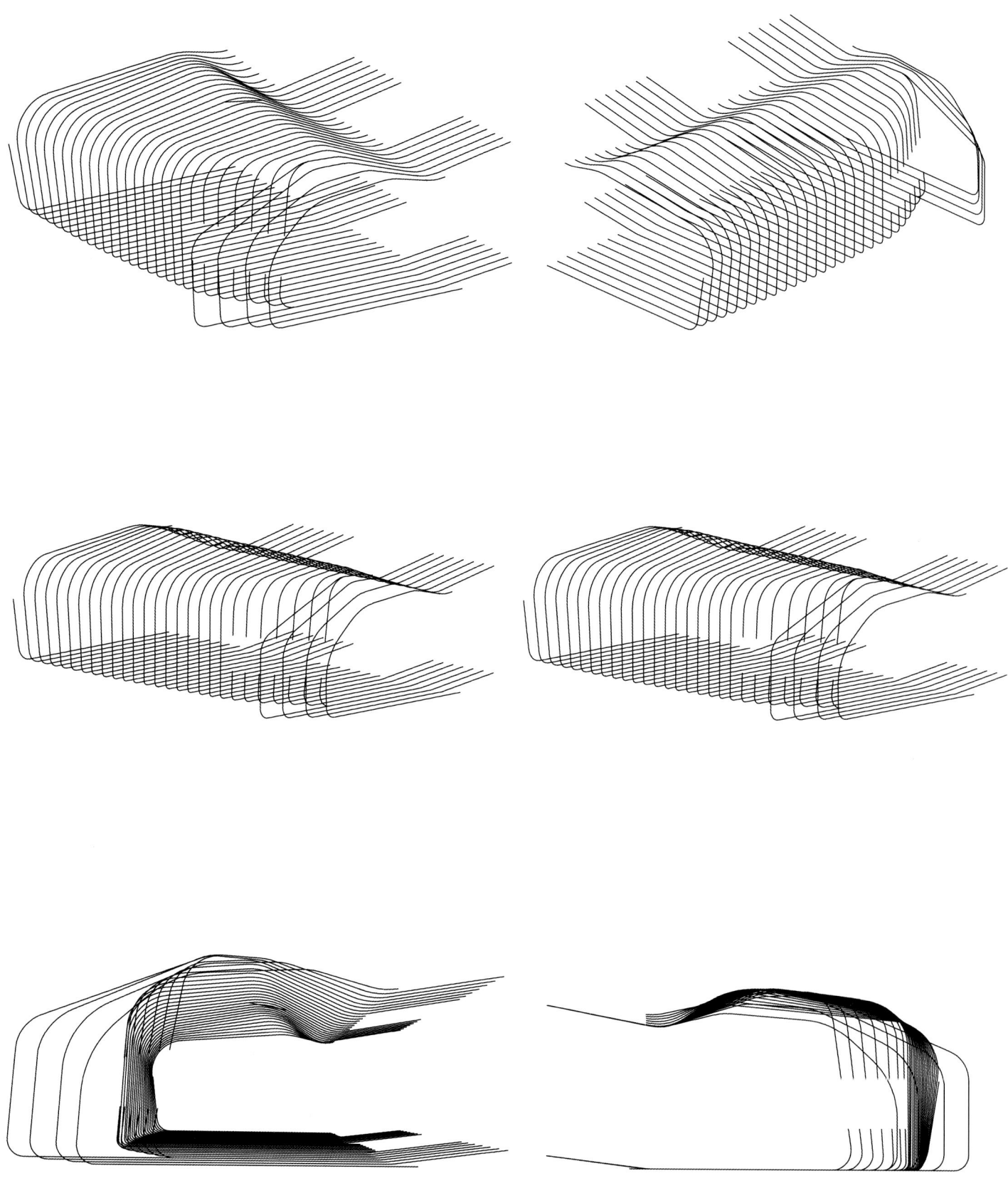

The resulting composition of sensitive and gently rounded forms establishes an apparently simplified, but in fact geometrically complicated continuum that unifies the floor, the walls and the ceiling.

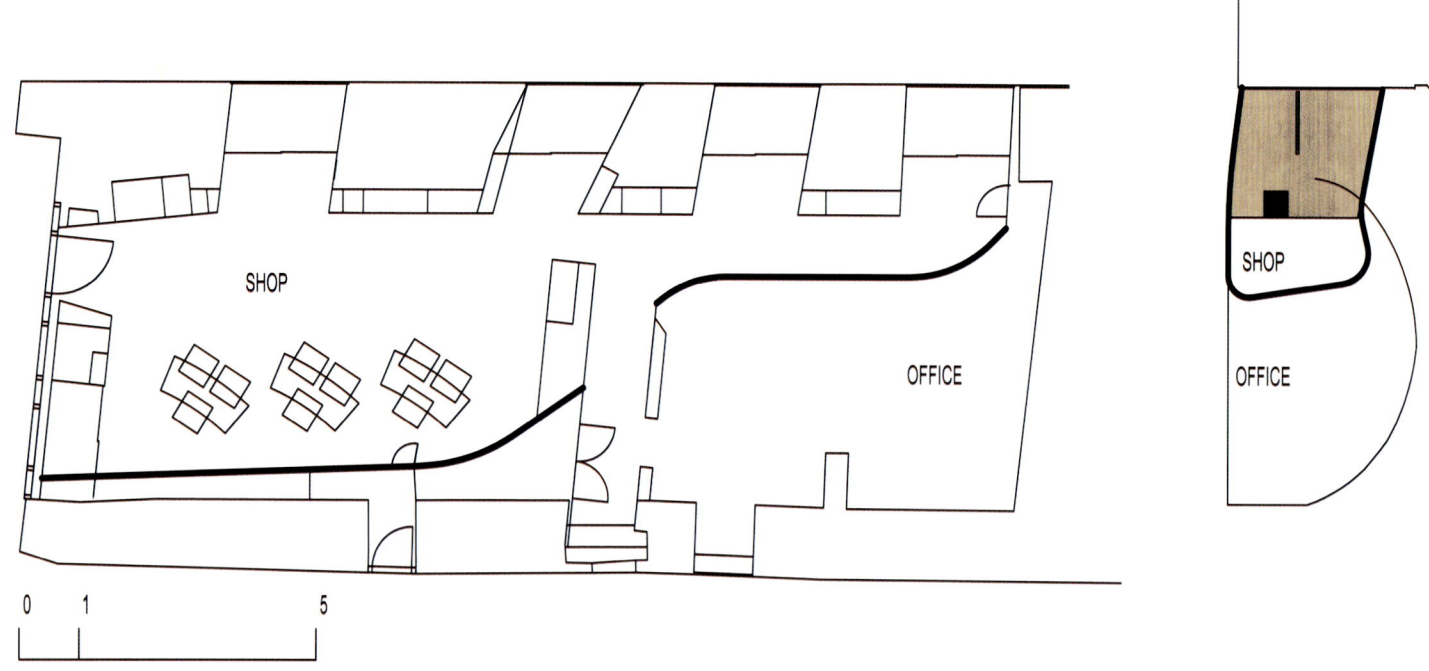

SHOP

OFFICE

SHOP

OFFICE

0 1 5

Floor plan

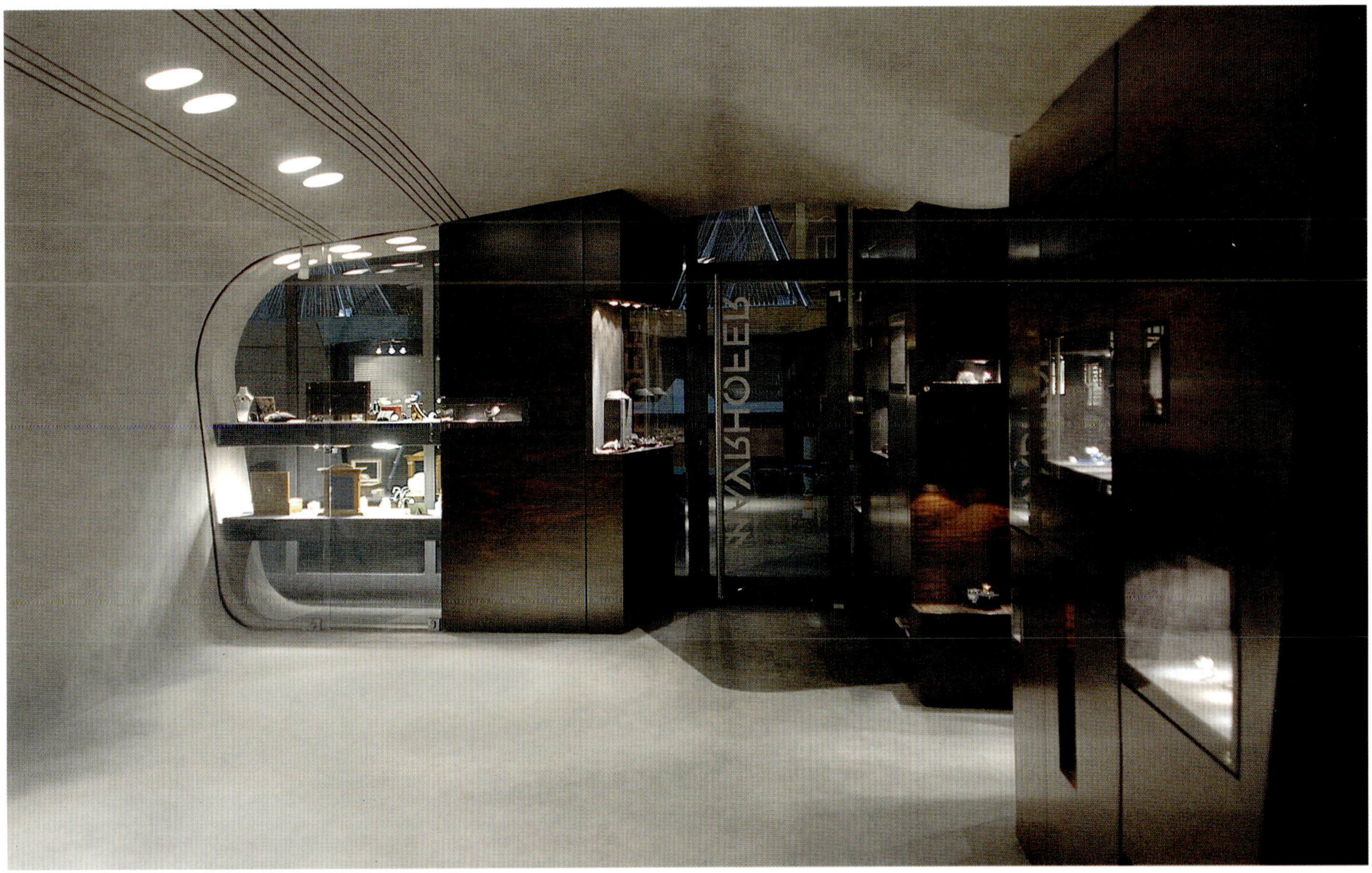

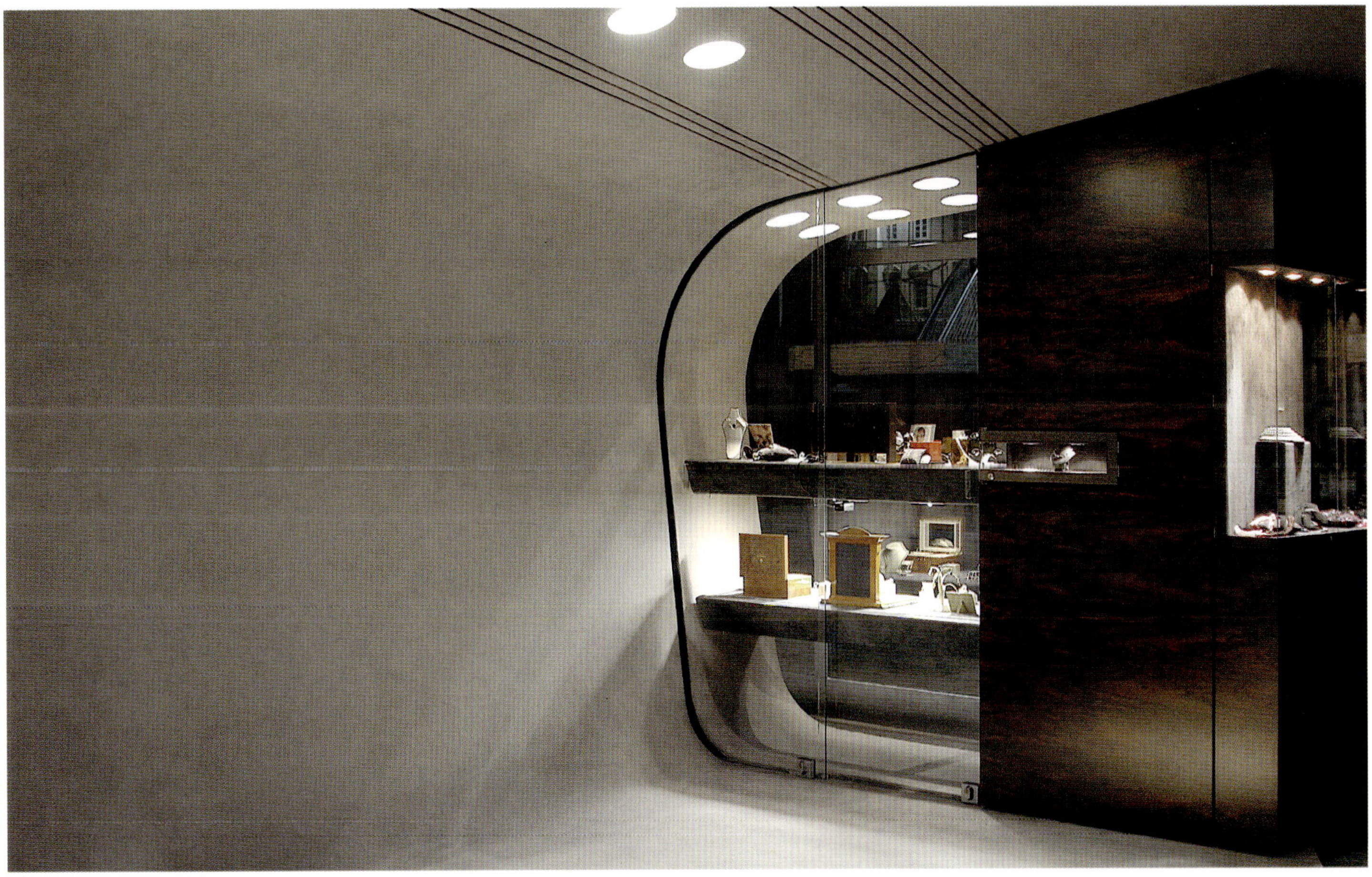

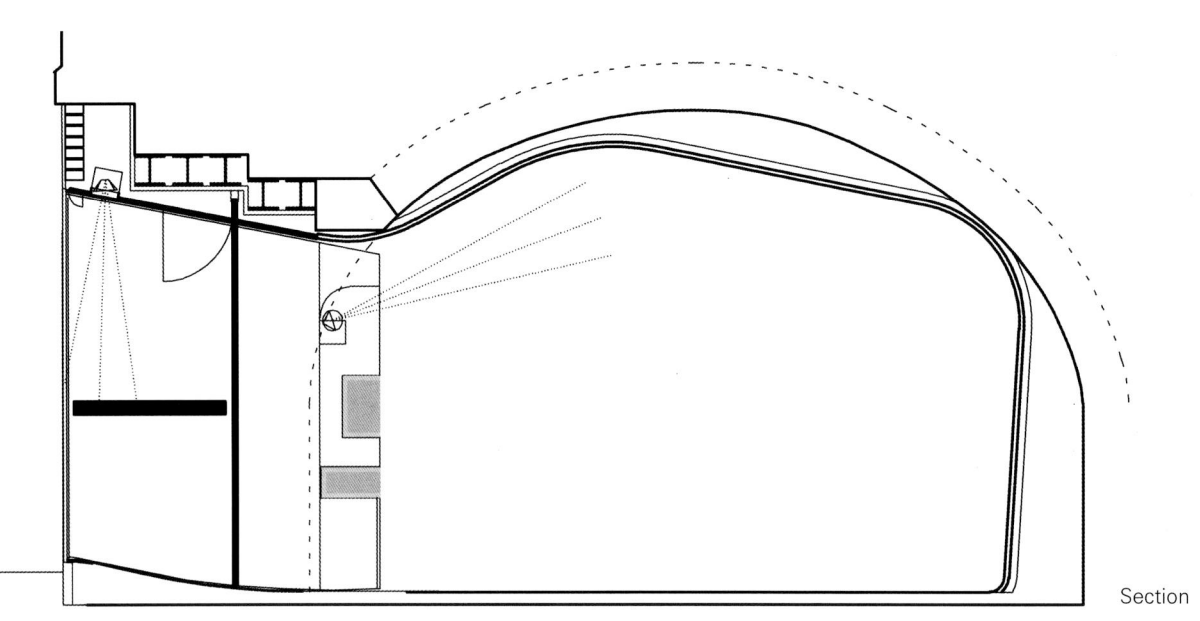

Section